Complex Responsive Processes in Organizations

Over the past decade, practicing managers and organizational theorists have been drawing attention to the centrality of information and knowledge in economic and social processes, the so-called "knowledge economy." This is reflected in the popularity of notions of learning, sense-making, knowledge creation, knowledge management and intellectual capital in organizations. More recently, attention has been drawn to emotional intelligence as an important management skill in these processes of learning and knowledge creation.

Complex Responsive Processes in Organizations argues that most of the literature on these matters, and the ways in which most practitioners now talk about them, reflect systems thinking and that its information processing view of knowledge creation is no longer tenable. The purpose of this book is to develop a different perspective, that of Complex Responsive Processes of relating, which draws on the complexity sciences as a source domain for analogies with human action. This alternative perspective places self-organizing interaction, with its intrinsic capacity to produce emergent coherence, at the center of the knowledge creating process in organizations. Learning and knowledge creation are seen as qualitative processes of power relating that are emotional as well as intellectual, creative as well as destructive, enabling as well as constraining. The result is a radical questioning of the belief that organizational knowledge is essentially codified and centralized. Instead, organizational knowledge is understood to be in the relationships between people in an organization and has to do with the qualities of those relationships. From this perspective, it makes no sense to talk about measuring intellectual capital and managing knowledge.

Ralph D. Stacey is Professor of Management and Director of the Complexity and Management Centre at the Business School of the University of Hertfordshire, and a member of the Institute of Group Analysis. He is also a consultant to managers at many levels across a range of organizations and the author of a number of books and articles on strategy and complexity theory in management.

Complexity and Emergence in Organizations

Series Editors:
Ralph D. Stacey, Douglas Griffin and **Patricia Shaw**
Complexity and Management Centre, University of Hertfordshire

The books in this series each give expression to a particular way of speaking about complexity in organizations. Drawing on insights from the complexity sciences, psychology and sociology, this series aims to develop theories of human organization, including ethics.

Complex Responsive Processes in Organizations

Learning and knowledge creation

Ralph D. Stacey

Routledge
Taylor & Francis Group

LONDON AND NEW YORK

First published 2001
by Routledge
2 Park Square, Milton Park, Abingdon, Oxon, OX14 4RN

Simultaneously published in the USA and Canada
by Routledge
270 Madison Avenue, New York, NY 10016

Reprinted 2001, 2002 (twice), 2004, 2005, 2006

Routledge is an imprint of the Taylor & Francis Group

Typeset in Times New Roman by Keystroke, Jacaranda Lodge, Wolverhampton
Printed and bound in Great Britain by MPG Books Ltd, Bodmin

British Library Cataloguing in Publication Data
A catalogue record for this book is available from the British Library

Library of Congress Cataloging in Publication Data
Stacey, Ralph D.
   Complex responsive processes in organizations : learning and knowledge creation /
Ralph D. Stacey
      p. cm. – (Complexity and emergence in organizations)
   Includes index.
      1. Organizational effectiveness.   2. Complex organizations–Management.
   3. Interorganizational relations.   I. Title.   II. Series.

   HD58.9 .S734 2001
   658.4′038–dc21   00-045939

   ISBN 0–415–24918–X (hbk)
   ISBN 0–415–24919–8 (pbk)

Contents

List of illustrations

Boxes

Figures

Series preface
Complexity and Emergence in Organizations

The aim of this series is to give expression to a particular way of speaking about complexity in organizations, one that emphasizes the self-referential, reflexive nature of humans, the essentially responsive and participative nature of human processes of relating and the radical unpredictability of their evolution. It draws on the complexity sciences, which can be brought together with psychology and sociology in many different ways to form a whole spectrum of theories of human organization.

At one end of this spectrum there is the dominant voice in organization and management theory, which speaks in the language of design, regularity and control. In this language, managers stand outside the organizational system, which is thought of as an objective, pre-given reality that can be modeled and designed, and they control it. Managers here are concerned with the functional aspects of a system as they search for causal links that promise sophisticated tools for predicting its behavior. The dominant voice talks about the individual as autonomous, self-contained, masterful and at the center of an organization. Many complexity theorists talk in a language that is immediately compatible with this dominant voice. They talk about complex adaptive systems as networks of autonomous agents that behave on the basis of regularities extracted from their environments. They talk about complex systems as objective realities that scientists can stand outside of and model. They emphasize the predictable aspects of these systems and see their modeling work as a route to increasing the ability of humans to control complex worlds.

At the other end of the spectrum there are voices from the fringes of organizational theory, complexity sciences, psychology and sociology who are defining a participative perspective. They argue that humans are themselves members of the complex networks that they form and are drawing attention to the impossibility of standing outside of them in order to objectify and model them. With this intersubjective voice people speak as subjects interacting with others in the co-evolution of a jointly constructed reality. These voices emphasize the radically unpredictable aspects of self-organizing processes and their creative potential. These are the voices of decentered agency, which talk about agents and the social world in which they live as mutually created and sustained. This way of thinking weaves together relationship psychologies and the work of complexity theorists who focus on the emergent and radically unpredictable aspects of complex systems. The result is a participative approach to understanding the complexities of organizational life.

This series is intended to give expression to the second of these voices, defining a participative perspective.

Series editors
Ralph D. Stacey, Douglas Griffin, Patricia Shaw
Complexity and Management Centre,
University of Hertfordshire

Acknowledgements

Although this book is written in my words I cannot claim that they simply articulate my ideas. These ideas were developed over a number of years in many conversations in which I participated. Particularly important, for me, were the conversations with the co-editors of this series, Doug Griffin and Patricia Shaw. Many of these conversations took place in the context of a doctoral group I ran with my colleague, Dorothea Noble, at the Business School of the University of Hertfordshire. Other participants in this group are also contributors to this series, namely, Phil Streatfield and José Fonseca. They were important contributors to the thinking I try to express in this book. I also want to thank other long-standing members of the doctoral group: Eliat Aram, Peter Fraser and David Bentley. An experience of major importance for me was my training as a group analyst at the Institute of Group Analysis and I want to thank the many group analysts who contributed to this experience. My participation in conversations with group analysts, particularly my former supervisor, Farhad Dalal, were important in shaping what I have written in this book. I am very grateful to my colleagues at the University of Hertfordshire. They create an institution which makes my work possible. Others have contributed to this book in ways that they are not even aware of and in particular I have in mind the neurosurgeon, Mr Dorward, and his team. Finally, and most important of all, I am grateful to my family.

1 Introduction: can learning and knowledge creation in organizations really be managed?

- The historical context
- Moving on from systems thinking
- Outline of the book

It is now widely thought that the world economy has left behind the industrial age and is moving into a new age of knowledge work in the information society. This global pattern of change is said to require new forms of organization and different ways of managing them. Many argue for a move away from bureaucratic, hierarchical forms of organizing and extol the virtues of more flexible, flatter, leaner structures modeled on networks in which authority, responsibility and decision-making are decentralized and distributed. Attention is drawn to the very different ways in which professional knowledge workers must be managed, compared to the manual workers of the industrial age. It is said that knowledge workers must be empowered so that they can participate more fully in the development of the organization. It is supposed that this will unleash the creativity of the organization.

The global change toward the knowledge economy is also said to have major implications for the nature of an organization's assets. In the industrial age, the main assets were physical resources, plant and equipment, which were traded in markets and could thus be valued. Measures of asset value coincided to a significant extent with the valuation of the organization by the capital markets. Managing the value of a corporation could then be understood as managing physical assets and the workers, the "human resources," who used them. Now, in the new knowledge economy, knowledge is the major asset and since it is not directly traded in markets, it is not measured and recorded in corporate balance sheets. As a result, enormous gaps have opened up between the asset values recorded by a corporation and the value capital markets place on the corporation itself. This clearly creates problems if the aim is to manage assets so as to produce shareholder value. This is the motivation behind the Intellectual Capital movement and its call to measure the intellectual capital of a corporation and manage its knowledge assets.

The new management task, then, is to manage the creation of knowledge. However, knowledge is thought to arise in individual heads, largely in tacit form and this creates significant management problems. First, the professional experts who possess knowledge could leave, taking it with them. One requirement, then, is to adopt management styles encouraging the professional elite to stay, such as empowerment. Another requirement, one that takes up a great deal of the literature on knowledge management, is to extract tacit knowledge from individual heads and convert it into explicit knowledge. In this form, so it is said, knowledge can be stored and manipulated using information technology and thus owned and controlled by the corporation. A second problem to be faced in the management of knowledge is that individuals, it is assumed, are reluctant to share the knowledge they possess. This requires management styles that encourage and persuade people to share knowledge and spread it around the corporation. A call is made for rediscovering the lost art of dialogue.

What I have briefly outlined above is a sketch of what I will be calling mainstream thinking about knowledge in organizations. I call it mainstream because views of this kind form the central message of most books I have come across that are directed at practitioners. Such views are also much in evidence in the academic literature on the subject. There are, of course, criticisms of this mainstream thinking particularly in the academic literature. Some have pointed to the importance of communities of practice in the generation of knowledge, and closely linked to this, there is the view of organizations as sense-making systems. Both place importance on narrative forms of knowledge and the role of storytelling and informal conversations in creating and storing knowledge. It is recognized that these forms of communication are important in using and spreading knowledge, and thus are to be encouraged.

The historical context: extending the sphere of control

Consider the place of this call for the management of knowledge in its historical context. In the first part of the last century, management was thought to be essentially the function of controlling the performance of tasks, that is, the particular actions members of an organization were required to undertake in order to produce its goods and services. It was the motivation and the actions of people that were to be managed. In the second half of the last century systems thinking led to an important shift to managing not just tasks but whole systems of roles required to carry out the tasks. In other words, it was no longer just the details of task performance but the whole inter-related system of tasks and roles that was to be managed. It was people's relationships that were to be managed. Then in the 1980s, the emphasis shifted once more. It was thought insufficient to manage the system of tasks and relationships. In addition, the system of values and beliefs, the culture, was also to be designed, managed and controlled. By this time the focus of control had widened from the detail of tasks, to systems of relationships, to systems of beliefs. Not long after this, the learning organization became a popular concept. The scope of management was extended to the learning process. It was assumed that learning was primarily individual in nature, meaning changes in the mental models that were thought to comprise an individual's mind. In other words, it was changes in people's minds that was now to be managed. It was thought to be possible for people to engineer changes in their own minds and in the minds of others.

The last century, then, witnessed a steady expansion in the scope of what was to be designed, managed and controlled. When that extension of control is couched in systems language it sounds innocuous enough. It is the extension of control from systems of tasks, relationships, values and beliefs to systems of learning and mental functioning. However, when one remembers that one is talking about human persons the flavor changes. During the twentieth century the extension of control was from the actions of a human person at work, to the relationships between human persons, to the beliefs and values of human persons and then to the very minds of human persons. Now, with the movement to measure intellectual capital and manage knowledge, the focus of what is to be controlled is shifting to knowledge itself. Again, if this is thought of as another system, it does not sound too bad. But when it is recalled how close knowledge is to the very identity of human persons, it sounds far more ominous to me. To talk of a corporation owning knowledge, managing knowledge, controlling knowledge, is to talk of corporations controlling the very identities of human persons. Some even talk about measuring "human capital" as a component of intellectual capital, referring to it as the "soul" of the organization. At this point, there is nothing left of the human person that falls outside the ambit of organizational control.

The irony is that one of the fundamental assumptions of this whole way of thinking is that of the primacy of the individual. It is assumed that an individual's mind is in his or her head and that knowledge is possessed by the individual in tacit form in his or her mind. It is the heroic individual who has the visions driving corporations. It is the heroic leader who achieves organizational success. Having placed the individual at the center of everything, however, we then talk about "human capital" as the "soul" of the organization and come to take it for granted that knowledge can be owned, measured and controlled. In the process, we reduce the human person to insignificance. I think that a very important reason why this has happened is the way we are thinking. We think that the human mind is a system, that human relationships are systems, that knowledge itself is a system. Running through mainstream thinking, and also through much of the criticism of it, there is a taken-for-granted view that there is a category called organizational knowledge and that it can and must be managed. This reflects an underlying way of thinking in which knowledge is reified, treated like a "thing" that can be possessed, that corporations can own. Knowledge creation is thought to be a system and it this view that makes it even remotely plausible, let alone ethical, to talk about managing knowledge and measuring intellectual capital.

Moving on from systems thinking

This book aims to move on from systems thinking about learning and knowledge creation in organizations to argue that knowledge arises in complex responsive processes of relating between human bodies, that knowledge itself is continuously reproduced and potentially transformed. Knowledge is not a "thing," or a system, but an ephemeral, active process of relating. If one takes this view then no one, let alone a corporation, can own knowledge. Knowledge itself cannot be stored, nor can intellectual capital be measured, and certainly neither of them can be managed. From this perspective, the mind is not a system and neither are the relationships between human persons. Instead of thinking about human acting and human relating in systemic terms, this book will be exploring a way of thinking in which individual minds, relating between people, organizations and societies are all transient processes in which human futures are perpetually constructed. The human self-conscious mind is not an "it" located and stored in an individual. Rather, individual mind arises continuously and transiently in relationships between people. Strangely enough, thinking that decenters the individual in this way actually restores the dignity of the human person and points to the capacity human relating has to pattern itself in the absence of global forms of control. Knowledge cannot be managed, and there is no need to manage it, because knowledge is participative self-organizing processes patterning themselves in coherent ways. This is the perspective of complex responsive process of relating to be explored in this book. It is not a perspective in which human agency is located *either* in the individual *or* the group/social, nor is it one in which agency is located in *both* the individual *and* the social. Human agency is not located anywhere because it is not an "it." Instead, in the perspective to be developed in this book, human agency is processes of interaction between human bodies and those processes perpetually construct themselves as continuity and potential transformation.

The first volume in this series of books (Stacey *et al.*, 2000) outlined the sources of this way of thinking. One source is *analogies* drawn from the natural complexity sciences. The first volume distinguished between two strands of thinking in the complexity sciences on the basis of their underlying theories of causality. One strand takes a Kantian view of causality in nature in which nature is assumed to unfold already enfolded forms. This causal framework was referred to as Formative Teleology, one that does not encompass an explanation of the emergence of truly novel forms. This strand of complexity thinking is an extension of systems thinking about nature. Transformative Teleology is an alternative causal framework derived from Hegel as interpreted by Mead, in which the future is understood to be under perpetual construction. This does encompass the possibility of emergent novelty and the second strand of thinking in the complexity sciences points toward it. It is this second strand of the complexity sciences that is used in this book as a source domain for analogies with human action. The main analogy to be drawn on is that of interaction. The second strand in the complexity sciences works with abstract models of interaction between abstract entities and convincingly demonstrates the possibility that interaction has the intrinsic capacity to spontaneously pattern itself in coherent ways. What if this is true of interaction, that is, relating, between human bodies? What if relating between human bodies also has the intrinsic capacity to spontaneously pattern itself in coherent ways? This book will argue that abstract interaction is analogous to human relating as understood from the perspective of a number of social psychologists, principally Mead and Elias. From this perspective, human futures are under perpetual construction through the detail of interaction between human bodies in the living present, namely, complex responsive processes of relating. This perspective represents a departure from, and a challenge to, systems thinking.

It is the purpose of this book to explore just what complex responsive processes mean and how they perpetually construct human futures, particularly how they perpetually construct human knowledge in organizations. Relating between diverse people in their local situations is understood as the process in which knowledge is perpetually reproduced and potentially transformed at the same time. This relating is understood as communicative interaction in which power relations emerge. Individual minds/selves and social relationships, individual and collective identities, are all understood as aspects of the same phenomenon, namely, relating. There is no separation between individuals as one level and groups, organizations and societies as another level. Knowledge creation is then understood as an active process of communication between humans. It follows that knowledge is not stored, but perpetually constructed. Knowledge is not shared as mental contents but perpetually arises in action. Knowledge is not transmitted from one mind to another but is the process of relating. What I am trying to do in this book, therefore, is to point to an alternative to systems thinking when it comes to understanding learning and knowledge in organizations. The shift is from whole systems to local processes in the living present.

The perspective to be explored in this book, then, focuses attention on relationships. However, it does so in a different way to some other responses that contest the extension of control ideology. Some of those others call for a return to ancient wisdom and closer links with nature, for finding a simpler way, for more caring in organizations. The perspective I will be exploring, however, is not about returning to the past and moving back to nature. Rather, it is an attempt to understand what people are currently doing in the complex, sophisticated organizations of the twenty-first century, with all their promise of increased wealth and their disturbing potential for destruction. The perspective I will be exploring is not a prescription for more caring relationships but an attempt to understand the multiple aspects of human relating as caring and not caring, and even worse, as disrespect and aggression. Yet others who focus on relationships are concerned with whole systems and seek to understand organizations as wholes. The perspective this book explores, however, is a move away from systems thinking and is, therefore, not about understanding and working with whole systems. On the contrary, it advocates focusing attention on local interactions between people. This book is not about a search for deeper levels and structures, or contact with transcendental wholes. On the contrary, it explores how we might understand the ordinary, observable communicative interactions between people in local situations in the living present.

Outline of the book

The two chapters in Part I outline the basic assumptions underlying mainstream thinking about learning and knowledge creation in organizations. The frame of reference here is that of systems thinking, including the psychological form of systems thinking, namely, cognitivism. One of the key assumptions is that the individual and the organization are different kinds of phenomenon. Although the group, team or organizational level is granted important motivational effects, it is usually assumed that it is ultimately the individual who learns and thus creates knowledge. That knowledge is thought to be located in individual heads in largely tacit form and expressed as professional skills. For knowledge to exist at the organizational level it must be shared by individuals. The issue of organizational knowledge then becomes one of transmission from one individual to another and to constitute organizational knowledge it must be extracted from individuals and stored in explicit form. Others downplay the importance of formally sanctioned, designed rules and codes of practice and elevate the role of informal stories as the location and means of sharing what an organization "knows." However, this approach mostly continues to make the same underlying assumption that individuals and organizations are different phenomena to be explained at different levels of aggregation. All that changes is the mode of transmission of knowledge between individuals and the location of organizational knowledge.

Throughout, knowledge is thought of as representations, models and maps, stored either in individual heads or in shared stories, practices and codes. Thinking, talking and acting are taken to be separate with acting flowing from talk and talk flowing from thought. Chapter 3 will argue that the split between individual and group/organization is an inappropriate one when it comes to thinking about organizational learning and knowledge creation. It will argue that individual and group are fractal processes that require to be understood at the same explanatory level. From this starting point, attention is focused upon the nature of relationships between people in an organization and the concern with sharing and transmission between individuals, with codification and technology, slips into the background. It becomes highly problematic to talk about extracting knowledge from individual heads as an activity that can be designed or managed. The whole of idea of designing the learning organization or managing organizational knowledge is called into question.

The chapters in Part II of the book develop a different theory of learning and knowledge creation in organizations, presenting an explanation of human action that is not built upon a split between the individual and the social. These chapters will argue that individual mind and the social are the same process. Mind is the action of a body, just as social relationships are and individual minds and social relationships arise together, simultaneously. Knowledge is under perpetual construction in the detail of relationships between people. It is only already formed rather than new knowledge that can be captured in explicit form, codified and stored as an organizational asset. It becomes meaningless to talk about managing the learning and knowledge creation process.

The two chapters in Part III compare the complex responsive process perspective with mainstream thinking and explore the implications of the differences. Finally, because a number of writers on knowledge management turn to the notion of autopoiesis, the Appendix explains why the theory of autopoiesis is an inappropriate source of analogy for human action.

The key conclusions are these. It is not possible to measure intellectual "capital" in any meaningful way. Even more, it is an illusion to imagine that "you," some powerful person in an organization, can manage learning and knowledge creation, quite simply because no one can manage human minds and human relationships of which knowledge is an essential aspect. The ideas of measuring and managing knowledge arise from a particular way of thinking about organizational life, which it is one of the aims of this book to question. What "you" can do, including the most powerful, is become more skillful in participating in the relationships you already participate in, in generating the knowledge you already generate with others, by paying attention in a different way. The main aim of this book is to point to ways of thinking that direct attention to different matters in different ways, that direct attention toward the complex responsive processes of relating in which knowledge is created.

Part I
The foundations of mainstream views on learning and knowledge creation in organizations: systems thinking

The two chapters in this Part outline the key assumptions, usually unquestioned, upon which reasoning about learning and knowledge creation in organizations is generally based.

First, the *organization* and its *individual* members are thought of as two *different explanatory levels* so that the question of knowledge has to be dealt with at two levels. Second, organizations themselves, as well as learning and knowledge creation by, or within them, are all thought of as *systems*. This focuses attention on interactions between sub-systems of which organizations are composed and between organizations as systems. Groups and individual members of an organization are also thought of as sub-systems, where individuals are mental systems. Third, interaction between systems and sub-systems is largely thought of in terms of the transmission of mental contents stored in the minds of individuals and then shared by them. The considerable problems inhering in these concepts of *storing, transmission* and *sharing of mental contents* are rarely addressed. Fourth, the explanation of transmission usually distinguishes between *tacit* and *explicit* mental contents as distinct categories of knowledge. The shaky foundations of this distinction are not normally subject to much scrutiny. Chapter 2 will explore these assumptions in mainstream thinking and how they are developed and critiqued.

Chapter 3 will be concerned with further exploration of the fundamental assumption, namely, the distinction between individual and organizational levels of explanation. A key concern will be that of human agency. At which level is agency to be located? In other words, where does the capacity for, the cause of, human action lie? Is it at the individual level? Or is it at the social level? Chapter 3 will question the whole idea of splitting the social and the individual and suggest that such a split creates problems that can only be overcome by abandoning it and thinking about the individual and social as one explanatory level.

This conclusion sets the scene for Part II of the book, where arguments will be presented for thinking about the social-individual as one ontological level and agency as processes, complex responsive processes of relating, that pattern themselves in the perpetual construction of the future as continuity and potential transformation. This perspective presents a significant challenge to system-based mainstream thinking about learning and knowledge creation in organizations. Such a challenge has major implications for the notion that knowledge creation can be managed.

2 Mainstream thinking about learning and knowledge creation in organizations

- Transmitting knowledge between individuals, diffusing it across an organization, and storing it in explicit forms
- Constructing knowledge and making sense in communities of practice
- Conclusion

As Chapter 1 has pointed out, the past few decades have witnessed a dramatic increase in the popularity of notions of learning and the creation and management of knowledge/intellectual capital in organizations. Two writers have played a prominent role in this growing popularity, namely, Senge's (1990) exposition of the learning organization and Nonaka's (1991; Nonaka and Takeuchi, 1995) model of knowledge creation in organizations. Senge's framework draws heavily on systems dynamics (Forrester, 1961, 1969, 1971; Meadows, 1982) in presenting the learning organization as a system; on Argyris and Schön (Argyris and Schön, 1978; Argyris 1982; Argyris *et al.*, 1985; Schön, 1983) for notions of individual mental models as well as single and double loop learning; and Bohm (1965, 1983) for the treatment of dialogue. Like Senge, Nonaka also draws on systems thinking, including some concepts from chaos and complexity theories (Gleick, 1987; Prigogine and Stengers, 1984), which he treats as extensions of that thinking, and Argyris and Schön whose learning theories he traces back to Bateson (1973). In addition, he relies heavily on Polanyi's (1958, 1960) distinction between tacit and explicit knowledge. All of these writers are widely quoted in many academic papers and also in the more popular books directed at practicing managers, leaders and consultants in organizations. I will refer to this body of work as the mainstream literature on organizational learning/knowledge creation because it has now become commonplace for academics, managers, leaders and consultants to think and talk either within its terms or in critique of it.

The main purpose of this chapter is to spell out what I see as the underlying frame of reference in mainstream literature. I will be arguing that mainstream thinking about learning and knowledge in organizations is at best limited in that, in the end, it cannot explain, within its own terms, how new knowledge is created. At best, it focuses attention on surface aspects of learning and knowledge in organizations and at worst it encourages what I see as the illusion that knowledge can be measured, captured, controlled and managed. This mainstream literature, however, does have its critics and the second purpose of this chapter is to outline the main points of critique to be found in the academic literature. I will be arguing that while some of the critiques point beyond the mainstream's underlying frame of reference, none of them actually make a fundamental move away from it. As a consequence, therefore, they do not hold out much prospect of overcoming the limitations of mainstream thinking, in my view. In the rest of the book I will be arguing for a perspective, that of complex responsive processes of relating, which seems to me to offer a way of dealing with the explanatory limitations of mainstream thinking. How one thinks about these matters is of great practical importance in the light of the time, money and effort now being directed toward the development of learning and knowledge creating organizations.

Let us now consider the principal features of mainstream thinking about learning and knowledge creation in organizations.

Transmitting knowledge between individuals, diffusing it across an organization, and storing it in explicit forms

In drawing out the main features of the underlying frame of reference in mainstream thinking, I turn to the literature already referred to above and to a sample of writers for practitioners who rely on concepts from that literature (Brown, 1991; Burton-Jones, 1999; Davenport and Prusak, 1998; Garven, 1993; Kleiner and Roth, 1997; Leonard and Strauss, 1997; Quinn *et al.*, 1996; Sveiby, 1997).

The first point to note throughout this body of work is the fundamental split it posits between the individual and the organization, or the social. The individual and the organizational/social are always treated as two distinct phenomenal levels requiring different explanations of how learning and knowledge creation take place. The connection between the two levels is usually understood as follows. Individuals in interaction with each other together create the levels of organization and society, and those collective levels constitute the context within which individuals act. In other words, individuals construct organizational/social levels, which then act back to affect those individuals. It is usually explicitly stated that it is individuals who learn and create knowledge, although this is almost always coupled with an emphasis on the importance of the teams within which that individual learning takes place. A key question then becomes whether a team, group or organization can be said to learn or whether it is just their individual members who do so. In mainstream thinking, in the end, it is usually individuals who learn and create knowledge and the principal concern from an organizational perspective is, then, how that individual learning and knowledge might be shared across an organization and how it might be captured, stored and retained by the organization. Sometimes, the group/social level is treated as a kind of transcendental group mind, common pool of meaning, or flow of a larger intelligence, for example, in Senge's treatment of Bohm's notion of dialogue.

In Figure 2.1, I have summarized in graphical form what I understand to be the key elements of explanations of learning and knowledge creation in mainstream thinking, taking account of both individual and organizational levels. This is of course a gross simplification of rather sophisticated concepts that have certainly taken thinking about organizations forward. That sophistication is inevitably lost in the simplification I put forward but, I would argue, there is a gain in the form of clarity about the underlying frame of reference and the usually implicit assumptions upon which it is built. The rest of this section consists of a description of the key features depicted in Figure 2.1.

As I have said, mainstream explanations usually assume that it is individuals who learn and that they learn most effectively in teams having particular characteristics. Figure 2.1 simplifies this view by depicting two individuals, A and B, engaged in some form of learning together. At the center of Figure 2.1 there is the action each takes in relation to the other. It is a central assumption of mainstream thinking that learning and knowledge creation involve the transmission of knowledge. This notion derives from information theory (Shannon and Weaver, 1949) and it posits a sender–receiver model of knowledge transmission in which individual A sends some kind of signal to individual B, who receives it and then sends a responding signal back to individual A. It is usual to classify these signals into a number of categories distinguishing between data, information, knowledge, insight or wisdom, and action (for example, see Davenport and Prusak, 1998). The definitions of these

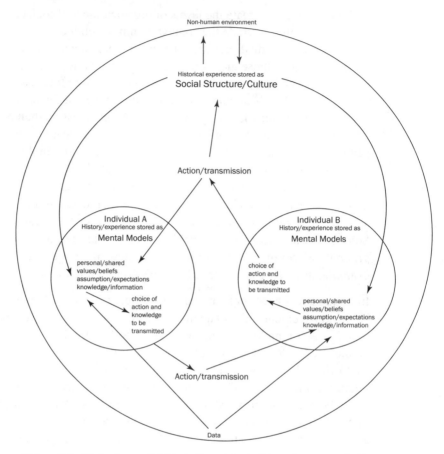

Figure 2.1 *Mainstream thinking: the system of learning and knowledge creation*

categories reveal a great deal about the underlying frame of reference in mainstream thinking:

- Data are usually defined as a set of discrete objective facts about events.
- Information is then data that make a difference. It is a message passed from a sender to a receiver that shapes the perception of the receiver. Information has a meaning; it has a shape and it is organized for some purpose. Data become information when the creator of information adds meaning to the data.
- Knowledge is taken to be a framework for evaluating and incorporating new experiences and information. This framework originates in the mind of the knower and it is formed by past experience as well as by

current values and beliefs. It is stored as memory in fluid and structured forms. It may be explicit or tacit, a distinction to be examined later on in this section, and it is transmitted from one knower to another. Insight and wisdom are sometimes classified under knowledge and sometimes regarded as higher forms of more intuitive knowing. In other words, knowledge is equated with the notion of mental models to be described below.

- Action is a choice made on the basis of knowledge and that knowledge is evaluated in the light of the consequences of the decisions and actions it leads to. This is a systemic, error-activated notion of learning.

The next point to note is how it is assumed that data, information and knowledge are transmitted from one individual to another and it is here that the distinction between explicit and tacit knowledge (Nonaka and Takeuchi, 1995) becomes particularly important:

- Explicit knowledge is formal, systematic knowledge, easily transmitted from one person to another in the form of language (verbal, mathematical and numerical). What is transmitted is thought of as a translation of already existing tacit knowledge into language, that is, into a codified form. Immediately, a particular assumption is being made about the nature of language, namely, that it is a formal, objective system of symbols located outside people and employed by them as a tool to translate already existing ideas and concepts into a form that can be readily transmitted to others. Criticisms of this view will be taken up in Chapter 5.
- Tacit knowledge is particularly important in this way of thinking. It is personal in the sense of being located in the minds of individuals. It is, therefore, a subjective phenomenon of insight, intuition and hunches, below the level of awareness. It is, therefore, hard to formalize and communicate. It is rooted in action and shows itself as skill or know-how, lying in the beliefs and perspectives ingrained in the way people understand their world and act in it. In other words, tacit knowledge takes the form of mental models that are below the level of awareness.

New knowledge

New knowledge is said to come from tapping the tacit knowledge located in individual heads and this process of tapping is understood as one of translating the tacit knowledge in individual heads into explicit forms.

Mainstream thinking focuses attention on this process of translation but does not explain how completely new tacit knowledge comes to arise in individual heads. The explanation starts from the point where some individual already possesses important tacit knowledge. For an approach claiming to explain the creation of knowledge, this is a major limitation. What is explained is how some novelty arising in an unexplained way is subsequently transmitted to others so that it can become organizational knowledge. This knowledge may be "new" to the organization but it is not "new" *per se*. The transfer of knowledge is said to take place as movement between tacit and explicit forms.

New knowledge, arising in an unexplained way in some individual, is transferred as movement in tacit form from one individual to another. This movement takes place through a process of mimicry. The possessor of tacit knowledge expresses it in the form of skilled action, that is, as the professional, expert, mentor or teacher. The acquirer of this tacit knowledge observes, copies and practices the skilled action of the expert, thus internalizing and learning it. Having acquired the tacit knowledge through this process of mimicry, the now skilled novice may translate it into explicit form for communication to others. This step of translating tacit into explicit knowledge is recognized as being problematic because it requires expressing the inexpressible. The translation therefore requires the figurative language of metaphor and analogy to bring what is below the level of awareness into awareness.

This is where it becomes important to work and learn in teams. How members of those teams relate to each other, how they converse with each other and what kind of language they use, all become important matters. Once tacit knowledge has been made explicit, then others must internalize it so that it becomes part of their tacit store. Or the explicit knowledge may be embodied in working models and prototypes of one form or another, in cultural artifacts, or in written and unwritten codes and procedures. As knowledge is dispersed through an organization by this process of movement between tacit and explicit, it must be tested and this requires discussion, dialogue and disagreement. Some distinguish between discussion and dialogue, where the former is a competitive form of conversation and the latter a cooperative one in which people suspend their assumptions and learn collectively far more than they can learn individually (Senge, 1990; Bohm, 1983).

Transmitting knowledge

From a mainstream perspective, therefore, learning and knowledge creation are basically a process of transmission between individuals in which data is converted into information through the medium of knowledge, which may be explicit but, far more importantly, may be tacit. The transmission of knowledge between people is a process of conversion between tacit and explicit forms based on mimicry in tacit–tacit transfers, group dialogue and discussion in metaphorical and analogical language in tacit–explicit transfers, formalization and codification in explicit–explicit transfers, and internalization in explicit–tacit transfers. Knowledge is understood to move in this way through the interplay of individual and group/organizational/social levels.

The individual level: mental models

Figure 2.1 depicts the individual level as two circles labeled individual A and individual B. In mainstream thinking, an individual mind is understood in terms of mental models. These are an individual's assumptions, expectations, knowledge and information about the world of other people and relationships with them, as well as about the non-human world in which the individual lives and acts. They are values and beliefs of the individual, some of which may be shared with others and some of which may be unique to that individual. They are representations of the world and the individual self in that world, which are historically determined by the experience of the individual and lie largely below the level of awareness.

This understanding of mind is drawn from cognitivist psychology, which holds mind to be a function of the human brain (McCulloch and Pitts, 1943; Gardner, 1985). The brain, according to this approach, forms representations of external reality, structures them into patterns, or models, which are stored in memory, and then later retrieved in order to process new sense data encountered by the individual. Mental models, then, provide the means for an individual to process data about the world and the means for making a choice of actions to take. Mainstream thinking, therefore, is based on a very particular view of the nature of mind and of the functioning of the brain. It is a view in which the mind and the brain of which it is a function, form representations, store them in memory, process information and data and then make a choice. It is a theory in which thought and choice precede action. All of these assumptions are taken for granted.

A particular theory of learning flows from this view of individual mind and in mainstream thinking this is derived through Argyris and Schön (1978) and Bateson (1973). An individual learns in a single loop manner when choices of action, or choices of information and knowledge to be transmitted to others, are made on the basis of given mental models. Learning here consists of the error-activated adjusting of choice in the light of its consequences. However, as the world changes, given mental models may become inappropriate and action choices will consequently be faulty. This situation requires double loop learning, which means that it is not simply choice that is adjusted but also the basis for choice, namely, the mental models. This error-activated process of changing mental models is one of raising tacit assumptions, values and beliefs to the level of awareness and changing them. However, this is a difficult process that normally requires interaction with others, hence the importance attached to learning in teams through discussion and dialogue. Such learning is also performed on the basis of mental models; this time models of the learning process itself. According to Argyris and Schön there are typically two different models of learning. Learning Model I is a set of tacit assumptions that lead individuals into a debating mode in which they seek to win and not lose and in which they withhold information in order not to hurt others or embarrass themselves. Learning Model I blocks the process of double loop learning. When Learning Model II is deployed, however, people enter into true dialogue and this enables double loop learning.

The social level: routines and sharing knowledge

The process of learning and knowledge creation also involves the group/organizational/social level. Figure 2.1 depicts a loop in which the actions of individuals toward each other and the knowledge, information and data they transmit to each other, become shared routines, that is, stored in the form of culture, social structure, organizational procedures, traditions, habits and group norms. These are historically built up in past experience. They may be stored in cultural artifacts as well as written or unwritten forms. They are usually understood to be explicit, although they are sometimes talked about as a group mind, implying something tacit as well. They constitute a level above that of the individual, which forms the social context within which individuals live, act and relate to each other. That higher level consists of sets of shared assumptions, beliefs and behaviors which are internalized by individuals as part of their individual mental models, depicted as the loops running from social structure to the mental models of individuals A and B. Sometimes, as in Bohm's discussion of dialogue, it is a kind of group mind or larger intelligence that shapes mental maps.

The split between the individual and the social

In mainstream thinking, then, there is a circular, systemic interaction between individuals at one level and the group/organization/society at a higher level. The nature of this circular interaction is considered to be of central importance to the possibility of learning and knowledge creation. It is widely held that effective learning and knowledge creation require widespread sharing of values to do with openness, trust, affirmation, dialogue and empowerment. Effectiveness of these processes is also said to require particular forms of leadership that establish values of this kind and provide a central vision to guide the learning and knowledge creation process. It is recognized that it is difficult to establish and sustain group, organizational and societal relationships of this kind, and mainstream thinking is concerned with some of the obstacles to the required leadership and value formations required.

Political activity is usually regarded as an obstacle and Argyris's (1990) views on how organizational politics obstruct learning and knowledge creation are now widely accepted. He argues that behavior according to Learning Model I amounts to what he calls organizational defense routines. In order to defend against the fear of embarrassing themselves or hurting others, people have a strong tendency to render contentious matters undiscussable. They have a tendency to espouse values conducive to learning while acting in accordance with their opposite. Instead of open disclosure, people only reveal what they really think and feel in informal settings behind closed doors and engage in personal politicking, which is said to be antithetical to learning and knowledge creation. The remedy is greater openness and true dialogue requiring concerted action to overcome the natural disinclination of individuals to share knowledge.

The circular, systemic interaction between individuals and group/organizational/social contexts, takes place within a non-human environment, depicted in Figure 2.1 as the outer circle. This environment generates data that are understood in terms of individual mental models and, of course, that environment is also affected by the group/ organization/society level.

Over the past few years, developments in the natural complexity sciences have attracted the attention of some writers concerned with organizational knowledge. The tendency, however, is to regard the complexity sciences as an extension of systems thinking. This way of thinking about the implications of the complexity sciences for human action does not lead to any significant change in the underlying frame of reference described in this section (for the development of this argument see Stacey *et al.*, 2000). As an example, let us take the work of Boisot (1998).

A perspective on complexity and knowledge creation

Boisot adopts the mainstream definition of knowledge as the capacity to act and says that it is built on information that is extracted from data. Effective action is dependent upon representations that connect with the real world and those representations are formed into schemata (mental models) to make sense of the world. Knowledge creation is a process of generating insight by extracting information from data and the application of knowledge is the testing of these insights. Knowledge constitutes an asset that yields a stream of useful services. Its distinctive feature is that it can be shared with others and retained at the same time. There is no questioning of, or departure from mainstream thinking here.

One of Boisot's principal concerns is with the conditions in which knowledge will flow, that is, be shared with others, and those in which it will not. In some circumstances, knowledge diffuses naturally, while in others it does not, and understanding these circumstances is essential to mastering knowledge. He claims that knowledge flows between people, that is, it is fluid, when it is context-free, codified, abstract and stripped of unnecessary data. When knowledge is data rich, qualitative, ambiguous and context-dependent, then it is viscous and flows hardly at all. Over time, as one gets to understand something, viscous knowledge becomes more fluid knowledge, enhanced by personal experience and idiosyncratic interpretation as it is embedded in individual minds. However, people find this fluid knowledge hard to share. Codification is then required to diffuse the knowledge in an organization. However, this makes it more accessible to competitors and thus less valuable.

Knowledge assets, therefore, have this paradoxical aspect: they must be codified if they are to become an asset but once this happens, they lose value. Effective strategies must, therefore, be developed to manage this paradox. Knowledge assets are built through learning, that is, an ability to exploit knowledge flows, both fluid and viscous, in adaptive ways. The extent to which knowledge is shared defines culture: bureaucracies do not share knowledge but markets do. Clearly, Boisot adopts a sender–receiver view of knowledge and his main concern is with how top managers should manage an organization's knowledge assets. Again, these arguments are well within the frame of reference of mainstream thinking.

Boisot then draws on notions from the complexity sciences, which he understands as extensions of systems thinking. For him, individuals are information processors who pay an evolutionary price for complexity production, where complexity is an increase in data. Below a certain level of complexity, human information processing capacity is fossilized and an increased intake of data is required. Boisot calls this complexity absorption. However, above a certain limit, the human processor runs into processing and storage limits and faces the chaos of processing breakdown. Here complexity reduction is required, that is, shedding some data and incorporating other data into information structures by acts of insight. If the capacity to learn is to be maintained, "ingested" data must be "metabolized" so as to reduce the complexity, or discharge entropy. Boisot then defines the state between complexity absorption and complexity reduction as the "edge of chaos."

Complexity absorption leads to a steady flow of tacit, experiential knowledge locked up in people's heads, while complexity reduction produces a flow of codified, or explicit, knowledge. Innovative knowledge creation occurs in-between, at the "edge of chaos." Boisot uses a phase space metaphor to talk about the Information Space. This is a three-dimensional space defined by a movement from abstract to concrete on one axis, undiffused to diffused along the second axis, and uncodified to codified along the third axis. Knowledge moves around this space from personal (concrete, undiffused and uncodified) to proprietary (abstract, undiffused but codified), textbook (abstract, diffused and codified) and common sense (concrete, diffused and codified). Proprietary knowledge controlled by the center of an organization is defined as order while personal knowledge is defined as chaos. In between there is complexity or dissipative structures of knowledge.

What Boisot is doing here, it seems to me, is taking some terminology from the natural complexity sciences to describe exactly the same system of knowledge flow as that found in mainstream thinking, which does not appeal at all to the complexity sciences. There is the same system of flows between tacit and explicit knowledge, now relabeled with terms taken from the complexity sciences. Not surprisingly, much the same conclusions follow.

If value is to be extracted from knowledge assets, then they must be managed as they emerge, wax and wane. To do this, complexity and uncertainty must be reduced; otherwise tacit knowledge remains in people's heads and cannot be transferred into an organizational asset. Managers can choose learning orientations for an organization to prevent this happening. The Information Space of an organization can be mapped in order to analyze its technological posture, that is, the configuration of its knowledge assets. Having interpreted the Information Space map, managers can then take action to alter it in beneficial ways.

How mainstream thinking focuses attention: prescriptions for managing learning and knowledge

In the mainstream thinking briefly summarized above, organizations are taken to be learning, knowledge-generating systems of individuals interacting with each other in group/social contexts. Individuals and contexts are taken to be two distinct phenomenological levels interacting with each other to form the whole system. It is then taken for granted that these whole knowledge-generating systems must be managed in some way in order to optimize, or at least improve, their functioning.

This perspective quite naturally focuses attention in two ways. First, the immediate concern is with explicit knowledge since it is clearly difficult to talk about directly managing tacit knowledge. However, since mainstream thinking locates the origination of knowledge in tacit forms located in individual minds, the second concern is with the indirect management of tacit knowledge through managing the individuals who possess it. Consider each of these concerns and the kinds of prescriptions that they lead to.

Since knowledge is ultimately located in individual minds, organizational management requires the conversion of this individual knowledge into explicit forms and their location at the level of the organization. This leads to prescriptions to do with codifying and proceduralizing knowledge so that it is available to all members of the organization and not susceptible to loss when individuals leave it. Informal relationships as a means of generating and retaining knowledge are mistrusted and dismissed because they are so fragile and susceptible to loss through people leaving. Knowledge generated in informal ways is not regarded as being really organizational knowledge but purely personal knowledge. This is felt to be a problem because of the link mainstream thinking draws between organizational knowledge, regarded as intellectual capital, and the stock market valuation of corporations. Organizational knowledge, then, is considered to be that which can be codified, measured in some way and stored in databases accessible to those who need to use it. This leads to a great interest in information technology and information systems. It also leads to interest in measuring intellectual capital and presenting the measurements to stock market analysts in the hope of managing corporate valuations.

In the end, however, the organizational level cannot avoid dependency on the individual for knowledge generation. The second strand of prescriptions, therefore, is concerned with how to manage the individuals who possess tacit knowledge. This is expressed in prescriptions for managing professionals and experts (for example, see Quinn *et al.*, 1996). Attention is focused on recruiting the best people in the belief that a small elite can make all the difference. Once recruited, however, these professionals and experts must be frequently appraised and evaluated in order to weed out those who are not performing well. This requires systems for appraisal and feedback. It is quite usual to link these prescriptions with ones to do with designing incentive systems, forcing the development of professionals and pushing them beyond their comfort zones in the belief that this promotes creativity. This is sometimes supported by appeals to the notion of the "edge of chaos," implicitly understood as crisis. Challenges should be increased in demanding environments that are intolerant of non-optimal performance, which is to be frequently revealed by audits. Visionary leadership is called for to motivate professionals in such demanding environments and overcome their reluctance to share their knowledge. Dialogue, as a special form of relating, is to be used as a tool to develop knowledge.

These forms of management control are frequently linked to calls for a shift in organizational design from hierarchical structures to network organizations consisting of webs of self-managing professionals with shared interests and common values.

Review of mainstream thinking: the learning/knowledge creating system and its underlying assumptions

The underlying frame of reference in mainstream theory and application with regard to learning and knowledge creation in organizations is clearly that of systems thinking. Mainstream theory postulates a circular interaction between the level of the individuals and the level of the group/organization/social, all functioning within a non-human environment, with which there is also a circular connection. At the individual sub-system level there is interaction between individuals, where each individual mind is also thought of in systems terms as mental models that process sense data, converting them into information and knowledge. This view of the mind is based upon a theory of brain functioning in which the brain also is thought of as a system for processing and storing information. The psychological assumptions are drawn from cognitivist psychology, which is a systems theory of human action that has close intellectual links with systems theories of the cybernetic kind. The underlying theory of learning is a systems view of learning as basically an error correcting process. Knowledge creation is thought of as a sender–receiver system in which knowledge is created by converting tacit knowledge into explicit, transmitting that explicit knowledge to others, who convert it back into tacit knowledge. Language is understood as a system used for translating tacit concepts into words and other symbols.

The prescriptions are all to do with designing and installing systems: those to store explicit knowledge in routines and procedures, artifacts and databases; those to monitor, evaluate and provide incentives for individuals who possess the tacit knowledge required by an organization; those to design special forms of conversation called dialogue. Throughout the discussion on theory and prescription, there are frequent appeals to systems theories, explicitly and implicitly, as writers describe and prescribe stocks and flows of knowledge, feedback processes and other features of systems.

The first volume in this series, *Complexity and Management: Fad or Radical Challenge to Systems Thinking?*, argued that systems theories amount to an explication of Kantian notions of causality. Drawing on Kantian philosophy, that volume presented a dual theory of causality and argued that it is this dual theory that underlies systems thinking. The first element of this duality is Rationalist Teleology, which basically holds that the cause of human action is human motivation expressed in autonomously chosen goals and means of achieving them, arrived at through rational reasoning expressing ethical universals. The second element of this duality is Formative Teleology, which is a systemic theory of causality in which a system unfolds patterns of behavior that are already enfolded in its structure in movement to a mature state that can be known in advance. The main features of these two theories of causality are summarized in Box 2.1.

Box 2.1 Definitions of Rationalist Teleology and Formative Teleology

	Rationalist Teleology	*Formative Teleology*
Movement toward a future that is:	a goal chosen by reasoning autonomous humans	a mature form implied at the start of movement or in the movement. Implies a final state that can be known in advance
Movement for the sake of:	realizing chosen goals	revealing, realizing or sustaining a mature or final form of identity, of self. This is actualization of form or self that is already there in some sense
The process of movement or construction, that is, the cause is:	the rational process of human reason, expressing ethical universals, reflected as human values. Cause is human motivation	the process of unfolding a whole already enfolded in the nature, principles or rules of interaction. This is a macro-process of iteration, that is, formative cause
Kind of self-organization implied:	none	repetitive unfolding of macro-pattern already enfolded in micro-interaction
Nature and origin of variation/change is:	designed change through rational exercise of human choice to get it right in terms of universals	shift from one given form to another due to context. Change is stages of development given in advance
Origin of freedom and nature of constraint:	human freedom finds concrete expression on the basis of ethical universals	no intrinsic freedom, constrained by given forms

The mainstream theory of learning and knowledge creation in organizations is a systems theory and like other systems theories it implicitly assumes the dual causal structure of Rationalist and Formative Teleology. The learning and knowledge creating system depicted in Figure 2.1 is basically one in which tacit knowledge already stored in the heads of some individuals, already enfolded as it were, is unfolded by processes of conversion. Mental models are already there, as are the learning models according to which they are supposed to be changed and so are the visions that are supposed to guide the learning and knowledge creation of the whole system. System archetypes (Senge, 1990) are already there. Bohm's "common pool of meaning" is an implicate, hidden order that is already there.

However, by definition, this systems perspective cannot succeed on its own as an explanation of how new knowledge is created. It can only explain how already enfolded knowledge is unfolded by the system. Within its own terms this systems view does not, indeed cannot, explain how completely novel knowledge arises. It simply assumes that it arises as tacit knowledge in the heads of some individuals, or exists in a common pool of meaning, and the explanation starts from there. The same point applies to the requirement for a vision to guide the functioning of the system. There, too, there is no explanation within systems thinking itself of how such a guiding vision is formed. It follows that the origin of novel knowledge, and of the vision supposed to guide it, lies outside the system and it is here that Rationalist Teleology is relied upon. It is special individuals, an elite, standing outside the system, who make autonomous choices. This becomes very clear when one considers the prescriptions since they mainly have to do with designing systems of one kind or another by individuals who stand outside the systems and choose their designs. The choices arise in dialogue that employs metaphor and analogy as well as rational reasoning but there is little explanation of the origins of creativity within that dialogue. In the end, even the move from Formative to Rationalist Teleology fails to explain how truly new knowledge is created.

The frame of reference underlying mainstream thinking about learning and knowledge creation, then, is systems thinking with its dual causal framework of Formative and Rationalist Teleology. I summarize these implicit assumptions below in a way that suggests a unified, tidy consensus. However, within mainstream thinking there are, of course, differences and contradictions. Furthermore, in listing the assumptions below I am giving my interpretation of what seems to me to be the implicit assumptions. Mainstream thinkers do not normally reflect upon the underlying causal framework, or the "both/and" thinking with its split between individual and social that this implies. To summarize, then, the main underlying assumptions implicit in the mainstream frame of reference seem to me to be the following:

- *Assumption 1.* The human brain makes representations of a pre-given external reality and forms them into neural maps that are stored and later retrieved to process subsequent data.
- *Assumption 2.* Individual mind is a function of the individual brain consisting of representations of reality structured into mental models.
- *Assumption 3.* Mental contents are translated into language and transmitted to others so that they can be shared through the process of mimicry. In other words, the model of communication is that of the sender–receiver kind.
- *Assumption 4.* Thought comes before action and is a form of processing information in accordance with mental models.
- *Assumption 5.* Individual learning and knowledge creation are equated with changes in individual mental models.
- *Assumption 6.* Knowledge takes either a tacit or an explicit form and knowledge creation is essentially a system of flows between the two categories. For organizations it is the explicit form that is of primary importance, that is, knowledge that is codified and proceduralized. Mimicry is essential to the process of transmitting knowledge from one person to another.
- *Assumption 7.* The social is assumed to be a separate phenomenon created by individual interactions and acting back on those interactions in the form of their context. The social level consists of routines, procedures, cultures, and so on, which are shared by individuals, that is, which feature in their individual mental models. Or, an assumption is made of some kind of group mind.
- *Assumption 8.* In this split between the individual and the social as different levels of phenomena, it is the individual that is primary in the sense that it is ultimately in individual minds that new knowledge is created.
- *Assumption 9.* Linked to the split between the individual and the social is the dual causality typical of systems thinking. Both the social and the individual mind are understood as systems subject to Formative Teleology in that the system unfolds a future enfolded in it. However, any change in the system is due to some action taken outside it by autonomous humans governed by Rationalist Teleology.

- *Assumption 10*. Emotion is thought of as separate from reason. Feelings tend to be thought of as either negative, in which case they block knowledge creation, or as positive, in which case they motivate learning. Feelings are treated in normative prescriptive ways expressing a call for the abolition of negative feelings and the fostering of positive ones of togetherness, caring and community. Emotion and feelings are not understood as essentially paradoxical, positive and negative at the same time, or as essential aspects of the process of learning and knowledge creation. Similarly, power, politics and informal personal relationships are usually all thought of as obstacles to learning and knowledge creation, rather than aspects of one process of knowledge creation and destruction.

These assumptions have been challenged in the literature on management and organizations in a number of ways. What the challenges have in common is that they all take issue with Assumptions 1 and 2 listed above, proposing that instead of simply representing reality, individual minds actively construct the worlds they perceive and act on.

Constructing knowledge and making sense in communities of practice

There are a number of significant developments and criticisms of the mainstream thinking outlined in the previous section:

- First, there is psychoanalytic thinking about organizations. This emphasizes the importance of unconscious processes, emotion, fantasy and informal personal relationships in the construction of perceptions. These are mainly understood to constitute obstacles to learning and knowledge creation. What is being challenged or developed here relates to Assumptions 1, 2 and 10 above.
- Second, there are critics of the notion of mental models as representations and the suggestion that brain–mind is an autopoietic system. This leads to the notion that individual minds actively create, or enact, a world. This is a direct challenge to Assumptions 1 and 2 in mainstream thinking.
- Third, there are those who point to the individual-centered learning theory expressed in mainstream literature and move toward more socially constructed views of learning and knowledge creation. Similar to this in some respects is the perspective of sense-making in

organizations and the enactment of organizational realities. Again, it is Assumptions 1 and 2 above that are being developed or challenged. Some also question Assumptions 8 and 10 above.

Each of these developments and critiques is reviewed in the following sub-sections. I will be making the point that although some of the assumptions underlying the mainstream frame of reference are seriously questioned, none of the developments reviewed here challenge Assumptions 7 and 9. In other words, all these developments and critiques proceed within the framework of systems thinking, arguing on the basis of the assumed split between social and individual and thus implicitly assuming the dual causality of Formative and Rationalist Teleology.

Unconscious processes as obstacles to learning and knowledge creation

A number of writers (for example, Hirschhorn, 1990; Shapiro and Carr, 1991; Oberholzer and Roberts, 1994; Gabriel, 1999) adopt a psychoanalytic view of organizations in which they stress the importance of unconscious group processes in blocking the learning and knowledge creation process in organizations. Mainstream thinking ignores processes of this kind and thus presents a picture that ignores potential obstacles of great importance. Psychoanalytic writers point to how individuals elaborate their perceptions of reality in fantasy and so distort their perceptions of reality as a basis for action. In other words, this is an argument against some fundamental assumptions of mainstream thinking (Assumptions 1 and 2 above) that minds accurately represent reality. The psychoanalytic argument is one in which minds unconsciously create, in fantasy, what they respond to.

The early developers of this perspective worked together at the Tavistock Institute and the work of Miller and Rice (1967) was particularly influential in this development. Miller and Rice thought of a group of people as an open system (von Bertalanffy, 1968) in which individuals, also seen as open systems, interact with each other at two levels. At one level they contribute to the group's purpose, thus constituting a sophisticated (work) group, and at the other level, they develop feelings and attitudes about each other, the group and its environment, thus constituting a more primitive group, driven by unconscious basic assumptions of fight–flight, dependency and pairing (Bion, 1961a). Both of these modes of relating are operative at the same time: when the basic assumption mode takes the form of a background emotional atmosphere, it may well support the work of the group but when it predominates, it is destructive of the group's work. Individuals, then, are thought of as open systems relating to each across their individual boundary regions, thus constituting a group, which is also thought of as an open system with a permeable boundary region. Furthermore, an intersystemic perspective is adopted in which an organization is thought of as one open system interacting with individuals and groupings of them as other open systems.

Organizations are seen as task systems in that they have primary tasks, which they must perform if they are to survive. Learning and knowledge creation could be thought of as such a primary task. The primary task requires people to take up roles in order for it to be carried out and the enterprise, or task system, imports these roles across its boundary with the system consisting of individuals and groupings of them. Roles and relationship between roles fall within the boundary of the task system but groups and individuals, with their personal relationships, personal power plays and human needs not derived from the task system's primary task, fall outside it, constituting individual/group systems. The latter always operate in two modes at the same time: work mode and basic assumption mode.

When the individual/group systems have the characteristics of a sophisticated group with basic assumption behavior as a supportive background atmosphere, then they export functional roles to the task system and the latter can perform its primary task. When, however, the individual/group systems are flooded with basic assumption behavior, they export that behavior into the task system thus disrupting the performance of primary task. Part of the organization as task system, a sub-system of it, might be set up to contain imported basic assumption behavior such as fight. Its primary task is then to operate as an organizational defense that allows the rest of the task system to carry out its primary task. In the absence of such organizational defenses, the task system imports fantasies and behaviors that are destructive of the primary task. These undesirable imports may be reduced by: clarity of task; clearly defined roles and authority relationships between them, all related to task; appropriate leadership regulation at the boundary of the task system; procedures and structures that form social defenses against anxiety; and high levels of individual maturity and autonomy.

This psychoanalytic perspective, therefore, takes issue with Assumption 10 above by incorporating the effects of emotion, fantasy, unconscious group processes and informal relationships as obstacles to learning and knowledge creation seen as primary tasks. It also takes a different view of the nature of mind (Assumptions 1 and 2 above), understanding mind not simply as processes of representing an external reality but as processes of fantasy, repression, and so on, which construct an "inner world" in which perceptions of reality may well be distorted. In other words, individuals are constructing much of the world in which they act. Clearly, however, this argument applied to organizations proceeds within the framework of systems thinking, splits the individual and the social, accords primacy to the individual and implicitly assumes the dual causality of Formative and Rationalist Teleology.

Autopoiesis, enactment, and sense-making in organizations

Other ways of thinking also move away from the notion that the mind accurately represents reality and then stores those representations for later use in perception. Some neuroscientists (for example, Freeman 1994, 1995; Freeman and Schneider, 1982; Freeman and Barrie, 1994; Skarda and Freeman, 1990; Barrie et al., 1994; Kelso, 1995) question the notion that the brain represents and stores in the way assumed by mainstream thinking. I will take their criticisms up again in Chapter 4 but here I want to point to the work of the biologists, Maturana and Varela (1992), since their work has been taken up by a number of writers on organizational knowledge (for example, Roos et al., 1997).

Maturana and Varela present evidence for their view that the brain does not simply register stimuli but creates patterns associated with them. The brain does not process information or act as a passive mirror of reality to form more or less accurate representations of the world. Instead, it is perturbed, or triggered, by external stimuli into actively constructing global patterns of electrochemical activity. Furthermore, these patterns are not stored in specific parts of the brain because each time a stimulus is presented to the body, the brain constructs a pattern anew that involves whole ensembles of neurons in many different parts of the brain. This leads Maturana and Varela to conclude that the nervous system does not simply represent a world; rather, it creates, calls forth, or enacts a world. The world people act in is the world they have created by acting in it. This is the notion of enactment, namely, a process of selecting, or calling forth a world. Humans do not simply perceive a pre-given world in the only possible way, building up more and more accurate representations of it but, rather, they select those sense perceptions they are biologically and socially enabled to select. In other words, Maturana and Varela adopt a constructivist, or at times a social constructivist, perspective rather than the cognitivist one underlying mainstream thinking.

This view of brain functioning is linked to Maturana and Varela's notion of autopoietic systems (see Appendix for a review and critique of this concept in relation to organizations). An autopoietic system consists of components whose behaviour, or structure, is formed by the system's "organization" or "identity." Such systems have no task, goal or purpose other than maintaining their own identity. The identity defines and limits the interrelations between, and the nature of, the system's essential components in accordance with what is necessary to reproduce or replace that identity. In this way the system is closed, self-referential, self-producing, self-contained, and self-sustaining. It maintains the same identity, unity, and autonomy. Although an autopoietic system can change its structure, any change in identity amounts to a disintegration or destruction of the system. Structural change in autopoietic systems is possible because they are structurally coupled, that is open, to other systems that constitute their environment. However, the way in which the structural components are rearranged is completely determined by the system's own internal processes, that is, its organizationally closed identity.

The perspective presented by Maturana and Varela is important to thinking about knowledge creation in a number of ways. It provides a serious challenge to the cognitivist underpinnings of mainstream thinking, questioning Assumptions 1 and 2. As an alternative, it presents a view of mental process as one of perpetual construction, thereby moving away from the notion that brains faithfully represent an external reality and also any idea of the brain as storing and retrieving representations in any simple way. The Maturana and Varela perspective brings bodily action to the forefront and develops the notion of enactment, that is, of humans acting into what they have constructed. However, the individual is still held to be primary and the theory is still a systems theory. The constructivist position is not inconsistent with the notion of mental models since it can be taken to be an alternative way of understanding how mental models are constructed. The social is still another level compared to the individual and the same dual causality continues to be implicitly assumed. The autopoietic system of mind, and of the social, unfolds a future enfolded in the identity of the system.

Some have incorporated the work of Maturana and Varela into their thinking about knowledge creation and the management of intellectual capital (for example, Roos *et al.*, 1997). They draw on this work to conclude that knowledge is always located in the individual and created within autopoietic brains. For them, knowledge is always tacit and what is called explicit knowledge is data that helps other to create their own knowledge. These writers, then, take up the points made about brain functioning to argue against a view of knowledge as the structuring of representations about an external pre-given reality. This leads them to focus their attention even more firmly on the individual and they then proceed very much within mainstream thinking.

Toward socially constructed perspectives on learning and knowledge creation in organizations

The tacit–explicit distinction is central to the mainstream systems perspective on learning and knowledge creation in organizations. Double loop learning is a process of bringing into awareness, that is, making explicit, mental models that are below the level of awareness, that is implicit or tacit, and changing them by a conscious act of choice. Double loop learning, therefore, is a process of conversion between tacit and explicit knowledge. Knowledge creation is also thought of as a process of conversion: from tacit to tacit through mimicry; from tacit to explicit and from explicit to explicit through articulation in the form of prototypes and models; from explicit to tacit through processes of teaching and learning. Serious critique of the plausibility of this conversion process, therefore, amounts to a significant undermining of the whole mainstream framework.

Tsoukas (1997) shows how Polanyi (Polanyi, 1958, 1960; Polanyi and Prosch, 1975) actually argued that tacit and explicit knowledge are not two separate forms of knowledge, but rather, inseparable and necessary components of all knowledge. It therefore makes little sense to talk about converting one form into the other and back again. Linked to this point, Tsoukas also takes issue with the way in which mainstream thinking privileges propositional knowledge over narrative knowledge. Propositional knowledge takes the form of if-then statements of the kind found, for example, in the natural sciences, in the design of technologies and in the procedures of organizations. In emphasizing the articulation of explicit knowledge in the form of models, prototypes, codes and procedures, mainstream thinking privileges propositional knowledge. Narrative knowledge takes the form of anecdotes and stories, interspersed with evaluations of them. Tsoukas argues that narrative knowledge is just as important as propositional knowledge, if not more so, when it comes to life in organizations. Focusing attention on narrative and storytelling immediately brings the relational aspect of knowledge to the fore because narratives and stories are socially constructed between people rather than being simply located in individual minds.

Those taking up this line of criticism emphasize the importance of narrative and storytelling (for example, Boje, 1991, 1994, 1995), as well as conversation in organizations (for example, Shotter, 1993; Boden, 1994; Grant et al., 1998). Linked to these ideas is the notion of communities of practice (Lave and Wenger, 1991; Brown and Duguid, 1991). Here knowledge is created in the stories a community of practitioners tell each other. Looked at in this way, knowledge is embedded in the ordinary everyday conversation between people. It is primarily localized and contextual, distributed through an organization rather than centralized in data banks, and embedded in the stories people tell each other about their experience, stories that interactively create their experience. Socially constructed views of this kind also stress power differentials and politics in organizations.

Similar to the above, is the approach of writers in the tradition of organizational sense-making, most notably by Weick (1979; 1995), who takes a view in some ways similar to those of Maturana and Varela when they emphasize enactment and a view similar to those in the previous paragraph who emphasize the role of storytelling and communities of practice. For Weick (1995), sense-making has the following features:

- Active agents place stimuli in some kind of framework so that they can comprehend, explain, attribute, extrapolate and predict. Weick often uses the metaphor of a map and talks about individual mental models.
- Individuals form conscious and unconscious anticipations and assumptions as predictions of what they expect to encounter and sense-making is triggered when there is a discrepancy between such expectations and what they encounter. The need for explanation is triggered by surprise and takes the form of retrospective accounts to explain those surprises. Meaning is ascribed retrospectively as an output of a sense-making process and does not arise concurrently with the detection of difference.
- Sense-making is the process people employ to cope with interruptions of ongoing activity.
- It is a process of reciprocal interaction of information seeking and meaning ascription, that is, it includes environmental scanning, interpretation and associated responses.

- A distinction may be drawn between generic (collective) and intersubjective (individual relating) forms of sense-making.

Weick regards sense-making as both an individual and a social activity and argues that it attends to both how a "text" is constructed and interpreted, to both creation/invention and discovery. He argues that sense-making is grounded in identity construction, where identities are constructed in the process of interaction between people. He emphasizes its retrospective nature, where meaning is the kind of attention directed to experience. Sense-making is a process of relating in which people co-create, or enact, their environment. This leads him to place particular emphasis on talk, discourse, conversation, storytelling and narrative. In this process, people notice, extract and embellish cues, which he regards as the simple, familiar structures from which people develop a larger sense of what may be occurring. For him, the metaphor of a "seed" captures the open-ended quality of sense-making because a seed produces a form. He quotes Shotter (1983), who describes how an acorn limits the tree that grows from it to an oak tree but does not specify it exactly. Rather, it grows unpredictably. Notice here how this assumes the causal framework of Formative Teleology.

Weick ascribes particular importance to novel moments in the process of sense-making. He locates the origins of novelty in dissonance, surprise, gaps, differences, disruptions, unexpected failures and uncertainty. For him it is events of this kind that trigger sense-making, which could produce novel explanations. He describes the process as one that involves emotion and is necessarily confusing.

The developments described in this sub-section all take issue with mainstream thinking with regard to Assumptions 6 and 10. Assumption 6 relates to the distinction between tacit and explicit knowledge and the privileging of the latter. Assumption 10 refers to the exclusion of emotion, power and personal relationships as creative forces in knowledge creation. In their emphasis on conversation and narrative knowledge the writers referred to above present a very different view to mainstream thinking but they also retain some of its features, such as the concept of mental models, for example, Weick. Some, however, go further and avoid thinking in terms of mental models (Assumptions 1, 2, and 5 above), for example, Shotter (1993). Some question the mainstream primacy accorded to the individual in the knowledge creation process (Assumption 8), for example, Shotter (1993), but most do not. What none of them questions, it seems to me, are Assumptions 7 and 9 of mainstream thinking, those to do with the split between individual and social and the dual causality that goes with it. It seems to me that all of the developments and critiques of mainstream thinking presented here argue within the assumption that the individual and the social are systems at separate levels of being or explanation. All of them implicitly assume the causal framework of Formative Teleology applied to the individual and social systems and some kind of Rationalist Teleology applied to the outside individual who changes the system.

What the developments and criticisms amount to

The developments and critiques of mainstream thinking described above point to important challenges to, or extensions of, that mainstream thinking. There is the challenge to the view that the mind is a processor of information that stores accurate representations of external reality and the suggestion that the brain-mind perpetually constructs meaning and knowledge. The emphasis on narrative, storytelling and the dramatic in the construction of knowledge, as well as the importance of politics, power and emotion provide important understanding of the micro detail of interaction between individuals and its importance in the construction of knowledge. Weick's linking of difference/discrepancy and the origin of novelty is a highly important one to be taken up in Part II of this book.

However, they all continue to argue within the framework of systems thinking. They all conceptualize the individual as one level and the social as another level in a system in which one level impacts on the other sequentially. It is a "both/and" approach in that both the social and the individual are regarded as important and the argument with mainstream thinking is just how important each is and which is to be regarded as prior to the other. As a consequence, the critics implicitly retain the underlying split causality of mainstream thinking. The system is assumed to unfold that which is already enfolded, that is, Formative Teleology, whether it be the system of the social or the system of the mind. However, the origin of change is then understood from a perspective outside the system, where causality is that of Rationalist Teleology.

Conclusion

The literature exploring learning and knowledge creation in organizations derives from a number of different disciplines such as sociology, psychology, and organizational and management theory. Some argue that these diverse origins have led to an undesirable fragmentation of the whole field of study and call for efforts aimed at integration (Huber, 1991; Prange, 1999). Others argue that the different perspectives cannot be integrated because they are distinct and incompatible, and that this plurality of views should be seen as a strength (Easterby-Smith, 1997; Easterby-Smith and Araujo, 1999). The argument in this chapter has been that while there are indeed many different perspectives, they largely fall within a particular underlying frame of reference. That frame of reference is provided by systems thinking. Underlying this thinking is the split causal framework of Rationalist and Formative Teleology, reflected in the taken-for-granted analysis of human action, learning and knowledge creation into levels: the individual and the social. This book argues that the split between the individual and the social is a major limitation when it comes to thinking about knowledge creation in organizations. The next chapter, therefore, looks at the way in which this split has been dealt with in a number of literatures and then Part II of this book develops a perspective that avoids such a split.

3 Different levels of learning and knowledge creation in organizations: the individual and the social

- The endless debate about priority and primacy
- The individual and the social as separate mutually influencing levels
- Moving away from the split between individual and social
- Conclusion

As described in the previous chapter, a key assumption underlying mainstream thinking about knowledge creation in organizations is that the individual and the organization are different kinds of phenomena. It is taken for granted that they constitute different ontological levels requiring different explanations. Although the group, team or organizational level is granted important motivational effects, it is usually assumed that it is ultimately the individual who learns and so creates knowledge. The underlying way of thinking about the nature of the individual is cognitivism in which individual minds are assumed to form representations of external reality, build them into models and store them in memory. Knowledge is localized in individual heads and is largely tacit, being expressed in professional skills. For knowledge to exist at the organizational level it must be shared by individuals and it is usual to assume that individuals are reluctant to share their personal knowledge with each other. A central concern, therefore, is that of how knowledge is transmitted from one individual to another so that it is shared and how it might be retained when individuals leave the organization. The view is that knowledge must be extracted from individuals and preserved for the organization in the form of practices, routines and codes of one kind or another, in which organizational knowledge is said to be stored. This perspective focuses attention on the codification of practices, the embedding of knowledge in artifacts and the use of information technology.

Mainstream thinking has been developed and critiqued in a number of ways reviewed in the previous chapter. Some depart from cognitivism and take a psychoanalytic perspective in which unconscious individual and collective group processes distort perceptions of reality and undermine learning and knowledge creation. Others challenge cognitivism in a different way. They contest the notion that knowledge is representations, models and maps, stored in individual heads. Instead, they propose a constructivist perspective in which individual minds actively select, or enact perceptions and perpetually construct patterns of meaning. Others take the constructivist perspective further to emphasize the importance of the social in the construction of knowledge. For example, they take a sense-making approach to think about organizational knowledge in the context of communities of practice in which individuals convey what they know about their practice to each other through storytelling. This perspective downplays the importance of formally sanctioned, designed rules and codes of practice (propositional knowledge) and elevates the role of informal stories (narrative knowledge) as the location and means of sharing what an organization "knows." Others go even further and take a social constructionist position in which the role of the individual in the creation of knowledge is reduced while that of relationships between them is taken to be central. What changes in the development and critique of mainstream thinking is:

- the view taken of individual mind, moving from cognitivist to psychoanalytic, constructivist and constructionist perspectives;
- the location of knowledge, moving from location in the individual to location in the social and from propositional to narrative forms;
- the mode of knowledge transmission from sharing through mimicry to conversational relating and participation in storytelling and conversation.

However, all these approaches continue to make the same underlying assumption that the individual and the organization are different levels of phenomena. This immediately leads to the debate about which comes first and which is more important. These questions have aroused interest for a long time, giving rise to the agency–structure debate in sociology and economics and in the discussion of the individual–group relationship in psychology and social psychology. It is important to be clear on the position one takes in these debates because so much of the subsequent framework for thinking about organizational knowledge flows from it. This chapter will take a brief look at typical positions taken in this debate and then argue that the conceptual split between individual and group/organization is an inappropriate one to make when it comes to the matter of organizational learning and knowledge creation. I will argue that individual and group/social need to be understood at the same explanatory level. From this perspective, it becomes highly problematic to talk about extracting knowledge from individual heads, sharing knowledge between people, or managing knowledge.

The endless debate about priority and primacy

In the agency–structure debate, the term agency refers to the capacity of the individual human for making choices and taking action on those choices. It refers to the freedom of the individual to act and denotes those causes of human action to be found in the individual. Structure refers to the causes of human action to be found in society, institutions, organizations and groups. Social structure is defined as the pattern of recurring relations between people in their ongoing dealings with each other, usually those that are repetitive and enduring, although some writers include ephemeral contacts between people in their definition of social structure.

Examples of social structures are economic phenomena such as patterns of relationships between the owners of capital and the providers of labor. All markets are social structures, being patterns of relationship between suppliers and demanders of goods and services. Other examples of social structures are state and government functions; legal relationships; technological development; the family; religious practices; language; demography. All these social structures are characterized by repetition and endurance.

Some writers draw a distinction between institutions and other social structures. Institutions are those social structures for which, in addition to repetition and endurance, there are:

● descriptions in language;
● representations in the minds of individuals;
● shared views that are widely accepted;
● practical manifestations, often in material terms.

A social structure that is not an institution would, for example, be the demographic pattern of a population that is not talked about and does not feature in thought and policies. Organizations may be thought of as institutions with a significant element of formal description and design, that is, where roles, relationships between members and the tasks they perform are more defined than they are in institutions that are not also organizations. For example, the family is clearly an institution but one may not want to refer to it as an organization.

Closely linked to the ideas of social structure, institutions and organizations are the notions of habits, customs, traditions, routines, mores, values, cultures, paradigms, beliefs, missions and visions. These are all ideas about the repetitive, enduring, shared practices of people in their ongoing dealings with each other in institutional life.

An important question arises as soon as this distinction is made between the individual and his or her habits of thinking and acting, on the one hand, and the group/organization/institution characterized by shared beliefs, values, paradigms, customs, traditions and culture, on the other. The question has to do with what the connection between the individual actor and the institution is. This is usually understood as a question about the cause of human action and the beliefs, customs and traditions that underlie it. Does this cause lie within the individual agent or is it to be found in the social structure? How do individuals and institutions affect each other?

The connection between the individual and the social can be understood from one of three perspectives:

● individualism;
● collectivism;
● mutual influence.

From the perspective of individualism, all agency is located in the individual, with institutions and other social structures taken to be the result of individual actions (for example, Popper, 1945; Hayek, 1948). In its most extreme form this view denies any role for social structure in the determination of human action. An understanding of the social is sought purely in terms of the behavior of individuals. However, such an extreme position is rarely taken and the most notable proponents of this view accord some importance to the impact of the social in determining the nature of the individual action, generally without exploring how this happens. A purely individualist perspective, therefore, does not get one very far.

Collectivism moves to the other extreme and ascribes all agency to social structure, usually understanding this in terms of impersonal social forces, such as the class struggle, which are taken to determine the behavior of individuals. This approach reduces the individual to a passive victim of impersonal social forces where individuals are stripped of any freedom to choose. Nowadays, this perspective attracts much less attention than it used to, although notions of the collective unconscious, group mind, or transpersonal processes come close to a collectivist perspective.

If one leaves behind the extremes of individualism and collectivism, there are a number of ways of thinking about the manner in which social structure and individual mind mutually influence each other.

The individual and the social as separate mutually influencing levels

This section briefly reviews how the mutual influence of social and individual are thought about in psychoanalysis, critical realism, institutional economics, and social constructionism. In each case I will be concerned with a number of questions:

- First, what is the nature of the connection between the individual and the social?
- Second, which is regarded as temporally prior and which is regarded as primary?
- Third, where the connection between the two involves individuals sharing something, just what is it that they are sharing and how do they come to share it?
- Fourth, what theory of causality is assumed?
- Fifth, how do repetitive enduring institutions and their individual members change?
- Sixth, how do novel developments in institutions and individual minds arise?

Psychoanalysis and the connection between the individual and the social

This section briefly summarizes some key concepts in Freudian theory and its later development as object relations theory without taking account of more recent developments in psychoanalytic thinking (for example, intersubjectivity theory, Stolorow, *et al.*, 1994) because it is largely in these earlier forms that psychoanalysis has been taken up in organizational theory (for example, see Gabriel, 1999).

The basis of Freudian theory (1923) is universal principles that explain the structuring of the individual psyche. The psyche is thought of as a mechanism, nowadays as a system or process, consisting at an individual's birth of the id. The id is the source of psychic energy taking the form of drives, which are individual mental ideas of inherited aggressive and libidinous instincts. There is, therefore, a strong link with the biological level. The drives blindly seek discharge according to the pleasure principle but the id-driven newborn soon encounters prohibition of such blind discharge provided by the parents as representatives of the social. It is this clash with the social that structures the mind as the ego emerges to regulate the id so that the individual's behavior becomes acceptable in the social situation. Part of this regulatory function involves the repression of the id's unacceptable wishes so that these become unconscious. This central concept of the individual unconscious is therefore closely connected with the mechanism of repression. However, what is repressed returns as action caused by wishes, or fantasies, of which the individual is unconscious. Later in the development of the psyche, the individual introjects the prohibitions of the father to form a superego, also an agency of regulation and repression. A group comes into existence as a psychological phenomenon when people identify with a leader, in effect replacing their own superego with that of the leader (Freud, 1921).

The later development of object relations theory by Klein (1946) added the notion of inherited unconscious fantasies that also clashed with social reality. Here individual mind is thought of as a process of representing, not a pre-given reality as in cognitivism, but relationships with others as objects in which these representations of others are taken into the psyche as introjections that are internally elaborated in fantasy. An individual mind is then thought of as an "inner world" of interacting fantasies and conflictual processes involving the splitting of internally represented objects into good and bad and their projection onto others, thereby distorting reality. Furthermore, there is the process of projective identification in which an individual puts feelings into others, thus unconsciously manipulating them to play particular roles.

Groups form through this process, one of role suction as people are sucked into performing roles on behalf of, and speak as voices for, the group (Bion, 1961a). The group-as-a-whole is thought of as a separate phenomenon to individuals, one to which they anonymously donate mental contents. Individuals unconsciously contribute their personal mental contents to a group pool of mental contents, according to which they all then behave. When the anxiety of being in a group becomes too great, the individuals in it collectively regress and collectively employ the same defensive mechanisms that each individually employed as an infant. Unconscious processes of splitting, projection, denial and repression, taking the form of basic assumption behavior and group fantasies, then characterize group behavior. In other words, unconscious group processes are an extension of, and take the same form as, personal unconscious processes. The function of unconscious group and personal processes is also the same, namely, that of defense against anxiety and repression of drive-dominated and fantasy-driven behavior. There is the frequently implicit, and occasionally explicit, reference to the group as an illusion of the individual mind and to individuals being at war with their "groupishness."

The key questions

Turning now to the questions posed above, the connection between the individual and the social is such that the social operates as prohibition and as source of introjected representations of relationships that structure the individual mind, which originates in biological instincts and inherited unconscious fantasies. In turn, individual minds create the social through a process of identification with leaders, role suction, unconscious donation of mental contents and projective mechanisms of a defensive kind. The individual is primary in that both psychic and social processes arise in the individual as ways of dealing with drives and unconscious fantasies. In evolutionary time the individual as a biological entity comes before the social but in any individual's lifetime the social comes before the individual and acts to structure the individual mind. As for the third question posed above, individuals share mental contents through unconscious processes of projection, projective identification and introjection. The implicit theory of causality can be understood in two ways. The Freudian formulation implies a form of efficient causality in that all behavior is understood to be determined by specific causes, usually a number of them so that behavior is overdetermined. Every act is due to a number of causes, either conscious reasoning or unconscious wish fulfillment. The object relations formulation can be understood as Formative Teleology in that mental development is the unfolding of universal unconscious fantasies through the processes of projection and introjection.

The fifth and sixth questions posed above have to do with how change occurs and how novelty arises. In psychoanalysis, change is generally thought of as a process in which unconscious material is brought to consciousness. This is believed to prompt changes in behavior. However, a fuller answer to this question of change, and to the one to do with how novelty arises, requires a brief account of how the process of thinking is understood in psychoanalysis. I will take as an example some of Bion's ideas on the nature of thinking.

For Bion (1961b), thoughts arise in the individual as inherited preconceptions, that is, raw elements of sensuous and emotional experience in which the physical and the psychical are indistinguishable and lend themselves only to projective identification. The development of a thinking apparatus to think the thoughts requires a relationship with another. He uses the infant–mother relationship as the model for the kind of relating that creates the thinking rather than the purely projective apparatus. If the mother can accept the feelings that the infant wishes to get rid of and can transform them into a form that the infant can re-introject, then a thinking apparatus is created. He describes this capacity of the mother as the container and the infant's projections as the contained. This particular view of relating, then, is one in which one person transmits unwanted feelings, the contained, so that they lodge in another who contains them, detoxifies them and transmits them back to the first. As an individual matures, he or she develops, through introjection, his or her own internal-containing capacity. When the container, external or internal, cannot contain the contained, then projective identification occurs.

Thought, therefore, arises in inherited preconceptions originating in the individual outside of relationships with others. The individual then relates to another, transmitting feelings that are arising in him or herself, which may be contained by the other and then transmitted back again. Successful accomplishment of the process enables thought. This is a sender–receiver model of communication in which inarticulate thoughts are put into words leading to conscious action. Furthermore, can an inherited preconception be said to be novel?

Outside the psychoanalytic community, many dismiss out of hand the elaborate unconscious modes of transmission between people (for example, Turner, 1994). Even within the psychoanalytic community many find at least aspects of the classical theories unconvincing (for example, see the Stolorow et al.'s 1998 dismissal of projective identification, Gedo's (1999) rejection of the notion of psychic energy, and Leader's (2000) questioning of the notion of an "inner world"). I now turn to discussions of the connection between the individual and the social that do not rely on unconscious processes of transmission. The next section turns to the critical realist perspective, which is similar in some ways to that of classical psychoanalysis but does not rely on mechanisms of unconscious transmission.

Critical realism and the connection between the individual and the social

Critical realists (Bhaskar, 1975, 1989; Archer, 1995) distinguish three layers of reality: that of the natural world, that of the individual mind, and that of the social. Each layer of reality is differentiated from the one below it by emergent properties that cannot be reduced to the lower level nor predicted from it.

At the lowest level, the natural world is governed by material and efficient cause, that is, connections between cause and effect of the law-like "if-then" type. Traditional natural science and its notion of causality applies here.

At the next level, are the consciousness, mind and agency of the human individual, which all emerge from the complex neurosystem of the biological individual and these emergent properties constitute the individual's freedom to choose goals and the means to achieve them. A different kind of causality applies at this level, namely, final or teleological causality, in which the actions individuals choose to achieve their goals depend upon, but cannot be reduced to, the properties of the biological level. This psychological level is governed by the laws of reason, that is, the actions of the human individual are caused by reasons, intentions and plans. Bhaskar argues that human intention is always caused by reasons, or states of mind, but the cause of reasons is not identified. Individual human action therefore ends up being caused by uncaused reasons. No appeal is made to the biological level, to the genetic effects on behavior or to concepts such as instincts, because the level of the human individual is thought to emerge from the biological, then to be governed by a different form of causality. In the terms used in Chapter 2, this is Rationalist Teleology.

The social level emerges from these actions of individuals and these actions are taken to be the only efficient cause of social structure. Social structure is caused by the actions of individuals in which by their actions they reproduce and change the social, that is, the rules, relationships and positions constituting social structure. These actions are caused by the reasons and intentions people have to take such actions. However, although institutions do not exist independently of individuals, they are not simply the product of human activity. The social level is governed by its own laws, which cannot be reduced to or predicted from individual psychology. In the terms used in Chapter 2, causality at the social level is Formative Teleology.

The social level constitutes the situations within which individuals have to act and, therefore, constrains individual action, although it does not, as in psychoanalysis, structure individual minds, which are emergent properties of the biological level. Social structure provides the stability in human life while the actions of the individual are uncertain and unpredictable because the individual is free to act within social constraints.

The key questions

Turning to the questions posed on p. 44, the answer to the first question about connection provided by critical realists is as follows. Individuals form the social in their intentional actions caused by reasons and in so doing they create a system that constrains their freedom. As to the second question posed above, critical realists insist that social structure always exists prior to any individual actor. Infants are born into social structures and institutions, that is, systems of signs and symbols, or language, that already exist in the sense that they are past rules and relationships that are currently being reproduced by the individual family into which an infant is born. It is also clearly the individual who is primary because individual actions are required to construct the social, which is then only a constraint on individual action. It is not at all clear how individuals come to share the rules and systems of social structure. However, it is clear how the critical realist argument falls into the dual causality of Formative Teleology and Rationalist Teleology. The source of change and novelty is located in human freedom and intention but there is no explanation of how humans form such intentions. The answer is always reason as an uncaused cause.

Institutionalism and the connection between the individual and the social

Hodgson (1999b) draws on notions in institutional and evolutionary economics (Veblen, 1899, 1934; Commons, 1934) to draw different conclusions about the connection between the individual agent and social structure to those of the critical realists. He disagrees with the sharp distinction they make between the biological, individual, and social levels because it leads to ignoring the biological and limiting the social impact on individual action. Hodgson maintains the distinction between these levels, arguing that each emerges from the other and that this emergence means that each higher level has additional causal powers not found at the lower levels. However, unlike critical realists, he argues that the lower level of biology continues to have a causative impact on individual action, as does the higher social level.

Taking the social level first, Hodgson draws on Veblen's argument that institutions are habitual methods of carrying out the life processes of a community within a material environment. Veblen also argued that institutions are shared habits of thought that cannot be reduced to individual habits of thought because of their practical manifestation in a material environment. This view of institutions as shared habits of thought is the source of the greater impact of the social on the individual than critical realists recognize. Institutions do not simply form the constraining situation within which individuals take action, they shape the very habits of thought that give rise to the actions through which institutions are reproduced and changed. Social structures depend upon individuals because they come into being and change in the habits of thought of individuals. Institutions are the outcome of the conduct of individuals. They are the enduring social relations based on elementary psychic capacities of individuals. However, they are not simply the effect of individual beliefs because they are also partly the cause of individual beliefs in the sense of shaping those beliefs. This leads Hodgson to propose the notion of reconstitutive downward causation. Individual goals, aims and habits of thought are reconstituted by institutions, shaped by them. For example, the desire for wealth is not innate but is shaped by the community and its history. This means that institutions operate as causal factors in the development of the individual mind just as individual actions operate as causal factors in the development of institutions, even though they remain separate levels of being, in which the social emerges from the individual and cannot be reduced to it.

The process of evolution is brought in to explain how this mutual causation operates. Institutions and individuals are both held to be subject to the laws of natural selection. The fittest mental habits of individuals are competitively selected to form the patterns of institutional habits. Institutions compete with each other and the process of competitive selection determines which institutions survive and which become extinct. Institutions also competitively select individuals with the fittest temperaments and habits, that is, those adapted to these institutional patterns. Through this process of competitively selecting individuals, institutions change individual minds, shaping their beliefs and habits. Institutional patterns subsequently change through the operation of competitive selection on newly arising individual mental habits. How do those new mental habits arise? The answer, as I understand it, has to do with the reasoning capacities of individuals. Reasoning individuals form new intentions and new mental habits.

This is where, as I understand it, the biological level comes in. Veblen argued that humans could not have suddenly acquired the capacity to reason and act intentionally. These capacities could not simply be taken as given, as uncaused cause, in the manner of the critical realists. Instead, he argued that intellectual functions arise through instinctive dispositions and continue to operate under their surveillance. The link with biology as a causal factor in individual behavior is therefore made through the idea of genetically determined instincts of reasoning. Evolutionary psychologists also maintain that rationality and intelligence are instincts (Pinker, 1997). This means that rationality, intelligence and the ability to use language are genetically programmed in much the same way as sex and aggression are assumed to be in psychoanalysis.

This perspective, then, maintains that individual minds emerge from the biological level as critical realists do, but unlike the latter, the institutionalist argument points to a continuing causal link between the biological and the individual human mental levels. Instead of having a causality (efficient) for the biological level, a causality (teleological) for the individual mind and another causality (social forces) for the social, the institutionalists propose that the biological operates as efficient cause in relation to the individual mind and so does the social level, and they do this through the evolutionary process of competitive selection, which operates at all three levels. In this way, a sharp split between causality between the three levels is said to be avoided.

The key questions

Consider now how this perspective deals with the questions posed on p. 44 about the connection between the individual and the social. Individual habits of mind, determined by biologically evolved reasoning instincts as efficient cause, compete with each other to form institutional habits. Those institutional habits then compete with each other for survival and then act as selective forces, which compel individuals to change their habits of mind. This view creates something of a difficulty for human freedom. If habits of mind are caused by biologically evolved reasoning instincts, on the one hand, and the selective force of social competition, on the other, then there appears to be little left of human freedom. Are the most important individual intentions genetically programmed, as full-blown evolutionary psychology would have it? Or is it just a generalized reasoning instinct that is so determined, leaving open the possibility of freely chosen reasons? If it is the latter, then the argument is very close to the critical realists and one has to ask how a particular reason or intention arises. As far as I can see, there is no more of an answer to this question in institutionalism than there is in critical realism.

Next comes the question of temporal priority. First, if evolutionary time is taken, then, from the intuitionalist perspective, individual reasoning instincts must have come first. Individuals, it is said, could not have suddenly started to replicate social practices without evolution first having produced reasoning instincts through random variations at the level of the genes subjected to competitive selection. The reasoning instinct, according to a neo-Darwinian perspective, must have gradually evolved to the point where individual members of the population displayed reasoning capacities. Only then could they have had the capacity to engage in repetitive and enduring social relations. So, in evolutionary time, individuals must have been prior. However, in the time frame of individual history, it is the social structure that is prior. Like the critical realists, Hodgson insists that institutions are temporally prior to individuals in that institutions reflect the past history of the community that an individual joins at birth.

There is a problem with this argument about temporal priority. In a discussion about the temporal priority of the constructs of "the generalized individual" and "the social structure," "a particular individual infant" is substituted for "the generalized individual." As soon as this is done, of course, the social structure is prior. In a sense, the point becomes trivial. It is quite obvious that particular parents must precede a particular infant. But this says nothing about the priority of the "generalized individual" in relation to the "social." In generalized terms, there can be no social structure without the "generalized individuals" engaging in social practices, nor can there be such "generalized individuals" without social relations. A family is "individuals" engaged in the social practices of "family." In this sense, neither the "individual" nor the "family" is prior in temporal terms since neither can exist without the other.

A similar difficulty applies when one shifts to evolutionary time. If human states of mind are shaped by social structures, how could typically human minds have evolved in the absence of such structures? The notion that first individual humans with reasoning instincts evolved and then they engaged in social practices amounts to a view in which social relationships are not essential to what it means to be human. If one retains the notion that the individual and the social are two separate levels of being, a debate ensues about which is temporally prior. That debate never produces a satisfactory conclusion.

As to the question of whether the individual or the social is primary, institutionalism takes a "both . . . and" position. Institutionalism is basically a theory of the evolution of habits and it argues that habits evolve through competitive selection at *both* the level of the individual *and* the level of the social separately, with evolution at one separate level affecting evolution at the other. Each is primary at its own separate level.

This point links to the question about sharing. The argument is that institutional habits shape or cause changes in individual mental habits through the process of competitive selection. Individuals are forced to comply with institutional habits if they want to survive. It is through this mechanism that downward reconstitutive cause is said to operate. However, all that the institutional pressure for conformity can ensure is that individuals will act compliantly. How could such pressure ensure that mental habits change? How do institutional habits become individual mental habits? As far as I can see, there is no answer to this question and like critical realism, the institutional perspective implicitly has to rely on mimicry, which again only ensures conformity of action. It too cannot explain how habits, as repetitive actions, can become mental contents. Turner (1994), arguing in a different tradition, proposes that institutions are not based on shared mental processes at all but rather on common practices that individuals emulate. He argues that individuals have different private mental states that it is impossible to share and that what is shared instead is common observances, performances and rituals. People come to share these common ways through emulation or mimicry.

Then there is the question of causality. The prime causal mechanism in institutionalism is that of competitive selection, applied to mental and social habits. The mental habits are either determined by biological evolution or by the autonomous employment of a general reasoning instinct that was biologically evolved. If it is the latter, then causality is of the same kind as in critical realism, that is, Rationalist Teleology, but this time circumscribed in some unidentified way by biologically evolved reasoning instincts. Social habits also evolve under competitive selection. The first volume in this series (Stacey *et al.*, 2000) pointed to the questions some strands of thinking in the complexity sciences pose for reliance on natural selection as the primary driver of evolution. Those strands propose instead the primary importance of intrinsic self-organization as the transformative cause of evolution. The heavy reliance of institutionalist thinking on the principle of competitive selection is thus open to challenge.

Finally, there is the question of change and novelty. Given the emphasis on competitive selection, change presumably arises as chance variations in mental habits that are competitively selected for survival as institutional change. Novelty here is purely a matter of chance at the level of the individual.

I argue, then, that the psychoanalytic, critical realist and institutionalist perspectives present rather different explanations of the connection between the individual and the social. The psychoanalytic and critical realist positions ultimately accord primacy to the individual, seeing the social as unfolding what is enfolded as inherited instinct and unconscious fantasy or as constraining the actions of the individual. The institutionalists, in a sense, accord greater agency to the social in that institutions, or social habits evolve independently of individual minds and then affect them. However, in the end, novelty presumably arises at the individual level. The three perspectives agree on the temporal priority of the individual in evolutionary time and the temporal priority of the social in terms of individual historical time. They propose very different theories of causality: the efficient cause of unconscious wishes in the case of psychoanalysis, the Formative and Rationalist Teleology of critical realism and the formative cause of competitive selection in the institutionalist argument. Psychoanalysis posits unconscious processes as the connection between the social and the individual mind, while critical realists and institutionalists avoid the hypothesis of unconscious process but fail to account for just how mental contents can be transmitted. None of them offers convincing explanations of how novel change can come about since psychoanalysis seems to suggest that thinking arises in inherited preconceptions, critical realists hardly address the matter, while institutionalists seem to ascribe novelty to chance.

I turn now to a way of thinking that differs from all of those so far discussed in the manner in which it accords primacy to the social.

Social constructionism and the connection between the individual and the social

Gergen (1999) presents what he calls the working assumptions of social constructionism:

- Language does not map or picture an independent world but, rather, a potentially unlimited number of descriptions and explanations with none being superior in terms of their capacity to map or picture reality. Everything humans have learned could be otherwise.
- Language and all other forms of representation gain their meaning from the ways in which they are used in relationships. The individual mind does not originate meaning, create language or discover the world. Relationships are prior to all that is intelligible.
- Relationships are based on wider patterns of practice, such as rituals and traditions. Relationships and reality are socially constructed and are limited by culture, history and human embeddedness in the physical world.
- Language constitutes social life and without shared language descriptions of social life are impossible. In the continuous generation of meaning together humans sustain life. Generative discourse transforms social life.
- The generation of the good is always from within a tradition and this requires reflexivity, that is, attempts to suspend the obvious and question assumptions.

Gergen points out that many participating in constructionist dialogues do not necessarily share these assumptions. He distinguishes social constructionism from constructivism, which focuses on the way in which the individual mind constructs what is taken to be reality, either with (Piaget, 1954) or without (von Glasersveld, 1991) a systematic relationship to the external world, and from social constructivism in which individual minds construct reality in a way significantly formed by relationships (Vygotsky, 1962; Bruner, 1990).

The social constructionist approach views the social as the process of articulating individual selves and the world. It is a challenge to the primacy and priority of the individual, in effect, placing relationship, the social, as prior and primary. There is a strong ideological underpinning in that a shift to this way of thinking is held to promise better forms of social life.

> And toward what kind of alternative should we strive? In what way can we conceptualize persons such that the individual ills are not duplicated, and the possibilities for more promising forms of social life are opened? . . .
>
> Social constructionism traces commitments to the real and the good to social processes. As proposed, what we take to be knowledge of the world grows from relationship, and is embedded not within individual minds but within interpretive and communal traditions. In effect, there is a way in which constructionist dialogues celebrate relationships as opposed to the individual, connection over isolation, and communion over antagonisms.
>
> (Gergen, 1999, p. 122)

Gergen's commitment to the removal of the individually located mind and the substitution of relationship is clearly revealed in his critique of others who have emphasized the importance of relationships.

While recognizing the substantial contribution made by what he calls the symbolic interactionism of Mead (1934, 1936, 1938) to understanding human interdependency and the inseparability of individual mind and the social, he identifies several problems (Gergen, 1999, pp. 124–125). First, he says that Mead retains a strong element of individualism in that the individual is born into the world as a private subject who comes to take the role of others and so Mead never abandons private subjectivity. In Chapter 4, I will argue that this is a strength of Mead's argument: he never loses either the individual or the social. Second, Gergen says that Mead does not provide an answer to the intractable problem of explaining how it is that a person is able to grasp another's states of mind from their gestures. In Chapter 4, I will argue that Mead does convincingly explain this.

Third, Gergen says that Mead displays a strong flavor of social determinism in arguing that there is a "temporal and logical pre-existence of the social process to the self-conscious individual that arises in it" (Mead, 1934, p. 186). I find this an odd criticism because it seems to me that this is just what Gergen does. However, the point I made above about a particular individual and "the generalized individual" applies here. In terms of a particular individual, of course, the social precedes the individual. In generalized terms, Mead clearly states that neither the individual nor the social is prior; they are simultaneous. Fourth, Gergen also holds that Mead's view of individual mind as private role play featuring others in social relationships implies that others determine what goes on in an individual mind. Again, I find this an odd criticism since it seems to me that this is Gergen's position, but not what I understand Mead to be saying. I will be taking this point up in Chapter 4. Here I want to point to how Gergen removes the individual and elevates relationship or the social. He argues within the tradition that poses a dualism of individual and social and dismisses the former in favor of the latter, so arriving at a very different position to the approaches already discussed above, which ultimately locate change in individual minds.

Gergen then turns to the cultural psychology of Vygotsky (1962) and Bruner (1990). He recognizes their contribution to focusing attention on narrative knowledge, relationship and action but holds that their work is subject to the same criticism as those made of Mead. He makes much the same points about the phenomenology of Husserl (1960) and Schutz (1967).

In taking his position on the primacy of the social, Gergen largely ignores the importance of the human body. However, the social constructionist, Shotter (1993) does regard living bodily responsiveness to events and features of the surroundings as crucial to human relating. He sees bodily responsiveness as the beginnings of intellectual and self-controlling skills. He argues that human bodies participate in a ceaseless flow of relational activity. For him, the most important form of responsive relating is spontaneous, effortless and performed without much self-consciousness. It is in the "once occurrent moments" of being in such relating that meaning and novelty arise. He describes this as joint activity, a third realm of human experience between subject and object, which is neither just action nor just behavior. Joint action takes place when one's act is shaped by the act of another, so that none can be held individually accountable. He uses a spatial metaphor to describe what he calls the "strange" third realm as a "dialogic space" situated at the boundary between one consciousness and another, the interweaving of unmerged consciousnesses, a space between them. Participants produce moments of mutual, or joint, encounter of a one-off kind in which their bodily senses are mixed together in a flow of interaction that is never fully orderly or fully disorderly and, therefore, never fully knowable. Already specified situations are always open to further specification. He describes the realm of joint action as one in which people jointly construct their actions, experienced as a "third agency" with its own specific demands and requirements. This "it," or responsive order, makes calls on participants.

So, unlike Gergen, Shotter retains the individual to some extent as a responsive body, a distinct unmerged consciousness but then postulates a third realm, a third agency, an "it" that acts upon those who participate in joint action. In the end, it seems to me, he subjugates the individual to the relational or social.

Responsibility

The difficulties created by this elevation of the social become evident in discussions on responsibility. If actions are joint, how can an individual be held accountable? Both Gergen and Shotter hold that he or she cannot. McNamee and Gergen (1999) strongly argue that individuals should not be held responsible and accountable for their actions. They call for a move to a notion of relational responsibility, a "we" that is to be held responsible for actions. In the same volume, Mary Gergen (1999) goes even further and suggests that the notion of "responsibility" be dropped altogether in favor of "relational appreciation." Other social constructionists argue against this position, pointing to the difficulty of dealing with power, dominance, duplicity, deception and self-seeking (Lannamann, 1999; Deetz and White, 1999). Lannamann argues that:

> Although this move to the "we" is consistent with their [McNamee's and Gergen's] interest in relational processes, it short circuits relational process because it ignores the fact that the individual "I" is always, necessarily, a social construction, one that plays a central role in the production of joint action . . .
>
> The difference between . . . [their] . . . orientation to joint action and Shotter's is that Shotter, by preserving space for socially constructed agents (social Is), leaves more room for the messy possibility of unintended consequences.
>
> (Ibid., p. 87)

In the end, however, Shotter also takes the "we" position when it comes to responsibility, holding that because individuals shape each other's actions, they cannot be held accountable for them. In the same volume as McNamee and Gergen, agreeing with their call for taking responsibility toward relational processes, he and Katz say: "we come to live our lives almost as if a bodily part of a much larger, collective agency, as if inside a living 'we'" (1999, p. 154).

Having retained a place for the individual, in the end, Shotter loses the individual in the spontaneous third realm, or so it seems to me.

The key questions

How does the social constructionist perspective deal with the questions posed about the nature of the connection between the individual and the social? For social constructionists, language constitutes social life, which is equated with relationships between individuals. It is relationships that articulate, in fact socially construct, individual minds and selves. Biology features little and the social as relationship is both prior to the individual and primary. Individuals share language and descriptions. In other words, they share common acts of speech, making it unnecessary to postulate the transmission of mental contents. Social constructionists argue that discourse transforms social life and Shotter, at least, locates novelty in once occurrent moment of being. Shotter is arguing that change and novelty arise in the detail of bodily relating between individuals in discourse. In developing this kind of argument, social constructionists are moving away from the theories of causality underlying the psychoanalytic, critical realist and institutionalist positions. I suggest that they are pointing to a causal framework that my co-authors and I called Transformative Teleology in the first volume of this series of books (Stacey *et al.*, 2000). This is a view of causality in which the future is under perpetual construction in the detail of interaction between entities. Box 3.1 summarizes the features of this view of causality and it can be seen how closely it resembles the social constructionist position.

This move to a very different causal framework is, it seems to me, the prime strength of the social constructionist argument. However, in making this move, social constructionists continue to argue on the basis of separate levels for the individual and the social. They then accord primacy to the social and so largely lose individual agency. This, it seems to me, is a serious loss because it destroys the notion of any individual responsibility, making ethics and morality a group matter. One might argue for this move as the basis of a call to a better society, but this loss of individual agency and responsibility renders social constructionism in its present form inadequate as an explanation of current individual and social situations. Western society today is built on the notion of individual responsibility so that an argument which excludes it cannot, it seems to me, adequately explain current conditions.

I have now briefly reviewed four different ways of thinking about the individual and the social as different ontological levels, pointing to the difficulties that each leads to. I argued in Chapter 2 that this splitting of the individual and the social into two levels is a central feature of

Box 3.1 Transformative Teleology

Movement is toward a future that is under perpetual construction by the movement itself. There is no mature or final state, only perpetual iteration of identity and difference, continuity and transformation, the known and the unknown, at the same time. The future is unknowable but yet recognizable, the known-unknown.

Movement is for the sake of expressing the continuity and transformation of individual and collective identity and difference at the same time. This is the creation of the novel, variations that have never been there before.

The process of movement or construction, that is, the cause, is the processes of micro interaction in the living present, forming and being formed by themselves. The iterative processes sustain continuity with potential transformation at the same time. Variation arises in micro diversity of interaction as transformative cause. Meaning arises in the present, as does choice and intention.

The kind of self-organization implied is diverse micro interaction of a paradoxical kind that sustains identity and potentially transforms it.

Changes in identity depend upon spontaneity and diversity of variations in micro interactions.

Both freedom and constraint arise in diversity of micro interactions as conflicting constraints.

mainstream thinking about learning and knowledge creation and of those who develop and critique it. This chapter has so far demonstrated just how problematic this split is. It leads to an endless debate about which is prior and primary. The question of whether agency lies at the individual or the social level is not easily resolved and each attempt to do so brings with it new problems. Key problems relate to just what it is, and how it comes about, that people share with each other; just how change, particularly of the novel kind, takes place; and just how individual freedom and responsibility are to be accounted for in social relating. My contention is that none of the approaches so far reviewed provides a satisfactory way of dealing with the key questions and that this is due, in large measure, to the starting assumption, namely, that the individual and the social are at different ontological levels. I now go on to revue an approach that starts from the assumption that the individual and the social are to be explained at the same level of being. If such a move provides more satisfactory explanations it will have major implications for mainstream thinking about learning and knowledge creation in organizations, undermining it at its roots.

Moving away from the split between individual and social

Structuration theory (Giddens, 1976, 1984) moves away from splitting the individual and the social. This theory does not accord priority or primacy to either individual minds and actions or to social structure. Instead, it argues that both are mutually constituted, at the same time, in recursive social practices. Social practices, that is, patterns in the ongoing dealings of individuals with each other, are sustained through time and across space in the medium of the very practices themselves. These practices are both the outcome and the medium of individual interactions in the process of which individual capacities for action are themselves formed. Human subjects and social institutions are jointly constituted through recurrent practices. The properties of the individual mind and of social practices do not exist outside action but are constituted in it. Individual and social are thus not separate levels of being but the same level, with each arising in the reproduction of patterns of interaction between people, in which reproduction there is the potential for transformation. This amounts to an argument that agency is forming itself; it is forming while being formed at the same time. This theory differs from social constructionism in that it does not accord either temporal priority or primacy to the social. It differs from the psychoanalytic and critical realist perspective in that it does not ultimately accord primacy to the individual. And it differs from institutionalism in that it does not explain transformation in terms of chance variations.

Hodgson (1999b) presents a number of criticisms of structuration theory from an institutionalist perspective. First, he objects to the view that individual and social are one level of being, arguing that this move conflates the two and ignores the process of emergence. Obviously structuration theory does not regard the social as emergent from the individual and therefore does not ascribe properties to the social level that are additional to the individual. However, there is more than one way of thinking about emergence. Hodgson defines emergence as the appearance of properties at one level that depend upon a lower level but cannot be reduced to that lower level.

Another definition of emergence, drawing on some strands of thinking in the complexity sciences (see Stacey et al., 2000), is the arising of pattern through the process of self-organization. Here, entities, components or agents interact with each other on the basis of their own local organizing themes and, in that interaction, their local organizing themes are reproduced and potentially transformed. This is the argument that connection, interaction, relationship between diverse entities have the intrinsic capacity for transformation (Allen, 1998a, 1998b). Another way of putting this is to say that individual relational practices replicate and potentially transform themselves. Individual relational practices are at the same time social practices simply because they are about interaction with others. Social practices are thus replicating and transforming at the same time as individual practices. Patterns of interaction are developing so that what is emerging is patterns of interaction from patterns of interaction. Agency is forming while being formed at the same time in paradoxical movement. This is very much a causal theory of Transformative Teleology (see Box 3.1). In other words, self-organization/emergence here is a transformative process in which patterns of social interaction transformatively cause themselves, just as in structuration theory. Although Giddens may not talk about emergence, I suggest that it is implicit in his argument in the form just described.

My criticism of structuration, therefore, would not be its avoidance of emergence defined as the appearance of additional properties at the social level compared to the individual level because it is implicitly built on emergence defined in what I take to be a more interesting and useful way for understanding human action. My criticism is, rather, that Giddens does not sufficiently develop the self-organizing notion of emergence and therefore does not fully develop his notion of social practices recursively forming themselves. In arguing at a macro level he does not pay sufficient attention to the detail of interaction between diverse individuals as the process in which transformation emerges. I will be taking this matter up in Part II of this book.

Hodgson's second criticism of structuration theory is that it ignores the biological nature of individuals and the material context in which they live. Hodgson argues that this means that structuration theory cannot explain where individual self-reflexivity and consciousness come from. This seems to me to be a valid criticism and is one that I will take up in Part II.

A third criticism presented by Hodgson (1999b) and others (Archer, 1995) relates to the importance of historical time. The four perspectives reviewed in the previous section all argue that social structure comes before the specific individual in historical time. The claim is that Giddens' insistence on the individual and the social being one level ignores this. However, it seems to me that structuration theory does incorporate historical time in an important sense. There is no claim in structuration theory that social practices are created anew every moment but, rather, that they are replicated or re-produced in the present. What is being re-produced in any time frame is a pattern of social practices engaged in during previous periods, but always with the potential for transformation. History is, therefore, of the essence. The criticism I would make of structuration theory is that it does not explain the transformation process. What is it that transforms social practices in their replication? Structuration theory has little to say about this, as far as I can see, because unlike social constructionist writers, it does not pay attention to the detail of interaction in the present. It does not recognize the intrinsic patterning and novelty-producing capacity of interaction between diverse entities. I will be taking this point up in Part II.

Finally, Hodgson (1999b) and others (Craib, 1992; Kilminster, 1991) are critical of Giddens' contention that social structure exists only in replicated social practices or actions and as memory traces that orient the actions of knowing individuals. Social structure, therefore, is carried as memory traces in individuals and transmitted through practice from one individual to another. This means, they say, that social structure ends up being internal to the minds of individual actors. Social structure, according to Giddens, persists in a stable way because individuals act in routine ways and they do this in order to control anxiety, a way of behaving that they learn through the caring and predictable routines established by parental figures. The critics argue that structuration theory, therefore, ultimately locates the social in individual psychology. I will be exploring this criticism in Part II.

The key questions

To conclude, consider how structuration theory deals with the questions posed on p. 44. First, the connection between the individual and the social is one where individuals form the social while being formed by it, and the social forms individuals while being formed by them, at the same time. Neither is temporally prior nor primary, and there is no need to posit the sharing of mental contents because the whole argument is conducted in terms of actions or practices. Structuration theory points to a causal framework of Transformative Teleology, which is completely different to that assumed by the perspectives discussed in the previous section. Since classical psychoanalytic theory is based on notions of efficient cause, it is deterministic and thus cannot explain novel change in its own terms.

Since critical realism assumes the split causal frameworks of Formative/Rationalist Teleology, it also cannot explain novel change in its own terms. Formative Teleology assumes the question away because it assumes the unfolding of what is already unfolded and Rationalist Teleology simply ascribes change to human reason as an uncaused cause. Institutionalism ascribes novel change to chance and competitive selection of mental and social habits. Social constructionism ascribes novel change to the detail of social relating in a somewhat similar way to structuration theory, but one which accords primacy to the social.

There are three important points made by critics of structuration theory. First, it does not pay attention to the biological body of individuals. Second, it pays little attention to the material context in which people live. Third, it implies that the social is stored as memory traces in individuals and so ends up regarding individuals as prior and primary. Part II will develop a perspective that is similar in many ways to structuration theory but pays attention to these criticisms. It is also similar in many ways to social constructionism but does not accord primacy to the social.

Conclusion

In this chapter I have been concerned with the problematic nature of the fundamental, taken-for-granted assumptions upon which current thinking about learning and knowledge creation in organizations is based. The fundamental assumption is that there is one level of explanation called the individual mind and another called the organization, which is a social structure or institution. On the basis of that assumption, knowledge creation in organizations is thought of as a system in which new knowledge arises in individual minds in a way that is taken for granted. It is also assumed that it is possible for humans to transmit mental contents to each other so that they can be shared as the basis of organization. The organization as an institution then influences individual minds in some way. This chapter has pointed to how all of these assumptions create considerable problems and I have argued that the basic problem is the assumed spilt between the individual and the social. The chapter concluded by pointing to a way of thinking that does not make this split. Structuration theory is built on the assumption that the individual and the social are one level of explanation. This theory also has problems but it points to the direction that Part II will develop. That section of the book will discuss other ways of thinking about the individual and the social as one level of explanation, ways that overcome, it seems to me, the problems raised with respect to structuration theory. I think this is a matter of major importance because of the significant challenge it presents to mainstream thinking about learning and knowledge creation in organizations.

Part II
Toward a complexity perspective: the emergence of knowledge in complex responsive processes of relating

The five chapters of Part II develop a view of human action within a causal theory of Transformative Teleology (see Box 3.1). From this perspective, the future is under perpetual construction through continuous processes of relating, which have the inherent, spontaneous capacity for coherent patterning, paradoxically displaying both continuity and potential transformation at the same time. This perspective draws on particular strands of thought in the complexity sciences as source domain for analogies with human action. These analogies are translated into human terms through concepts developed by Mead and others who hold that the individual and the social are one ontological level.

As an alternative to mainstream thinking about learning and knowledge creation in organizations, the chapters in Part II present an explanation of human action in which individual mind and the social are the same process. These chapters will explore what it might mean to say that the individual is social through and through as minds arise between people in their social relationships with each other. This is a perspective in which the individual in no way disappears from view or becomes the passive component of some social force or group mind, nor is it one in which minds somehow float between people. Rather, it is one in which mind is the action of a body just as social relationships are. It is a view in which individual minds and social relationships arise together, simultaneously. It does not lose sight of the individual but presents a perspective on how the individual mind arises, one in which neither the individual nor the social are prior or primary because both arise together.

This shift in perspective has important practical consequences, to be taken up in Part III. The most immediately obvious consequence is that if knowledge is under perpetual construction in the detail of relationships between people, then it is only already formed, rather than new, knowledge that can be captured in explicit form, codified and stored as an organizational asset. It becomes meaningless to talk about managing the learning and knowledge creation process. The practical outcome might be to stop wasting time and resources on efforts that cannot succeed, at least from the perspective I am presenting. Instead, attention might be directed at changing organizational actions and policies that disrupt and destroy patterns of relationship between people because these will destroy the learning and knowledge creating process. When considering mergers and acquisitions, a key question might be how such moves destroy the very reason for making the merger or acquisition.

4 The emergence of the individual and the social in communicative interaction

- Complex adaptive systems as a source domain for analogies of human acting and knowing
- The evolution of mind, self and society
- Back to the complexity sciences as source domain for analogies
- Conclusion

This chapter commences with a brief review of work done on complex adaptive systems by some scientists (Ray, 1992; Kauffman, 1993, 1995; Goodwin, 1994) at the Santa Fe Institute in the United States of America. I will explain below why I think that their work, and that of others (Prigogine, 1997; Allen, 1998a, 1998b) in the complexity sciences, serves as a source domain for analogies with human action despite claims made in this book that it is limiting to think about human action in systems terms, indeed inadequate when it comes to the creation of new knowledge. Having outlined some key features of the work on complex adaptive systems, the chapter then goes on to argue that Mead's (1934) theories of mind, self and society provide an insightful way of translating some insights from the complexity sciences into an understanding of human acting and knowing that does not rely upon a split between the individual and the social, which I have argued is the hallmark of both mainstream thinking and that of most of its critics.

Complex adaptive systems as a source domain for analogies of human acting and knowing

Although scientists who work with the concept of complex adaptive systems are clearly doing so within a systems framework, some of that work intriguingly points beyond systems thinking. Some are seeking to model phenomena that display the internal capacity to spontaneously produce coherence, as continuity and transformation, in the absence of any blueprint or external designer. For me, their work amounts to demonstrations of possibility. First, there is the possibility that both continuity and transformation can emerge spontaneously. Second, there is the possibility that it is the process of interaction that has the intrinsic capacity for patterning interaction as continuity and transformation at the same time.

Most systems theories envisage the systemic unfolding of that which is already enfolded, usually by a designer, in the system itself. They offer the prospect of control from outside the system, by a designer, and any transformation of the system must also be determined from outside by a designer. The complexity approach I am interested in, however, is one that is trying to simulate the process of evolution as a dynamic internal to evolution that expresses identity and difference at the same time. When this process of evolution is modeled as a "system" of interacting entities, that "system" has a life of its own that renders it much less susceptible to control from outside, if at all. This kind of systems modeling points toward Transformative Teleology in that a "system," with a life of its own, is perpetually constructing its own future as continuity and transformation. However, the modeling only points toward this kind of causality because it is all too easy to focus attention on the "system" and lose sight of the process of interaction, which is central to the notion of Transformative Teleology. I will be arguing that *the "system" does not provide an analogy for human action but that the process of interaction does*. The reasons for this claim and the meaning of Transformative Teleology are presented in the first volume (Stacey *et al.*, 2000) in the series of which this book is part and summarized in Box 3.1 on p. 60.

However, modeling of abstract interactive processes cannot directly say anything about human acting and knowing. The use of such modeling as source of analogy, therefore, requires caution for a number of reasons. The first is that the very act of modeling requires an external modeler and the specification of the model requires the initial design of a system, even though what is being modeled is an evolutionary process, one that is supposed not to depend upon any outside design and may not even be usefully thought of as a system. It requires an act of imagination, then, to avoid thinking about the model from an external perspective as a system and think, instead, about what the modeling of interaction might be saying *from a perspective within that interaction*. It is for this reason that complexity theories cannot simply be applied to human action; they can only serve as a source domain for analogies with it. Furthermore, the models of complex adaptive systems are nothing more than abstract sets of relationships that demonstrate possible properties of those relationships. These are relationships completely devoid of the attributes of any real processes and, therefore, their use as analogies requires imaginative acts of translation if they are to say anything about real processes. Later, this chapter will turn to such an act of translation in the human sphere but first consider some key aspects of complex adaptive system theory.

The structure of a complex adaptive system can be summarized in the following way:

- The system comprises large numbers of individual agents.
- These agents interact with each other according to rules that organize the interaction between them at a local level. In other words, an agent is a set of rules that determines how that agent will interact with a number of others and this interaction is "local" in the sense that there is no system-wide set of rules determining the interaction. The only rules are the rules located at the level of the agent itself.
- Agents endlessly repeat their interaction referring back to their rules, that is, interaction is iterative, recursive and self-referential.
- Agents' rules of interaction are such that the agents adapt to each other. The interaction is nonlinear and this nonlinearity is expressed in the variety of rules across the large numbers of agents.
- Ongoing variety in the rules is generated by random mutation and cross-over replication.

A number of hypotheses are put forward about the properties of interactive systems with this kind of structure:

- Coherent global patterns of order will emerge from the spontaneous self-organization of the agents as they interact according to their local rules, all in the absence of any overall blueprint. In other words, the iterative, recursive, nonlinear interactions constitute an attractor, that is, pattern of interaction.
- Those attractors may take a number of different dynamical forms

depending upon the state of important parameters, particularly the flow of energy, the number and strength of connections between agents and the degree of diversity of agents. For example, there may be stable equilibrium point or cyclical attractors, or unstable random patterns.

- At critical ranges of the parameters, a dynamic between stability and randomness arises and this takes the form of attractors that are paradoxically stable and unstable at the same time. This is the dynamic at the edge of chaos and it seems that attractors here are similar to the strange and fractal attractors of chaos theory.
- In the presence of random mutation and/or cross-over replication, the agents, that is, the diverse sets of local interaction rules, will evolve in an adaptive manner. In other words, in the presence of diversity, novel attractors will emerge. This evolution is radically unpredictable.
- One reason for the stability of the attractors at the edge of chaos is redundant interactions, while one reason for their instability is the amplification of small differences. The dynamic at the edge of chaos is characterized by a power law, which means that there are small numbers of large extinction events and large numbers of small ones. This power law provides another source of both stability, in that large extinctions are rare, and instability, in that there are extinction events at all. A further reason for stability lies in the constraints agents, as rules, place on interaction with each other and the fact that these constraints conflict with each other engenders instability. Since, in these systems, the rules evolve in an emergent way, so do the conflicting constraints.

What if human interaction is analogous in some way to the abstract interaction modeled by complex adaptive systems? What if the hypotheses outlined above provide some kind of analogy to human interaction? It could mean, for example, that human relating intrinsically patterns living human experience as the coherence of continuity and transformation. It could mean that this coherence arises without any blueprint, plan or vision. Perhaps the plans and visions are simply the form that the local interaction of the more powerful takes. It might mean that coherence in human action has to do with self-organizing conflicting constraints. If one starts to develop this line of thinking, it could lead to a very different understanding of human acting and knowing to that of the mainstream or most of its critics. Before pursuing this, however, consider how scientists working with ideas of complex adaptive systems demonstrate the possible plausibility of the above hypotheses.

Model interaction in the medium of digital symbols

The action of complex adaptive systems is explored using computer simulations in which each agent is a computer program, that is, a set of interaction rules expressed as computer instructions. Since each instruction is a bit string, a sequence of symbols taking the form of 0s and 1s, it follows that an agent is a sequence of symbols, arranged in a particular pattern specifying a number of algorithms. These algorithms determine how the agent will interact with other agents, which are also arrangements of symbols. In other words, the model is simply a large number of symbol patterns arranged so that they interact with each other. It is this local interaction between symbols patterns that organizes the pattern of interaction itself since there is no set of instructions organizing the global pattern of interaction across the system. The programmer specifies the initial rules, that is, symbol patterns, and then the computer program is run, or iterated, and the patterns of interaction across the system, the attractors, are observed. Simulations of this kind repeatedly produce patterns of behavior that are consistent with some or all of the hypotheses set out above. In other words, the models are a demonstration of the possibility of the hypotheses. They provide a "proof" of existence in the medium of digital symbols arranged into algorithmic rules.

For example, in his Tierra simulation, Ray (1992) designed one bit string, one symbol pattern, consisting of eighty instructions specifying how the bit string was to copy itself. He introduced random mutation into the bit string replication and limited computer time available for replicating as a selection criterion. In this way, he introduced chance, or instability, into the replicating process and imposed conditions that both enable and constrain that process. This instability within constraints made it possible for the system to generate novel attractors. The first attractor was that of exponentially increasing numbers, which eventually imposed a constraint on further replication. The overall pattern was a move from sparse occupation of the computer memory to overcrowding. However, during this process, the bit strings were gradually changing through random bit flipping, thus coming to differ from each other. Eventually, distinctively different kinds of bit strings emerged, namely, long ones and short ones. The constraints on computer time favored smaller ones so that the global pattern shifted from one of exponential increase, to one of stable numbers of long bit strings, to one of decline in long strings accompanied by an increase in short ones. The model spontaneously produced a new attractor, one that had not been programmed in. In other words, new forms of individual bit string and new overall global patterns emerged at the same time for there can be no global pattern of increase and decline without simultaneous change in the length of individual bit strings and there can be no sustained change in individual bit string lengths without the overall pattern of increase and decline. Individual bit string patterns, and the overall pattern of the system, are forming and being formed by each other, at the same time. To repeat, the new attractor is evident both at the level of the whole population and at the level of the individual bit strings themselves at the same time.

Furthermore, the new attractors are not designed but emerge as a self-organization process, where it is not individual agents that are organizing themselves but, rather, the pattern of interaction, and it is doing so simultaneously at the level of the individual agents and the population as a whole. It is problematic to separate them out as levels, since they are emerging simultaneously. No individual bit string can change in a coherent fashion on its own since random mutation in an isolated bit string would eventually lead to a completely random one. In interaction with other bit strings, however, advantageous mutations are selected and the others are weeded out. What is organizing itself, through interaction between symbol patterns, is changes in the symbol patterns themselves. Patterns of interacting are turning back on themselves, imperfectly replicating themselves, to yield changes in those patterns of interaction.

Ray, the objective observer external to this system, then interpreted the changes in symbol patterns in his simulation in terms of biology, in particular, the evolution of life. Using the model as an analogy, he argued that life has evolved in a similar, self-organizing and emergent manner. Other simulations have been used to suggest that this kind of emerging new attractor occurs only at the edge of chaos where there is a critical combination of both stability and instability.

The computer simulations thus demonstrate the possibility of the theory's hypotheses in the medium of digital symbols arranged as algorithmic rules. Digital symbols can quite clearly self-organize in the dynamics at the edge of chaos to produce emergent attractors of a novel kind, provided that those symbol patterns are richly connected and diverse enough. Natural scientists at the Santa Fe Institute and elsewhere then use this demonstration of possibility in the medium of digital symbols as a source of analogy to provide explanations of phenomena in particular areas of interest such as biology. There is no reason I can see why the same procedure should not be adopted in understanding human interaction, particularly given the importance of symbols in that interaction.

In the rest of this chapter, and in the others in this Part, I will argue that the interaction between patterns of digital symbols described above provides an abstract analogy for human interaction, if that interaction is understood from the perspective of Mead's thought on mind, self and society. In focusing on interaction as the point of analogy I am avoiding any analogy between complex adaptive systems and human action because that would immediately import the limitations of systems thinking referred to in the first part of this book. I am arguing that it is inappropriate to think of human interaction in systems terms, since that perspective reifies what is an ongoing process. I am taking the interaction of entities in the model as an analogy for relating between humans. *There is also no analogy between the programmer of the complex adaptive system model and anything in human interaction.* There is no possibility of standing outside human interaction to design a program for it since we are all participants in that interaction.

Consider now Mead's explanation of the evolution of mind, self and society and the way in which he understands human relating as a process of interaction in the medium of symbols.

The evolution of mind, self and society

To put Mead's views into perspective, consider explanations of how mind and society evolved according to evolutionary psychology (Pinker, 1997), a view already referred to in Chapter 3 in the discussion on how institutionalism sees the split between the individual and the social.

Evolutionary psychology

Evolutionary psychology presents a neo-Darwinian explanation, which focuses attention on biological individuals and holds that as these individuals reproduce, random mutations at the level of the genes result in new biological forms that are competitively selected for survival. Through this process, humans are held to have gradually evolved brains with increasingly sophisticated capacities for thinking, speaking and coordinating their interactions with each other in a purposeful manner.

Individuals with superior thinking capacities survived longer and so reproduced more, until unsophisticated thinkers gradually disappeared from the population. These thinking animals, equipped by evolution with language and reasoning instincts, then had the capacity to form sophisticated societies. It is the evolution of the genes, therefore, that produced consciousness and self-consciousness as properties of more sophisticated brains and it is these more sophisticated brains that made it possible to form human societies.

From this perspective, learning and knowledge creation first take place in an individual brain, which then communicates knowledge to other brains in a sender–receiver model of knowledge transmission. Minds, equated with brains, arise in the process of competitive selection operating on chance mutations of genes, and once minds have evolved, societies become possible. The process driving the evolution of both mind and society is the blind, selfish, competitive drive for survival on the part of the genes. First, there is chance and competition, and only later is there cooperation, where the motivating drive for the latter is that of survival value in competitive conditions.

This explanation immediately runs into the problem of how to explain cooperative behavior of an altruistic kind among humans. Evolutionary psychologists deal with this problem by arguing, in effect, that altruism does not exist and that individuals cooperate because it enhances the survival capacity of their genes. People are programmed by their genes to act "altruistically" toward their children and other family members because this enhances the chances that their genes will be reproduced and so continue to exist in the population.

Axelrod (1984) simulates this kind of process in his game of the prisoners' dilemma. In this game, two individuals are in competition with each other and a number of strategies are open to each of them. For example, they may cooperate with each other; or one may "defect" by withdrawing cooperation, while the other continues to cooperate; or they may both defect. Axelrod allocates points for cooperating and defecting: if both defect then they both lose a small number of points; if they both cooperate, then they both earn a small number of points; if one defects and the other cooperates, then the former earns a large number of points and the latter loses a large number of points.

In a one-off game, the risks of cooperation are so great that both are highly likely to defect. In other words, it is difficult to see how cooperation could arise in a one-off game of competition, given the strong survival incentive for selfish behavior. However, if the game is replayed many times, and both know that this will happen, then the winning strategy is not immediately obvious. Axelrod demonstrates that a conditional form of cooperation will evolve when the game is repeated over many periods. The winning strategy will be "tit-for-tat," that is, a strategy of cooperating until the other defects and then immediately defecting too. In this way, both parties learn that cooperation taking a conditional form gives an optimal outcome for both over the long run. Cooperation therefore evolves as the best survival strategy in an ongoing competitive game such as life.

The problem with this explanation of the evolution of cooperation is that a great many human interactions do not have the characteristics of the prisoners' dilemma game. First, the prisoners' dilemma is a zero sum game in that there are a fixed number of points and, furthermore, someone outside the interaction between the players sets the structure of the rewards. Human evolution could not have proceeded in this way, because in human interaction, people co-create their perspectives on rewards, and cooperation normally leads to an increase in the total reward pool. Second, one party to the game may be a great deal more powerful than the other, so that the former is simply not harmed by the defection of the latter, in which case cooperation would not evolve. One party may not care that another's defection will hurt him, or one party may actually enjoy it if his defection harms another, or one party might not even recognize the right of the other to exist, all with the same failure of cooperation to evolve. Third, both parties have to know, or to assume that the game will continue and this is not always true of human interaction. And if one locates evolution at the level of the genes, it is hard to see how a gene could "know" that it is not taking part in a one-off game. Fourth, this whole approach to understanding cooperation is devoid of any emotion, and anxiety has no impact in the purely individual, rational choice between strategies. Fifth, the human body, and the deep human need for relationships with others, are completely absent from the explanation. The result is a highly cognitivist explanation of how humans might have come to cooperate with each other, one that certainly does not resonate with my experience of life.

Mead's theory of the evolution of mind, self and society

Mead (1934), a social psychologist, took a very different tack. He held that it was not plausible to say that mind was suddenly there at some point in evolution, as the evolutionary psychologists would have it. He also held that it was not plausible to say that mind preceded society or vice versa, as simulations like the prisoners' dilemma suggest, because human societies are not possible without human minds and human minds are not possible in the absence of human societies. Many animals, certainly humans, cannot survive simply by competing. They must cooperate and they also have an intense, intrinsic need for relationship and attachment to others. Indeed, the human brain seems to be importantly shaped by the experience of attachment (Schore, 1994, 1997). Mead therefore sought an explanation of how mind and society, that is cooperative interaction, evolved together.

He adopted a phenomenological stance and argued that an explanation of the evolution of mind must start with the modes of interaction displayed by higher mammals that do not have minds in the human sense, and then identify a process through which human-like minds might have evolved from those modes of interaction. His was an essentially action-based account of how mind and society might have evolved. By human-like minds, he meant mammal behavior that displayed awareness on the part of the animal of what it was doing in relation to others, that is, an elementary form of consciousness. In other words, Mead was talking about a rudimentary capacity for reflection on, thought about, and prediction of, the response that an action by one was likely to evoke in another. He sought to derive an explanation of these capacities from observations of the interactive behavior of the higher mammals and he often used dogs in his examples.

He pointed to how dogs relate to each other in a responsive manner, with the act of one fitting into the act of the other in some way, thus constituting an aggressive or playful, competitive or cooperative interaction, for example. His focus was immediately on interaction between animals, that is, a rudimentary form of social behavior. This led him to define a social act as a gesture by one animal that calls forth a response from another, which together constitute meaning for both. Immediately, knowing and knowledge becomes a property of interaction, or relationship. For example, one dog makes the gesture of a snarl and this may call forth a counter-snarl, or flight, or submissive crouching on the part of the other. The meaning to both animals of the first social act of snarl and counter-snarl is a fight, while that of the second is victory of one over the other, and that of the third is immediate dominance and submission. Mead argued that meaning does not lie in the gesture alone but in the social act as a whole. In other words, meaning arises in the responsive interaction between actors. Meaning does not arise first in each individual, to be subsequently expressed in action. Meaning is not transmitted from one individual to another but, rather, arises in the interaction between them. Meaning is not attached to an object, or stored, but perpetually created in the interaction.

Mead described the gesture as a symbol in the sense that it is an action that points to a meaning. However, the meaning could not be located in the symbol taken on its own. The meaning only becomes apparent in the response to the gesture and therefore lies in the whole social act of gesture-response. The gesture, as symbol, points to how the meaning might emerge in the response. Here meaning is emerging in the action of the living present in which the immediate future (response) acts back on the past (gesture) to change its meaning. Meaning is not simply located in the past (gesture) or the future (response) but in the circular interaction between the two in the living present. In this way, the present is not simply a point but has a time structure.

Mead argued that the gesture-response patterns of competition and cooperation constituted the kind of society that is widely found in nature. Mostly, such societies rest on functional specialization. For example, ant societies are structured by specialization into workers and breeders, while mammals may tend to specialize into hunters and breeders and into those that are dominant and those that are submissive.

Mindless cooperation and competition

The argument so far is depicted in Figure 4.1, showing the continuous process of gesture and response. I want to stress the word *continuous*. As soon as I try to depict what Mead is saying in a diagram, it looks as if the only time frame is the present. However, this is not the case. What is being depicted is a micro snapshot in an ongoing process, preceded by a whole history of gestures and responses and to be followed by yet further gestures and responses. Every gesture is a response to some previous gesture, which is a response to an even earlier one, thereby constructing history.

Figure 4.1 makes another simplification in that it takes interaction between two animals but, of course, the process will actually take place between many. In addition to the two interacting individuals, Figure 4.1 depicts the context within which they are gesturing and responding. This

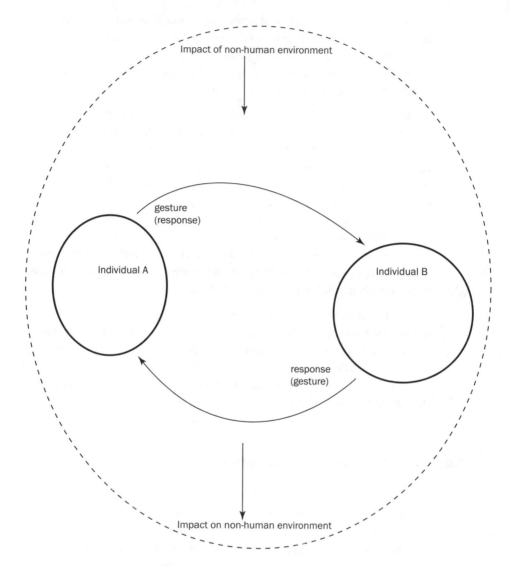

Figure 4.1 *Gesture and response*

context of physical environment and other organisms both enables and constrains the actions and interactions of the particular animals in the illustration. The acting and interacting of these animals also have an impact on the physical context. For example, large numbers of herbivores may denude particular kinds of vegetation, which might then be replaced by other kinds, thus altering the physical environment. This process of gesture and response between biological entities in a physical context constitutes simple cooperative, that is, social, activity of a mindless, reflex kind. The "conversation of gestures" is both enabling and constraining at the same time and it constitutes meaning. Cooperation here takes the form of functional specialization in which animals act in a meaningful way but are not aware of the meaning. At this stage, meaning is implicit in the social act itself and those acting are unaware of that implicit meaning.

This argument is suggesting that social, that is, simultaneously cooperative and competitive interaction, is fundamental in nature. Instead of adopting neo-Darwinian explanations that need to show how cooperation might have emerged from selfish competition, there is the notion of self-organizing processes that intrinsically produce emergent cooperative forms, which are only then subjected to competitive selection. Kauffman (1993, 1995), for example, shows how it is possible for autocatalytic chains to form in random interaction between molecules. In other words, molecules cooperate in the production of each other as the very basis of life. He argues that such connecting processes are typical of living forms in which simultaneously cooperative and competitive, self-organizing processes are far more important than random variations in producing variety in life forms. Cooperation is then as much to be expected as competition with neither being more fundamental than the other.

Mindful cooperation and competition

To continue with Mead's argument, he held that humans must have evolved from mammals with similar rudimentary social structures to those found in present-day species of mammals, as described in previous paragraphs and depicted in Figure 4.1. But how? His explanation ran along the following lines. The mammal ancestors of humans evolved central nervous systems that enabled them to gesture to others in a manner that was capable of calling forth in themselves the same range of responses as in those to whom they were gesturing. This would happen if, for example, the snarl of one called forth in itself the fleeting feelings associated with counter-snarl, flight or submissive posture, just as they did in the one to whom the gesture of snarl was being made. The gesture, as symbol, now has a substantially different role. Mead described such a gesture as a significant symbol, where a significant symbol is one that calls forth the same response in the gesturer as in the one to whom it is directed. Significant symbols, therefore, make it possible for the gesturer to "know" what he or she is doing.

This simple idea is, I think, a profound insight. If, when one makes a gesture to another, one is able to experience in one's own body a similar response to that which the gesture provokes in another body, then one can "know" what one is doing. It becomes possible to intuit something about the range of likely responses from the other. This ability to experience in the body something similar to that which another body experiences in response to a gesture becomes the basis of knowing and of consciousness.

In Chapter 3 I mentioned Gergen's criticism that Mead did not explain how one organism could know the potential response of another. In fact, Mead did provide an explanation, namely, that the central nervous system, or better still the biologically evolved whole body, has the capacity to call forth in itself feelings that are similar to those experienced by other bodies. The body, with its nervous system, becomes central to understanding how animals "know" anything.

The body and feelings

Mead was insistent on talking about interactions between bodies. He argued that any explanation of interaction had to be consistent with the capabilities of an animal's nervous system. The nervous system had to be such as to make it possible for the gesturer to call forth a response in his or her own body that is similar to that called forth by the gesture in another body. Mead himself did not develop this idea but recent research on the brain provides support for Mead's insight.

For example, the neuroscientist, Damasio (1994, 1999) argues that the human brain continuously monitors and integrates the rhythmical activity of the heart, lungs, gut, muscles and other organs, as well as the immune, visceral and other systems in the body. At each moment the brain is registering the internal state of the body and Damasio argues that these body states constitute feeling states. This continuous monitoring activity, that is, registration of feeling states, is taking place as a person selectively perceives external objects, such as a face or an aroma, and experience then forms an association between the two. Every perception of an object outside the body is associated, through acting in the world, with particular body states, that is, patterns of feeling. When a person encounters situations similar to previous ones, he or she experiences similar feeling states, or body rhythms, which orient that person to act in the situation. In this way, human worlds become affect-laden and the feeling states unconsciously narrow down the options to be considered in a situation. In other words, feelings unconsciously guide choice and when the capacity to feel is damaged, so is the capacity to rapidly select sensible action options. Damasio suggests that, from a neurological standpoint, the body's monitoring of its own rhythmic patterns is both the ground for its construction of the world it acts in and its unique sense of subjectivity.

Feelings, therefore, are rhythmic patterns in a body and they make it possible for the gesture of one body to call forth in itself a similar response, a similar feeling rhythm, to that called forth in the body to whom the gesture is made. In other words, there is some kind of resonance between the body rhythms of the two interacting individuals. Possessing this capacity, the maker of a gesture can intuit, perhaps even predict, the consequences of that gesture. In other words, he or she can know what he or she is doing, just before the other responds. That intuition may well take the form of one body's rhythmic patterns resonating with those of another in a form of direct communication. The whole social act, that is, meaning, can be experienced in advance of carrying out the whole act, opening up the possibility of reflection and choice in making a gesture. Furthermore, the one responding has the same opportunity for reflecting upon, and so choosing, from the range of responses. The first part of a gesture can be taken by the other as an indication of how further parts of the gesture will unfold from the response. In this way, the two can indicate to each other how they might respond to each other in the continuous circle in which a gesture by one calls forth a response from another, which is itself a gesture back to the first. Obviously, this capacity makes more sophisticated forms of cooperation possible.

Consciousness and meaning

The capacity to call forth the same response in oneself as in the other is thus a rudimentary form of awareness, or consciousness, and together with meaning, it emerges in the social conversation of gestures. At the same time as the emergence of conscious meaning, there also emerges the potential for more sophisticated cooperation. Human social forms and human consciousness thus both emerge at the same time, each forming the other, and there cannot be one without the other. As individuals interact with each other in this way, the possibility arises of a pause before making a gesture. In a kind of private role play, emerging in the repeated experience of public interaction, one individual learns to take the attitude of the other, enabling a kind of trial run in advance of actually completing or even starting the gesture. Will it call forth aggression, fright, flight or submission? What will be the consequences in each case?

In this way, *rudimentary forms of thinking develop, taking the form of private role playing*, that is, gestures made by a body to itself, calling forth responses in itself. Mead said that humans are fundamentally role playing animals. This argument emphasizes the importance of playing in the evolution of more sophisticated forms of cooperation, that is, more sophisticated forms of society. Note how the argument so far does not rely on the capacity for language. The simultaneous private and public role plays so far discussed all take place without verbal language. They take place in the medium of significant symbols, which are feelings, that is, body rhythms, and actions, and together they constitute what Mead called a "conversation of gestures" in significant symbols.

Mead then argued that the gesture that is particularly useful in calling forth the same attitude in oneself as in the other is the vocal gesture. This is because we can hear the sounds we make in much the same way as others hear them, while we cannot see the facial gestures we make as others see them, for example. The development of more sophisticated patterns of vocal gesturing, that is, of the language form of significant symbols, is thus of major importance in the development of consciousness and of sophisticated forms of society. Mind and society emerge together in the medium of language. However, I want to add that since speaking and listening are actions of bodies, and since bodies are never without feelings, the medium of language is also always the medium of feelings.

This development is depicted in Figure 4.2, which shows the continuous cycle of gesture and response between two individuals and the simultaneously occurring, private role play by each with him/herself. Figure 4.2 also makes the point that both the public conversations of gestures and the private role plays of each participant always have biological correlates in the form of body rhythms. Figure 4.2 also suggests that bodies directly resonate with each other as individuals interact.

Furthermore, these public and private role plays, or conversations, which constitute the experience of the interacting individuals, actually shape the patterns of connections in the plastic brains of each (Freeman, 1995). Both public and private conversations are shaping, while being shaped by the spatio-temporal patterns of brain and body. This simultaneous public and private conversation of gestures takes place in the medium of

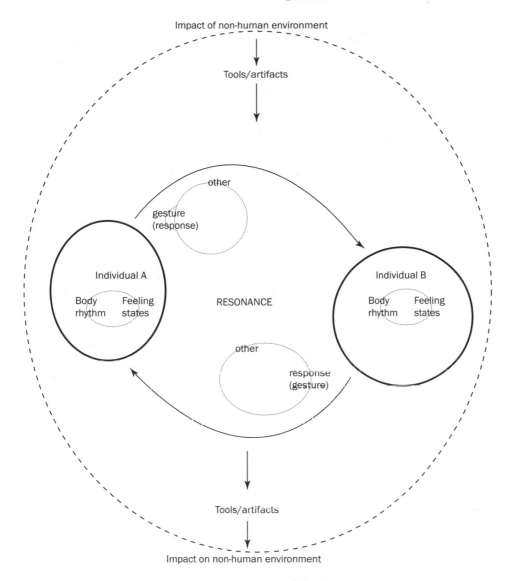

Figure 4.2 *Calling forth the same response in oneself as in the other*

significant symbols, particularly those of language, and it is this capacity for symbolic mediation of cooperative activity that is one of the key features distinguishing humans from other animals.

Vygotsky (1962) points to another key distinguishing feature of humans, namely, their possession of hands and thus their ability use tools. Human development has depended crucially on the ability to use tools cooperatively and that ability to use tools in ever more sophisticated ways is made possibly by the ability to speak. Figure 4.2, therefore, depicts the process in which humans act in relation to their material and non-human contexts using tools. In this way, human societies have a significant impact on the context, which simultaneously has both enabling and constraining effects on human activity.

As soon as one can take the attitude of the other, that is, as soon as one communicates in significant symbols, there is at least a rudimentary form of consciousness, that is, one can "know" the potential consequences of one's actions. The nature of the social has thus shifted from mindless cooperation through functional specialization to mindful, role playing interaction made more and more sophisticated by the use of language. Meaning is now particularly constituted in gesturing and responding in the medium of vocal symbols, but as I will argue in the next chapter, these vocal symbols are always aspects of a whole process that always includes the "symbols" of feeling. In other words, the principal enabling and constraining social process is conversation in words, but such conversation is always also in the medium of feelings. Mind, or consciousness, is the gesturing and responding action of a body directed toward itself as private role play and silent conversation, and society is the gesturing and responding actions of bodies directed toward each other. They are thus the same kind of process, characterized by interaction, that is, responsive communicative acts within and between individual bodies characterized by biological rhythms that constitute feelings, within an environment of other organisms and the material world within which people operate using tools in order to transform that environment.

The social attitude

Mead takes his argument further when he suggests how the private role play evolves in increasingly complex ways. As more and more interactions are experienced with others, so increasingly, more roles and wider ranges of possible responses enter into the role playing activity that precedes the gesture, or to be more accurate, is continuously intertwined with public gesturing and responding. In this way, the capacity to take the attitude of many others evolves and this becomes generalized. Each engaged in the conversation of gestures can now take the attitude of what Mead calls the generalized other. Eventually, individuals develop the capacity to take the attitude of the whole group, or what Mead calls the game. In other words, creatures have now evolved who are capable of taking the social attitude as they gesture and respond. The result is much more sophisticated processes of cooperative interaction. This is depicted in Figure 4.3.

There is now mindful, social behavior with increasingly sophisticated meaning and an increasing capacity to use tools more and more effectively to transform the context within which the interacting creatures live.

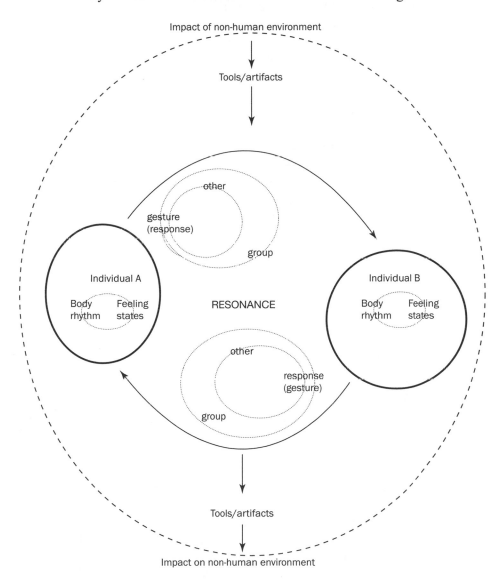

Figure 4.3 *Taking the attitude of the group*

The emergence of self

The next step in this evolutionary process is the linking of the attitude of specific and generalized others, even of the whole group, with a "me." In other words, there evolves a capacity to take the attitude of others not just toward one's gestures but also toward one's self. The "me" is the configuration of the gestures/responses of the others/society to one as a subject, or an "I." What has evolved here is the capacity to be an object to oneself, a "me," and this is the capacity to take the attitude of the group, not simply to one's gestures, but to one's self. A self, as the relationship between "me" and "I," has therefore emerged, as well as an awareness of that self, that is, self-consciousness. In this interaction, the "I" is the response to the gesture of the group/society to oneself, that is, the "me." The "me" is the attitude of others to the "I." Mead argues, very importantly, that this "I" response to the one's perception of the attitude of the group to oneself (the "me") is not a given but is always potentially unpredictable in that there is no predetermined way in which the "I" might respond to the "me." In other words, each of us may respond in many different ways to our perception of the views others have of us. Here, Mead is pointing to the importance of difference, or diversity, in the emergence of the new, that is, in the potential for transformation. I will take this up in Chapter 7, in a way Mead did not, when I deal with the role of fantasy in the development of unique individual role plays. Language plays a major role at this stage of evolution. Mead argues that without it, the emergence of human mind, self and society, as we know it, would be impossible.

At this point, a fully human society has emerged and simultaneously fully human minds, including selves. Mead consistently argued that one is not more fundamental than the other; that one could not exist without the other. The social, in human terms, is a highly sophisticated process of cooperative interaction between people in the medium of symbols in order to undertake joint action. Such sophisticated interaction could not take place without self-conscious minds but nor could those self-conscious minds exist without that sophisticated form of cooperation. In other words, there could be no private role play, including silent conversation, by a body with itself, if there were no public interaction of the same form. Mind/self and society are all logically equivalent processes of a conversational kind. Social interaction is a public conversation of gestures, particularly gestures of a vocal kind, while mind is a conversation of a gestures between "I," "me," "other," and "group" in a silent, private role play of public, social interaction. The result is self-referential, reflexive processes of sophisticated cooperation in the medium of symbols that constitute meaning. These processes, always involving the body and its feelings, both enable and constrain human experience and they are the basic forms of what I am calling complex responsive processes of relating.

Figure 4.4 depicts what has just been described, adding the point made before that all of these interactions, private and public, are processes in which humans act within a physical non-human context using tools and technology in a cooperative manner. In acting thus within the context, humans affect that context, which simultaneously affects them, enabling them to do what they do, and constraining them from doing other things. Figure 4.4 deliberately shows the processes of individual selves/minds outside individual bodies in order to indicate that mind/self emerges between people, in the relationship between them, and cannot be simply "located" within an individual body. In this way of thinking, individual minds/selves certainly exist, and very importantly so, but they emerge in relationships between people rather than arising within an individual.

However, the symbolic processes of mind/self are always actions, experienced within a body as rhythmic variations, that is, feeling states. Mind is action of the body, rather like walking is the action of the body. One would not talk about walking emerging from the body and it is no more appropriate to talk about mind emerging from the brain. Note how the private role play, including the silent conversation of mind/self, is not stored as representations of a pre-given reality. It is, rather, continuous spontaneous action in which patterns of action are continuously reproduced in repetitive forms as continuity, sameness and identity, and simultaneously as potential transformation of that identity. In other words, as with interaction between bodies, the social, so with interaction of a body with itself, mind, there is the experience of both familiar repetition of habit and the potential of spontaneous change. The process is not representing or storing but continuously reproducing and creating new meaningful experience. In this way, the fundamental importance of the individual self and identity is retained, along with the fundamental importance of the social. In this way too, both continuity and potential transformation are always simultaneously present.

In Chapter 3, I drew attention to Gergen's criticism of Mead's thought. He was critical of the way in which Mead never abandons private subjectivity. As I have already said, I regard this as a strength in that

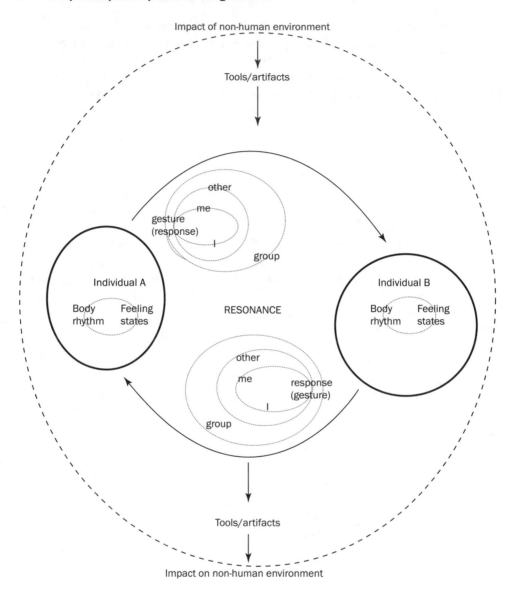

Figure 4.4 *Self-consciousness*

Mead is able to accord the same importance to individual subjectivity and the social, while Gergen abandons the former in favor of the latter. Next, Gergen says that Mead never explains how one person can grasp another's state of mind. Mead, however, never makes this claim. What he does argue is that one person can call forth in himself or herself a similar response to that called forth by a gesture in another. I understand this to be possible because one body can experience similar feeling rhythms to another's. This is not the same as grasping another's state of mind. Instead it is saying that one human body can empathize, can be attuned to another. This notion finds some support in studies of brain and body functioning.

Gergen also says that Mead's argument displays a whiff of social determinism. He points to the discussion on private role play in which the gesture of the other calls forth that role play. However, Mead's discussion of the "I" makes it clear that he was making no such suggestion. He says that the response of the "I" is not given. There is a notion of individual autonomy here. However, Gergen has a point, it seems to me. First, this "I" in Mead's argument sounds somewhat mysterious in that there is no explanation of the basis on which the "I" responds. Furthermore, saying that a response is called forth by the gesture of another does sound like the other determining the response. I want to suggest, therefore, that the response is simultaneously called forth by the gesture of the other and selected or enacted by the responder. In other words, the response of the "I" is both being called forth by the other and being enacted, or selected by the history, biological, individual and social of the responder. Your gesture calls forth a response in me but only a response I am capable of making and that depends upon my history. The constructivist argument mentioned in Chapter 2, therefore, brings an added dimension to Mead's argument. What I am suggesting is a tension of movement in the response, a tension of selection/enactment and evocation/provocation at the same time. In this way, the reproduction and potential transformation of historical responses in the living present are held in tension with the reproduction and potential transformation of evocation. In this way, Hodgson's criticism of structuration theory (see Chapter 3) does not apply to the argument being developed here because it features history, context and bodily interaction. The argument I am developing is one of emergence and it does not ultimately locate the source of change in the individual alone.

The perspective I am suggesting is similar to that of social constructionism in some respects, particularly in that both focus attention on the detail of human relating. However, there are important differences. First, there is no split between the individual and the social as there is in social constructionism and, therefore, no elevation of the social above the individual. There is no loss of the individual who therefore retains responsibility for his or her actions. If one has the capacity to call forth the attitude of the other in oneself, the capacity for private role play and silent conversation, the capacity for thought and reflection, then one has the duty to account for one's actions to others even if one cannot know what the consequences of these actions will be. Moral responsibility is simultaneously individual and social. There is no displacement of ethical responsibility from "I" to "we" as there is for many social constructionists. Mead was insistent on the social as moral order and the ethical responsibility of the individual in that order.

Back to the complexity sciences as source domain for analogies

What I have been describing in the previous section is a process of interaction between people in which their actions of gesturing and responding are understood as significant symbols. In other words, the process is an embodied one of interaction between embodied symbols of a particular kind, namely, the significant symbols of human gesturing, for example, in sounds called words. Scientists working with the idea of complex adaptive systems, mentioned at the beginning of this chapter, are exploring the properties of abstract models of interaction between symbols of a different kind, namely, digital symbols. The previous section suggests a way of thinking about human interaction as a continuous circular process of gesturing and responding between people in the medium of embodied symbols. The models of complex adaptive systems explore the nature of continuous circular processes of interaction between computer programs in the medium of digital symbols. It is possible that certain properties of interaction demonstrated in the abstract models might, therefore, offer analogies for human interaction, interpreted through Mead's thought. But why would one be looking for analogies in the first place? The reason, I think, is that Mead's powerful insights do not take us quite far enough, as I now go on to explain.

In the previous section, I presented Mead's basic ideas in a simplified form using interaction between two individuals as an example. As one imagines the process of gesturing and responding between larger and large numbers of individuals, the complexity of it all becomes mind-boggling. How could continuous circular processes of gesturing and responding between thousands, even millions of people produce any kind of coherence? This is not an issue that Mead dealt with, but it is one where the complexity sciences offer important insights, in my view.

The intrinsic ordering properties of interaction

As I mentioned earlier on in this chapter, a key insight from the complexity sciences relates to the intrinsic properties of interaction. The modeling of complex systems demonstrates the possibility that interactions between large numbers of entities, each entity responding to others on the basis of its own local organizing principles, will produce coherent patterns with the potential for novelty in certain conditions, namely, the paradoxical dynamics at the edge of chaos. In other words, the very process of self-organizing interaction, when richly connected enough, has the inherent capacity to spontaneously produce coherent pattern in itself, without any blueprint or program. Furthermore, when the interacting entities are different enough from each other, that capacity is one of spontaneously producing novel patterns in itself. In other words, abstract systems can pattern themselves where those patterns have the paradoxical feature of continuity and novelty, identity and difference, at the same time. By analogy, I understand the circular process of gesturing and responding between people who are different to be self-organizing relating in the medium of symbols with an intrinsic patterning capacity. In other words, patterns of relating pattern relating in ways that constitute both continuity and novelty, both identity and difference. This is what I mean by complex responsive process of relating and it amounts to a particular causal framework, namely, that of Transformative Teleology, where the process is one of perpetual construction of the future as both continuity and potential transformation at the same time. A single causal framework of Transformative Teleology here replaces the dual causal framework of Rationalist and Formative Teleology upon which mainstream thinking is founded.

If one takes this view of the emergence of coherent patterns of relating in the process of relating, then there is no need to look for the causes of coherent human action in concepts such as deep structures, archetypes, the collective unconscious, transcendental wholes, common pools of meaning, group minds, the group-as-a-whole, transpersonal processes, foundation matrix, the personal dynamic unconscious, inner worlds, mental models, and so on. Instead, one understands human relating to be inherently pattern forming. This leads to a very different notion of human agency. Agency means doing and human agency means human bodies doing something. Agency is concerned with what causes human bodies to do what they do. And what they do to survive is interact with each other. Humans are social animals and the cause of what they do cannot be simply located in their bodies. However, social structures and institutions cannot do anything because they are simply the routines and habits of human bodies. So one cannot locate agency there either. Nor can one split relationship off as an "it," a third realm of experience, and locate agency there because relating is not an "it" but an ephemeral process. If one holds that human doing and acting is a responsive process of relating between bodies perpetually patterning relating between bodies, then agency is patterning processes forming and being formed by patterning processes. Individual mind and social relating are patterning processes forming and being formed by patterning processes.

Fractal processes

I also want to suggest that complex responsive processes of relating can be understood, using a term from the complexity sciences, as fractal interaction. Fractal shapes are irregular shapes that display self-similarity, or scale invariance. This means that, no matter what the degree of detail of examination of the shape, it always reveals similar degrees of irregular patterning and no degree of detail is more fundamental than any other. For example, a branch on a tree has a similar irregular shape as the whole tree. A fractal process has a temporal aspect characterized by irregular fluctuations in multiple time scales. No matter what the time period within which the fluctuations are examined, they display a similar degree of irregularity. There is no time scale that is more fundamental than any other. The important point about fractal phenomena, therefore, is their self-similarity at all scales and the fact that no scale is more fundamental than any other.

Looking at Figure 4.4, and bearing in mind that it is a spatial representation of what is essentially temporal process, one can see that this is true of Mead's explanation of mind and society. From a macro perspective, Figure 4.4 depicts a process in which two people cooperatively operate within a physical context through the medium of tools and artifacts, while that context simultaneously enables and constrains their cooperative operation. In a sense they collectively make a gesture to the physical context, which responds so that the physical context is forming the cooperative human action while it is significantly being formed by it. Looking more closely at the cooperative interaction itself, one sees a self-similar process of public, largely vocal gesturing and responding between the interacting individual bodies as they resonate with each other. Looking even more closely at one of the individuals in the group, one sees a self-similar process of gesturing and responding in a private, silent role play, a mirror of the vocal public processes that is forming them while it is being formed by them. Looking even more closely, one sees that this silent role play, as well as the public interaction with other people, is also a self-similar process in that body rhythms are forming role plays and interactions while being formed by them (Dardik, 1997). This fractal perspective on individual and group in a physical context makes it clear that one is talking simply about levels of examination rather than anything fundamental. In fractal processes, no level is more fundamental than, or prior to, any other level. In Figure 4.4 one cannot say that the individual is more fundamental than the dyad or vice versa.

The complex responsive process of relating perspective, then, is one in which the individual, the group, the organization and the society are all the same kinds of phenomenon, at the same ontological level. There is no split and the question of which is prior or primary does not, therefore, even arise. The individual mind/self is an interactive role-playing process conducted privately and silently in the medium of symbols by a body with itself and the group, organization and society are all also interactive processes in the medium of the same symbols, this time publicly and often vocally between different bodies. The individual and the social, in this scheme, simply refer to the degree of detail in which the whole process is being examined.

Habits and systems

Chapter 3 described culture and social structure in terms of shared, repetitive and enduring values, beliefs, traditions, habits, routines and procedures. From a complex responsive process perspective, these are all social acts of a particular kind. They are couplings of gesture and response of a predictable, highly repetitive kind. They do not exist in any meaningful way in a store anywhere but, rather, they are continually reproduced in the interaction between people. However, even habits are rarely exactly the same. They may often vary as those with whom one interacts change and as the context of that interaction changes. In other words, there will usually be some spontaneous variation in the repetitive reproduction of patterns called habits.

Figure 4.5 depicts the addition of social habits and routines, values and beliefs, as aspects of repetition and variation in patterns of gesture and response. These habits and routines, values and beliefs are not at some higher ontological level. They are part of the pattern of interaction between people. Furthermore, there is no requirement here of any sharing of mental contents, or any requirement that people should be engaging in the same private role plays. The only requirement for the social understood as habits, routines and so on, is that people should be acting them out.

Figure 4.5 also depicts tools and cultural artifacts, a category that includes communication technology, books and other "stores" of knowledge. Although systems, databases, recorded and written artifacts are usually thought of as stores of knowledge, from the complex responsive process perspective they are simply records that can only become knowledge when people use them as tools in their processes of gesturing and responding to each other. What is captured in these artifacts is inevitably something about the meanings of social acts already performed. Since a social act is ephemeral and since knowledge is social acts, it can never be stored or captured. Habits here are understood not as shared mental contents but as history-based, repetitive actions, both private and public, reproduced in the living present with relatively little variation.

Knowledge creation

In mainstream thinking, knowledge is ultimately located in the mental models, the inner world, of individual minds, consisting of representations formed in past experience and stored in memory. When a new stimulus is encountered, relevant models are retrieved from memory to process the data and generate knowledge. From the alternative complex responsive process perspective, individual minds are continuously reproduced, that is historical, and potentially transformed private role plays and silent conversations mirroring public communicative interaction. Evolving public communicative interaction of gesture-response triggers shifts in private role plays and silent conversations. There is no storing and retrieving, only perpetual reproduction and transformation of themes made habitual by historical experience. Past experience has shaped the themes patterning both public and private role plays, but they are rarely reproduced in exactly the same way. Past experience has shaped brain–body patterning in particular ways and further relating is triggering reproduction and transformation. The shift here is from a notion of past

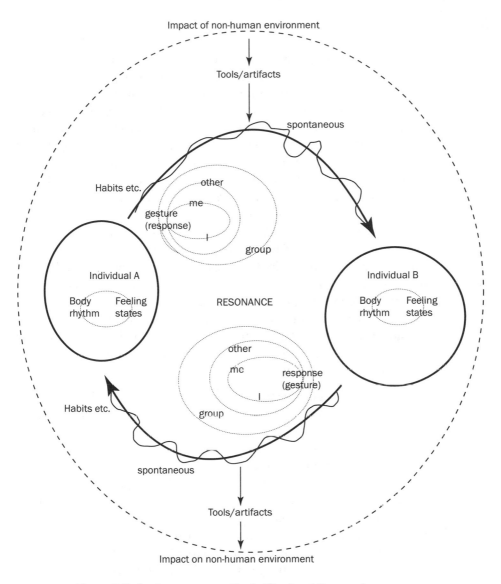

Figure 4.5 *Gesture-response: the habitual and the spontaneous*

experience being more or less accurately recorded and placed in storage, to past experience shaping current relating processes in the living present with its ever-present spontaneous potential for transformation. Chapter 9 will explain how this perspective is consistent with some views of how the brain functions. Knowledge, then, is not stored but perpetually created.

Conclusion

This chapter has set out the main features of a way of thinking about individuals and groups in terms of complex responsive processes of relating. These are processes of interaction between human bodies in the medium of symbols. They are processes of continuous reproduction and potential transformation of meaning arising in social action. The potential for transformation in Mead's scheme lies in the unpredictable response of the individual "I" to the "me." It is because an individual does not have a pre-programmed response to the perception she or he has of the attitude of others to her/himself that she/he can respond in novel ways. Note that although Mead sees the individual mind as logically the same process as relating between people in a group, he does not lose the notion of individual agency. Individuals can respond in individually novel ways, but their responses are always in the relationships they form and that form them. Agency is, thus, neither located in an individual, nor in the collective, nor in both. Instead it is patterning process, simultaneously individual and social. Furthermore, in this way of thinking, knowledge is not stored anywhere and then retrieved to form the basis of action. Rather, knowledge is continuously reproduced and transformed in relational interaction between individuals.

There are profound implications of this way of thinking for how one understands learning and knowledge creation in organizations. From the mainstream perspective, knowledge is thought to be stored in individual heads, largely in tacit form, and it can only become the asset of an organization when it is extracted from those individual heads and stored in some artifact as explicit knowledge. From the perspective being suggested here, knowledge is always a process, and a relational one at that, which cannot therefore be located simply in an individual head, to be extracted and shared as an organizational asset. Knowledge is the act of conversing, and learning occurs when ways of talking and therefore patterns of relationship, change. Knowledge in this sense cannot be stored and attempts to store it in artifacts of some kind will capture only its more trivial aspects. Organizational policies that disrupt relational patterns between people, however, could seriously damage its knowledge-generating capacity. The knowledge assets of an organization, then, lie in the pattern of relationships between its members and are destroyed when those relational patterns are destroyed. This begins to suggest very different ways of thinking about what it might mean to "manage" knowledge in an organization.

To develop further the perspective introduced in this chapter, the next chapter examines the nature of symbols and Chapter 6 looks at the patterning of symbolic interaction. I then turn to the enabling constraints that emerge in relating and finally to some ideas on the dynamics of relating.

5 Communicative action in the medium of symbols

- ● The importance of feelings
- ● The importance of reflection-in-action
- ● The importance of abstract thinking
- ● The multiple aspects of symbols
- ● Conclusion

The last chapter argued for a way of thinking about human acting and knowing that makes no fundamental separation between individual self-conscious minds and social interaction but, rather, sees them as different aspects of the same processes of cooperative, complex responsive relating between people. The distinctive features of this approach are as follows:

- ● Both the individual and the collective identities of human beings emerge in the complex interactions between human bodies as they responsively relate to each other. Meaning, that is, knowledge, also emerges in that interaction.
- ● In their responsive relating, people indicate to each other the potential evolution of their intended actions and it is this indication that makes it possible for them to cooperate in sophisticated ways. Responsive relating is a process in which people interweave their actions so that they can go on being and operating together. This circular, responsive process constitutes the joint action that is the social process and it is one in which human bodies act selectively in relation to other human bodies, thereby evoking selective responses from them.
- ● Bodies are uniquely individual and part of that uniqueness is an individual's self-conscious mind. Mind is the actions of an individual's body reflexively directed back to itself so as to call forth in itself bodily responses similar to those evoked by actions directed to other bodies. The responses that a body spontaneously calls forth in itself are simultaneously selected or enacted by that body's history of relating with others. In other words, the human mind is not separate in any way

from the body, but neither are the processes of mind located in the body. Mind and self are, rather, actions of a whole body, just as, say, walking is. The action of walking is performed by a body and that action is neither separate from the body, nor is it located in the body. The feature that distinguishes the action of mind and self from actions such as walking is that the former is directed back to that individual body while the action of walking is directed in the space around the body.

- The social is thus actions that are public and directed by one body to another, while individual mind/self is actions privately directed back to the body.
- Human action, then, simultaneously consists of both the private action directed back at the individual's body, that is, the individual mind/self, and the public action directed between individual bodies, that is, the social.
- A distinguishing feature of human action, both in its public and private forms, is that it is communication in the medium of symbols, which makes sophisticated cooperative activity possible.
- Another important distinguishing feature of cooperative human activity is that it is accomplished with the use of tools, essentially extensions of the body. The tools are the artifacts, technologies and designed systems human beings use to operate collectively in their non-human environment in order to "carn a living."
- Action itself, of either the public or the private kind, as communication or as operational use of tools, cannot be stored, only reproduced and potentially transformed. While the tools used in operational action usually take some physical form and thus can be stored, the question of storing becomes more complicated when it come to symbols. The symbols of communicative action can, of course, be recorded and stored in artifacts such as books. However, this record only becomes active symbols, that is, gestures calling forth responses, when used by someone, that is, when employed as part of an action. It is only in this action of using the artifact, reading the book, that meaning emerges. However, the symbol itself cannot be stored simply because it is an action, a gesture. Meaning, knowledge itself, therefore, cannot be stored. Any store of recorded symbols becomes simply a tool for potential use in communicative processes and their construction of meaning.
- All human action is history dependent. Any current action, whether in the medium of symbols or using tools is both enabled and constrained by the actions preceding it. Actions are patterned by both previous history and current context.

- Interaction, or relationship, has intrinsic pattern-forming properties, including the property of emergent novelty when interaction is diverse enough.

Central to the complex responsive process approach, then, is communicative interaction in the medium of symbols and the intrinsic patterning properties of such communicative relating. The purpose of this chapter is to further explore the nature of symbols and the purpose of the next chapter will be to consider the pattern-forming properties of communicative interaction.

The meaning of the word "symbol" is now most commonly taken to be a thing that represents something other than itself, such as the word "table" representing, perhaps, a wooden object upon which some other object might be placed. The word itself is derived from the Greek words *symbolon* meaning a mark or a token and *sym-ballein*, which means to throw together. Mead's use of the word is very different to common usage and more in line with the origins of the word in the sense that he takes symbols to be actions. For him, a gesture made by one animal that is responded to by another is a symbol. I understand this to mean that a gesture is thrown together with
a response and together they "stand for," or better still, constitute a meaning. Mead rejected the notion that symbols are independent of their meaning and said that they could not lie outside the field of action. He focused his attention on significant symbols but here I want to make a distinction between three kinds of symbol:

- protosymbols;
- significant symbols;
- reified symbols.

Each of these kinds of symbol will be discussed in the following sections.

The importance of feelings: protosymbols

In the last chapter, I pointed to the importance of time in bodily experience: the millisecond time scale of neuronal firing in the brain; the second by second time scale of the heart; the slower rhythms of the metabolic and endocrine systems; the hourly dynamics of the digestive system; and the daily, weekly, monthly and yearly rhythms of body energy. The suggestion is that these temporal dynamics, located in parts of the body, mesh into a symphony of rhythms having particular time contours marked by beat, duration and variations in intensity, constituting what Stern (1985, 1995) calls vitality affects, and Damasio (1994, 1999) calls background feelings. In other words, feelings are rhythmic variations of the body, its spatial and temporal dynamics. While all humans share these physiological characteristics in general, each individual seems to have their own unique pattern of bodily time contours (with reference to the heart, see Goldberger, 1997; Dardik, 1997). These unique bodily time contours constitute a person's feelings as unique experiences of self, or identity. A bodily sense of self, an identity, is actualized through the way in which others respond to that person's unique bodily time contours and the way in which such responses are experienced.

In other words, the bodily sense of a self emerges in a social process, one in which a self is co-created. It seems that these time contours, no matter what their sensing modality, are directly perceived by others. The capacity for cross-modal perception seems to be what enables humans to yoke together sight, sound, touch, smell and taste into the experience of some whole person or thing (Barrie *et al.*, 1994; Stern, 1995). This capacity is evident in music where the rhythms of sound are experienced in the body as feeling dynamics such as calmness or excitement. Similarly, one person's experience of being with another person has to do with the first's perception of the other's feeling dynamics through a process of transmutation from perceptions of timing, intensity and shape via cross-modal fluency into feeling dynamics in the first.

The key point is that humans seem to be biologically capable of selecting from an array of stimuli (images, sounds, touches, smells and tastes) impinging on the body, directly perceiving the amodal time/space qualities of that selection, and combining, matching, or even fusing these qualities with the time/space qualities experienced in the body. It seems, therefore, that it is the equivalence between the time/space contours of the stimuli and the time/space contours of feeling in the body that make possible the emergence of meaning in the stimuli that are being integrated. Indeed, it may not be going too far to say that the very possibility of mental development is based upon this temporal/spatial contour equivalence between inner physiologically based feeling dynamics and externally presented stimuli.

I would argue that this linking between qualitative aspects of perceived experience and similar qualitative aspects of felt bodily experience is the basis of human knowing. I refer to this linking, this throwing together of a stimulus with a bodily response, as a protosymbol and protosymbols provide humans with the means for protomental processes. It is important, I think, to note that these protomental processes are not mysterious inner essences, but rather, actions of the whole body. This is how I understand the process of communication Mead proposes, as described in Figure 4.1. A protosymbol is a gesture, which in relation to the response constitutes meaning for both of those involved but does not call forth a similar response in the one making the gesture as in the one responding to it.

This form of communication amounts to protoconversation but is in no way rudimentary or primitive. It does not underlie other forms of conversation as some lower layer but is, rather, simultaneously present in all other forms of conversation because all conversation involves a body and all bodies always have feeling dynamics. Protoconversation is the unconscious communication of feelings as bodily resonance, expressing the need to be met and understood at a deep existential level, in the realm of sensuous lived experience, which is ultimately what gives meaning to life. It seems to me that it is in the rhythmic, protoconversational exchange between us that a felt sense of reality, of existing, continually emerges. Protoconversations take a theme-and-variation format, with patterns of beat, rhythm, duration and intensity. Through them, we directly express, in our looking, vocalizing and touching, the rhythms and intensities of our bodily experience, our own temporal feeling dynamic, thereby evoking responses in terms of feeling rhythms from others. In essence, what we are doing is mirroring, echoing and resonating with each other's temporal feeling dynamic and thereby empathically attuning ourselves to each other. Furthermore, repeated experience of events of this kind are organized and integrated into protonarratives, which then organize and integrate further experiences of this kind.

Protoconversations are constructing protonarratives and this is the unconscious mental process of organizing and integrating experience into meaning, the ongoing construction of knowledge in the act of living together. Stern (1985, 1995) draws on his own and others' detailed observation of the relating between mother and infant to demonstrate how this process shapes an infant's self or identity.

What I have been describing is a continuous process of action and interaction that cannot be stored anywhere. It is a process in the living present and does not exist as a "thing" anywhere. However, this does not mean that what arises is completely new at each moment, arising from nothing, as it were. Interaction in the medium of protosymbols at any one moment takes place in a context of place and time, including the past history of interaction. Interaction in the living present is an extension of the historical experience of interaction, in which protosymbols trigger other protosymbols in a process of continuous reproduction that always has the potential for transformation.

In other words, habitual feeling dynamics of a repetitive kind are intertwined with spontaneous variations in them, in that even habits are rarely reproduced in exactly the same form. It is in this way that individuals amplify what is probably the inherited uniqueness of their bodily rhythm. Small variations in the experience of interaction and in the context of that interaction may be amplified into different patterns of bodily experienced identity, an example of the sensitive dependence on initial conditions typical of complex phenomena. This may well be the bodily basis of the unique sense of self people experience. Notice that this way of thinking about mind, self and communication does not require any notion of sharing. Each individual is bodily resonating in their own unique ways without sharing mental contents or putting feelings into each other. The possibility of bodily resonance is sufficient to explain empathy and attunement without anything being shared or transmitted from one to another.

Review: feelings, meaning and knowledge

Protosymbols are expressed in the medium of bodily rhythm as the throwing together of the rhythmic body pattern of a gesture by one individual body (A) with that of a response by another individual body (B) to constitute a meaning:

bodily gesture (A) – bodily response (B) = symbol = meaning.

This symbol is always social action in the context of the living present of time and place constituted by other humans, by their interactions, and by the non-human world, as well as by the historical experience of each of the interacting individuals, by the history of their own previous interactions with each other, and the history of the interactions between those around them. The meaning of the protosymbol, therefore, is always context dependent in both current and historical terms. Meaning, or knowledge, is reproduced and potentially transformed in interaction between individuals (A) and (B) in the medium of protosymbols in a specific context.

For example, without speaking at all, one person may stare fixedly at another who may then tremble with fear. The protosymbol is the throwing together of two very different bodily rhythms to mean fear. Or, a person may sit on a rock at the seaside and experience particular bodily rhythms that mean peacefulness. The gesture, or stimulus, is the rhythm of the sea thrown together with the slow rhythms of the person's body to mean peace. Protosymbols are directly experienced in the body as changes in rhythm and, therefore, as meaning in the form of feeling rhythms or emotions. This is a self-organizing process in which patterns of meaning emerge. Any breakdown in this process is a very serious breakdown in human communication. The most immediately obvious experience of the protosymbolic in adult life is the encounter with music: the rhythm of the music is immediately and obviously felt as changes in body rhythm.

The importance of reflection-in-action: significant symbols

In Mead's terms, a significant symbol is a gesture that calls forth a similar response in oneself as in another. While protosymbols are bodily gestures that call forth a bodily response in another to produce meaning for both, significant symbols have an additional feature: the bodily gesture of one calls forth a similar response in the maker of the gesture to the one called forth in the other. This enables the maker of the gesture to be aware, or mindful, of the meaning of the gesture he or she is making. There is, then, an added dimension to meaning, taking the form of potential awareness, or mindfulness, on the part of the maker of the gesture. I say potential, because the gesturer may not be aware of having a similar response, but the fact of having it opens up the possibility of becoming aware and so reflecting while acting.

A significant symbol could be a facial gesture or some other movement of the body, one that produces in the body of the maker a similar feeling dynamic to that produced in the body to which it is directed. However, it is the vocal gesture that opens up the greatest possibilities for communication in significant symbols because the maker of the vocal gesture can hear it in the same way as the one to whom it is directed. The most elaborated use of significant symbols, therefore, takes place in the action of speaking, that is, in the use of language. The action of speaking throws together a vocal gesture by one person with a similar response in that person as in the other. The meaning is in the dual nature of this response.

Significant symbols are usually expressed in the medium of ordinary, everyday conversation, in which people relate to each other, not as objects, but as each having their own subjectivity, that is, their own private, role plays or silent conversations. The vocalized and the silent conversations simultaneously taking place in significant symbols form themselves, into stories and narratives that organize the experience of being together, a matter to be taken up in the next chapter.

Both the vocalized and the silent conversations that are taking place simultaneously are, of course, the actions of a body. It follows that interaction is highly likely to be taking place in both significant symbols and protosymbols at the same time. Protosymbols are not more fundamental and they do not underlie significant symbols, nor are they earlier and thus more primitive. Protosymbols have a different structure to significant symbols and communication between bodies takes place in both throughout human life.

Review: reflection-in-action

Significant symbols throw together a gesture by one individual body (A) with a response of another individual body (B) and a similar response in individual body (A) at the same time to constitute meaning:

bodily gesture (A) – bodily response (A)/(B) = significant symbol = meaning.

The structure of a significant symbol is thus importantly different to that of a protosymbol and it is this that opens up the potential for individual (A) to be aware of the meaning, that is, to reflect in the action, and indicate to (B) how an act might evolve. These are symbols with the added feature of potentially pointing to the further evolution of an act. Significant symbols are always social actions in a context, just as protosymbols are. The context is, again, the living present of space and time and the historical experience of interaction, just as it is for protosymbols. The meaning of the significant symbol is also always context dependent in both current and historical terms. The significant symbol also points to a potential future in a way that the maker of the gesture could be aware of. Meaning or knowledge is, once again, reproduced with potential transformation in interaction between individuals (A) and (B) and it is possible for them to be aware of the meaning that they are reproducing and transforming.

The importance of abstract thinking: reified symbols

I want to distinguish protosymbols and significant symbols from another kind of symbol. Protosymbols and significant symbols are both actions of bodies having a gesture-response structure that take place in a context. The context for both is the living present and the historical background from which the gesture-response action evolves. In other words, the context is the time and place in the human and non-human world in which the action takes place and the history of the actors directly and indirectly involved. The context is the "real" lived in world and the history of lived experience. The gesture-response action is shaped and given meaning by this context even though the actions themselves do not directly make reference to it. Language, that is, vocal, verbal gestures and responses, is the most important example of significant symbols used in conversation as the medium of communication between people in their ordinary ongoing lives.

However, the usage of language in this way opens up another very important possibility for human communication, namely, the use of abstractions. Humans have developed abstract, systematic frameworks within which to talk about their worlds. For example, there is the framework of physics within which some talk about the material environment we live in and there is the framework of medical sciences within which others talk about the functioning of the human body. The historical development of abstract-systematic explanatory frameworks of all kinds has created a context additional to the kinds of current and historical contexts discussed in relation to protosymbols and significant symbols. That additional context is the abstract-systematic frameworks themselves. When one takes account of this aspect of context, I think it so substantially shifts the nature of gesture-response that it calls for the distinguishing of an additional category of symbol. I will call these reified symbols for the following reasons.

Consider what happens when people talk to each other with reference to an abstract explanatory framework, such as physics. The gesture of one takes the form of words or mathematical symbols that represent and directly refer to the abstract-systematic framework and so do the responding words. The interaction is now as follows:

bodily gesture (A) – abstract framework – bodily response (A)/(B)
= reified symbol = meaning.

If two people are talking about physics and one uses the words "gravity" and "relativity," those words immediately refer to a whole abstract-systematic framework and the responses those words call forth in each must also refer to that framework if they are to continue to discuss physics. The meaning of these words does not lie in those words, those gestures, themselves. It lies in the response that they call forth, just as for any other symbol, but those response are indirectly linked to the gesture through the framework. Furthermore, we seem to have developed a strong tendency, particularly in communication conditioned by abstract-systematic frameworks, to locate meaning in the word, in the gesture alone, and then proceed as if that word were the reality it stands for. We come easily to talk about words "gravity" and "relativity" as if they were things. This becomes even more prevalent when the words are written and the text replaces the conversation. It is for this reason that I am calling them reified symbols. A reified symbol throws together the gesture with an aspect of the context, that is an abstract-systematic framework, and in the process comes to represent and refer to it in a way that is identified or fused with the phenomenon being explained as though it were that phenomenon.

Reified symbols, then, are gestures that point to, or stand for, abstract-systematic frameworks of explanation. They represent a reality in an abstract way and then refer to that abstraction as reality. This is what a symbol is usually thought to be but it is a cognitivist definition that identifies the symbol with the word and thus ignores the gesture-response structure and, therefore, the proto and significant forms of symbol.

Abstract-systematic frameworks are constructed in reified symbols and have their own internal rules and procedures for processing and manipulating those symbols. Indeed, language, a system of symbols, itself can be explained in abstract-systematic ways in terms of syntax and grammar. The rules of mathematics and of logic are other examples. Each science, profession, discipline and community of practice has its own frameworks and its own conventions for manipulating and processing the associated reified symbols. Anyone who wants to join the community and participate in its communication has to do so within the framework of these rules and procedures, otherwise they will be excluded. These frameworks are taken to be meaning and knowledge and the essential gesture-response nature of meaning tends to be lost sight of, despite frequent reminders.

Review: abstract thinking

Reified symbols are verbal gestures (vocal or marks) that represent and refer to a particular aspect of context, namely, abstract-systematic explanatory frameworks so that the gesture alone becomes the symbol and meaning is identified with it in terms of the framework. The framework is easily fused with reality and the symbols become reified so that the response is no longer selected in relation to, provoked by the gesture in the wider context of lived current and historical experience, but in the context of an abstract explanatory framework. The contextual impact on the response thus becomes limiting and constraining. This point will be taken up in Chapter 8 in the discussion on power and legitimate systems in organizations.

Using symbols in this reified form can cut people off from their lived experience. They can be used to defend against feelings and the anxiety of changes in meaning and thus identity, commonly expressed as the duality of feeling and intellect. But they can also be used to transform the context of human action in highly creative and also very destructive ways. However, communication in reified symbols on their own is impossible because even when they discuss matters within an abstract-systematic framework, people will still be communicating in significant and protosymbols as well, simply because they are human bodies.

When people talk to each other in reified symbols, they talk about an objective, frequently quantified or quantifiable, phenomenon either outside of themselves or inside their bodies. They may talk about their own minds and experience in this way too. They employ a pattern of talking that is quite different to ordinary everyday conversation, in that narrative structures yield to propositional ones. Reified symbols represent a world external to subjective experience in the form of socially constructed propositions about it and they can be stored in artifacts. The medium in which reified symbols are expressed then becomes the written word. Reified symbols throw together a material stimulus, in the form of written marks, with a bodily response to produce meaning.

However, when a reified symbol is employed, in the sense that it is read or used in communication with another, it immediately acquires some of the quality of a significant symbol and perhaps also protosymbol. The reified symbol must call forth a similar response in the one directing it as in the one to whom it is directed otherwise there can be no communication. The use of reified symbols, therefore, can never be as objective as the definition I started with suggests. The vigor and emotion with which academics, and managers, defend their theories attest to this. This brings us to the linkage between the different kinds of symbol identified.

The multiple aspects of symbols

In the perspective I am taking, symbols are bodily interactions. They have the relational, responsive, associative and interlinked rhythm of bodily gesture-response. The protosymbol is a bodily action directly calling forth a selected bodily response in another; the significant symbol additionally calls forth a similar response in the gesturer; reified symbols call forth responses associated with an abstract frame of reference. The next point to note is that a communicative act is highly unlikely to call forth a single, simple response. Such acts will almost always call forth many responses at the same time and they are quite likely to be contradictory and conflicting. What someone says to me can quite easily call forth a response of interest attracting me to explore further and, simultaneously, a response of fear repelling me from further exploration. Only some of these responses may be called forth in the gesturer. In such interaction, then, some aspects of communicative interaction take the form of protosymbols and some take the form of significant symbols, at the same time. Furthermore, in technologically sophisticated societies, a great many communicative interactions will make some explicit or implicit references to abstract frameworks such as the law, organizational procedures, ways of using technology, and so on.

Most communicative interactions, therefore, take place in the medium of symbols having multiple aspects, simultaneously proto, significant and reified, and it is highly likely that these aspects will be contradictory, even conflictual. It is these multiple aspects of symbolic interaction that constitute its complexity. In other words, there is nothing automatic about a gesture calling forth a particular response in anyone and there is great scope for misunderstanding. However, it is this very complexity of symbolic interaction that generates the diversity that is an essential condition for the emergence of novelty. In other words, it is the complex nature of symbols, their responsive, relational features, that impart intrinsic pattern-forming and novelty-producing capacities. What I am talking about here is the emergence of knowledge in the bodily, symbolic relating of people.

Let me give an example. During a discussion I may say to you, "You are assuming Formative Teleology." This bodily gesture I make is a pattern of reified symbols that can only make any sense with reference to the kind of abstract discussion found, for example, in this book. However, I will have said those words in a particular tone of voice, while holding my body in a particular posture, in a particular place at a particular time. You will not respond to them simply in terms of the abstract frame they refer to, but in terms of my tone and posture and the context we are in. They may call forth in you a response of replying in abstract terms, while feeling attacked, aggrieved and aggressive. I may find some similar responses called forth in me by my words (significant symbol) but I may be surprised at some of the responses being called forth in you (protosymbol). This interaction between us, then, is at one and the same time an interaction in proto, significant and reified symbols.

Chapter 2 drew attention to a distinction between propositional and narrative forms of communication and knowledge (Tsoukas, 1997). In the terms I have been using above, propositional knowledge refers to reified symbols and narrative knowledge to significant and protosymbols. Although the distinction between propositional and narrative knowledge, like that between different kinds of symbol, may be a useful aid to understanding, some use it to create a duality between the two, elevating one or other to a superior status. Traditional science clearly elevates propositional knowledge to the only reliable form of knowledge and more recently, perhaps as a reaction, some of those concerned with social phenomena have been arguing for the elevation of narrative forms of knowledge.

For example, Shotter (1993, 1999, 2000) makes a distinction between words spoken in the first and second person and those spoken in the third person. The function of words spoken in the first or second person is rhetorical-responsive, or relational, that is, they are the words used in ordinary, everyday conversation as people account for their actions to each other so that they can go on relating and acting jointly. In the terms I have been using, the medium is protosymbols and significant symbols and the context is current time, place and body states as well as the experiential history of relating. When one speaks in the third person, however, one points to an object that is external to the direct interaction between the speaker and the one spoken to. A word is then used to represent an object being referred to in a representational-referential way. In the terms I have been using, the medium is reified symbols and the context is primarily that of abstract-systematic frameworks of explanation.

Shotter suggests that the responsive-relational and representational-referential forms of communication are different phases in the continuous flow of human interaction, with the former occurring "upstream" and the latter "downstream" in that process. Furthermore, he suggests that the process of understanding, or knowing, is substantially different for these two forms of interactional activity.

Knowing in the "upstream," relational-responsive form of human relating is described in terms of "ways of seeing." He defines "ways of seeing" as paradigms that unobtrusively shape and direct action. They are a background of anticipation that enables people to predict, to some extent, the responses their actions might provoke. They constitute a position of involvement from which certain kinds of event are noticed. "Ways of seeing" are open to further specification during the course of relating in ways that are structured by ongoing relations. When interacting in the responsive-relational form, people tell stories about themselves. Here, understanding is not a process of grasping the inner idea another has put into words and then putting the idea into practice. Instead, talk is seen as action rather than a precondition for action, or an unnecessary accompaniment to it.

Shotter contrasts "ways of seeing" with the abstract-systematic frameworks that emerge "downstream" in interaction and constitute knowing in interactions of a representational-referential kind. Here, interaction is based on abstract frameworks, in which thinkers stand aloof and present systematic models, expecting others to understand them in a passive manner that duplicates their own understanding. When people interact in the abstract-systematic mode, Shotter holds that they report on inner states, feelings, ideas, mental representations, progressively specifying their nature, step by step over time. In doing this they convey information and go about discovering something already existing, perhaps hidden behind appearances.

Shotter (1993; Shotter and Katz, 1996) makes it quite clear that he regards relational-responsive forms of interaction as primary, even superior, advocating this mode and tending to dismiss the other. The argument I am developing seeks to avoid this kind of dualism. I am arguing that human communicative interaction, nowadays at least, hardly ever takes one of these forms exclusively. Instead, Shotter's two modes of interaction are nearly always simultaneously present in communicative interaction between people. Even in ordinary, everyday family situations, where people are clearly communicating in the medium of protosymbols and significant symbols, that interaction is highly likely to be interwoven with the reified symbols of the legal system, organized religion, and membership of work and other organizations. In today's conditions of sophisticated technology and complex organizations it is difficult to avoid communication in the form of reified symbols and even the most abstract communication in reified symbolic form almost always provokes responses in the form of significant and protosymbols. The following anecdote illustrates my point.

Workshops at Inchcape

In 1995 I did some work on a management development program for the Inchcape group of companies, which has been described in a book called *Management and Mantras* (Butler and Keary, 2000). My recollection of some of the events is rather different to that of the authors, which is only to be expected when one bears in mind the reproduced and potentially transformed nature of human memory. Anyway, I will use some of my reconstructed recollections as an example. In April 1995, the executive directors on the Inchcape main board spent three days on a management development program and I was asked to conduct one of those days. On that day I presented some material on complexity theory and we discussed it in the Inchcape context. The reception was mixed but some of the directors felt that the senior directors of head office functions would benefit from a similar day.

Later that year, in November, I turned up to the second day of a two-day development program for those head office directors. At the start of the day, I sat listening to a discussion of what the participants were going to present to three of the main board executive directors on the next day. I was more than surprised at what they were proposing to say and even more surprised at how they seemed determined to say it. They pointed to a flip chart that they had prepared the previous day. This contained a number of bullet points of an abstract-systematic nature on key issues facing the business and how they ought to be addressed. However, the discussion about what they intended to say about these points was laced with anecdotes of how people were being treated and the whole manner of the proposed presentation was aggressive and highly confrontational. I remember thinking that the next day was bound to be a highly explosive one if they proceeded as outlined. Even before I began to speak, therefore, the experience of all of us was being organized by abstract-systematic themes about business issues, interlaced with narrative themes of aggression and attack. Interwoven with these themes, both propositional and narrative, were very strong feelings indeed.

I was then introduced and invited to talk about organizational learning and complexity. This is where I made my major mistake. Instead of picking up from where they had just left off and inviting some exploration of what was going on, I began to respond literally to the invitation by talking about learning in organizations as requested. To create some context for a discussion on the nature of learning in organizations, I began to present a brief outline of what Argyris (1990) had to say on single and double loop learning. In other words, I made a move to organize our experience along abstract-systematic themes. The participants, however, interrupted every second sentence, questioning the validity of everything I said. I pressed on and introduced Argyris' notion of "skilled incompetence," pointing to how the more skilled we are, the more likely we are to fall prey to "skilled incompetence." The participants' attacks became even more vociferous as they heard me accusing them of being incompetent. It was quite under-standable that they should hear an abstract point as a direct accusation, given the background of accusation and counter-accusation between them and their directors, a background I was largely in ignorance of.

By this point I was feeling at least as angry as the participants and I experienced a strong desire to be somewhere other than this particular room with these particular people, a desire I thought I would share with all of them. I then made another "mistake," angrily disclosing how I was feeling and proposing that we terminate the day and all go home, instead of inviting an exploration of what was going on. I suggested that we all break for coffee while we thought about what we would like to do. After coffee we returned and began to try to make sense of what we had created between us. We worked for the rest of the day with our experience, relating it to how and what they proposed to focus on with their directors, in the context of what was going on in their organization and how they felt about it. I felt that we had done valuable work together in what was a quite unexpected turn of events. Some others thought this too, but yet others thought that the day was a disaster. One referred to it as the collapse of management.

Note how the evolving relationship between us, the experience we were having, was being organized by abstract-systematic themes, interwoven with narrative themes of accusation and counter-accusation, and very strong feelings, all at the same time. Making sense of this experience is not assisted, I argue, by setting up a dualism between the abstract-systematic and the narrative forms of knowledge, but rather seeking to understand how they are simultaneous aspects of responsive associative patterns of communicating.

Conclusion

The central argument of this chapter is as follows. Humans communicate with each other in the medium of symbols, where these symbols are the responsive bodily interactions of relating. These active symbols are meaning and knowledge. Knowledge, therefore, is not an "it" but a process of action. Action is undertaken in the living present and is, therefore, ephemeral. Knowledge, it follows, cannot be stored nor shared simply because it is bodily action. In symbolic terms that bodily action has many aspects, taking the simultaneous form of proto, significant and reified symbols. Reified symbols can be expressed in the form of marks and so stored as artifacts. However, these artifacts are not knowledge. They are tools that people can use in their bodily communication with each other in which meaning and knowledge arise. This is clearly a notion of knowledge that differs fundamentally from that in mainstream thinking. The alternative notion I am suggesting leads to the conclusion that it is impossible to measure knowledge or manage it.

Knowledge is the process of patterning symbols and the next chapter turns to how coherent pattern arises in symbolic interaction between living bodies.

6 The organization of communicative action: rule-based or self-organizing knowledge?

- Global rules of language and the structuring of communication
- Narrative forms of communication
- Local rules and the structuring of communication
- Communicative action as patterning process
- The thematic patterning of experience
- Conclusion

The previous chapter argued that all human relationships are acts of communication between bodies in the medium of symbols having many aspects (reified, significant and proto) and it is in this communicative interaction that meaning is created and destroyed. In other words, communicative acts are embodied complex responsive processes of relating that create and destroy the knowledge enabling humans to act cooperatively in relation to the human and non-human world in order to "earn a living." This perspective places the actions of bodies, and the meaning-creation/destruction role of those actions, right at the center of any explanation of relationship, communication, knowledge creation and learning. It focuses attention on the medium in which human bodies relate, that is, communicate meaningfully with each other. In so doing they express their individual and collective identities, all as essential aspects of the joint actions they undertake to preserve the continuity of, and simultaneously transform, the contexts within which they go on being together. From this perspective, the underlying view of causality is one of Transformative Teleology (see Box 3.1, p. 60). In other words, complex responsive processes of relating are the transformative cause of themselves as a process of perpetually constructing the future as continuity and potential transformation at the same time. Furthermore, simultaneous continuity and transformation are participative self-organizing processes of interaction in which it is the local detailed nature of the interaction itself that gives rise to emergent patterning of itself in the living present.

The purpose of this chapter is to explore how human experience is patterned by communicative action in the medium of symbols. By experience, I mean current and historical participation of individuals and groupings of individuals in the bodily actions of both communication itself and of communication as the basis of the cooperative use of tools, including technologies and systems, in the transformation of the human and non-human contexts within which people live. The question, then, is how action, which includes communication, comes to display coherent, useful, meaningful patterns. In discussing this question, I will refer mainly to the most immediately evident, and in that sense the most prominent, form of human communication in the medium of symbols. This takes the form of talking and the extension of talking in writing and reading. In emphasizing verbal language in this way, as the primary example of communication in the medium of symbols, I do not wish to imply in any way that non-verbal communicative actions are less important or more primitive. On the contrary, since talking, reading and writing are bodily actions, they can only be accomplished in the medium of symbols with all their aspects (proto, significant and reified) at the same time. In other words, feelings and communicative actions in the medium of feelings are always part of any human interaction.

The actions of talking, reading and writing fall into the category of discursive practice, which takes a number of different forms. Perhaps the most common of these is ordinary conversation. The word "conversation" is sometimes defined very widely to include any language-based activity, in which case it is largely indistinguishable from discourse. Some, however, define conversation more narrowly to describe people talking directly to each other, in an ordinary, everyday way as they go about their lives together. Conversation in this sense might exclude discussions, that is, communication focusing on a given topic, and debates, that is, communication aimed at persuading others to move to a given position, and dialogues in which people advocate a position but hold themselves open to changing it. Other forms of discourse that could be excluded from the definition of conversation might be theories, scientific or otherwise, factual descriptions, and statements of opinion. Narratives and stories are also forms of discourse that might be distinguished from conversation. All the forms so far discussed may or may not include the written word, depending on who is making the definition.

Whatever the definition, all the forms of communication so far mentioned have a common feature. When people talk to each other, when they write and when they read what others have written, they participate in an active bodily experience of communication. The general question this chapter is concerned with, is how all such communicative experience is structured, or patterned. This general question will be explored in relation to how the experience of talking, particularly the use of language, is structured or patterned and a distinction will be made between a number of different ways of dealing with this question.

One approach, consistent with mainstream views on knowledge creation in organizations, posits that the experience of talking is structured by the rules of a language system and the rules for its use. It is argued that language is a system governed by global rules that exist before any experience takes place. Language, then, is an abstract system of communication, which, when adhered to by speakers, causes the coherent pattern experienced in people talking to each other. Another approach is more concerned with the form that talking takes, namely, whether it is structured along narrative lines or along propositional lines. From this perspective, the cause of structure in talking lies in the rules governing narrative or in the rules governing the development of propositions. Yet another approach focuses attention, not on global rules of a language system, or on general rules of narrative and other structures, but on local rules of communicative interaction. This latter perspective draws on the complexity sciences to argue that the rules governing communication are located at the individual, local level and that individuals use them in self-organizing processes from which the pattern of communicative experience emerges. All these approaches preserve the split between the individual and the social discussed in Chapter 3. As rule-based accounts of the structuring of communication they all also split theory from practice, ascribing the orderly structure of communication to pre-existing rules or theories, global or local, that govern communicative action. They imply Formative Teleology (see Box 2.1) in which the future structure of communication is an unfolding of the enfolded patterns already there, in some sense, in the rules.

After a brief exploration of the above three approaches, this chapter will argue for the complex responsive process perspective as an action-based approach that grants much less importance to rules of any kind and claims that the experience of talking is patterned by the action of talking itself. In other words, patterns in the experience of people talking together emerge in the very process of their talking to each other. I will also argue that this process of talking together structures human experience in narrative-like forms of themes and variations on those themes. These are fractal processes (see Chapter 4) in which there is no split between individual and social levels or between theory and practice. Here it is not so much the rules of a language system and the rules for its use, or rules about narrative and propositional structures, or local rules, that cause the coherence of communicative experience, but the process of participating in the use of language.

Consider first the global rule-based account of how human communication is structured and why this perspective is inadequate.

Global rules of language and the structuring of communication

The approach that I am pointing to here is most notably associated with the names of de Saussure (1974), Chomsky (1957) and Pinker (1994). I will not try to cover their arguments in any detail for it will suffice, in making the distinction I am interested in, to refer to two basic propositions.

The first basic proposition is this. If people are to talk to each other in a coherent way then they have to observe the syntactical and grammatical rules of the language that they are using. They have to put the words together according to rules in which nouns, adjectives, verbs, and so on, follow a prescribed sequence. If they string words together in any old way, then there is no structure, no meaning and no coherent talk. Attention is thus immediately focused on a global system of rules governing the coherent use of a language and it is assumed that individuals talking to each other possess those rules in some way and follow them when they talk coherently. This is another example of the prevalence of systems thinking. It is because people are following the systemic rules of grammar and syntax that their communicative experience has some structure. de Saussure and Chomsky were not much concerned with the semantic aspects of language, that is, with meaning and content. However, others extend the rule-based notion to the meaning and content of language when they talk about people sharing visions, values and cultural norms as the basis of structure in their interactions. Each individual language user is thus assumed to be a rule-following, information-processing entity in line with the cognitivist assumptions about human action that underlie mainstream theorizing about knowledge creation in organizations. Those writing in this tradition seem to have little to say about feelings, since individuals are assumed to use language in a rational, calculating sort of way.

Note, at this point, how the implicit causal framework underlying this view preserves the dual causality put forward by Kant. The cause of individual behavior is understood in terms of Rationalist Teleology (see Box 2.1) where individuals choose words to express their chosen aims of communication according to reasons. They make their choices in accordance with a global system of rules and this immediately implies Formative Teleology (see Box 2.1) in which the structure of their talking is an unfolding of what is enfolded in the rules. Chomsky talks about deep structure, an entirely syntactical system that accepts only those linguistic inputs that conform to it.

The question that then follows is how individuals come to possess the grammatical and syntactical rules that govern their use of language. For Chomsky, and even more explicitly for Pinker, the answer is inheritance. It is proposed that humans have evolved a language instinct in the sense that their genes program the hardwiring of their brains with the grammatical and syntactical rules of language. Again, the underlying assumption of Formative Teleology is clear. No one suggests that an individual need be aware of these rules in order to speak his or her mother tongue. Instead, the rules are taken to be wired into the brain in a way that the user is unaware of. The rules of the language system are unconscious or tacit.

Sampson (1997) has mounted a detailed refutation of the proposal that a genetic program largely determines language use. He proposes that individuals learn the rules of grammar and syntax and that the process is much the same as that scientists employ. In the manner suggested by Popper (1983), Sampson holds that as individuals experience life, they test hypotheses about language use, retaining those that are useful and rejecting those that are not. However, while he disagrees with Pinker and Chomsky on how humans acquire the rules of a language system, he retains all the other aspects of this essentially cognitivist approach. One of his principal criticisms of the Chomsky/Pinker approach is that their argument for genetic determination of language use cannot account for the human ability to produce a genuinely new idea. However, when he comes to explain how this is possible, he falls back on a dualism between mind and body, claiming that they are distinctly different kinds of entity.

While a body is genetically determined and cannot therefore produce anything new, other than through the very long process of biological evolution, a mind is not genetically determined and therefore can produce something new in a very short time. He does not provide an explanation of how the genuinely new comes about, ascribing it to individual flashes of intuition. He also does not explain how humans come to have these flashes of intuition through which they formulate new hypotheses for testing.

I would argue that this attempt to explain the coherence of the communicative experience in terms of a system of global rules existing outside the act of talking is inadequate. It is inadequate because it assumes that the rules are there in people's heads, when in fact these rules may simply be the constructions of linguists. The whole approach runs into the problem of how these rules ever get into people's heads and the answer, which has to do with both inheritance and learning, either cannot explain creativity or has to appeal to some split between mind and body to do so. In other words, there is no satisfactory account of how it is that people come to share the rules or just what it is that they are sharing. And there is a further drawback: the emphasis on rational calculation and the downplaying of the role of feelings easily lead to the unjustified privileging of particular types of talking and particular forms of knowledge, the abstract-systematic forms of talking and the propositional knowledge referred to in the previous chapter.

It does not matter much, therefore, whether one argues that the rules are genetically acquired or acquired through the process of learning, for in both cases the explanation is inadequate. It is the whole notion of human behavior driven by a global set of rules that is inadequate for the task of explaining how experience is patterned in both stable and novel forms at the same time. An alternative way of thinking about the system of syntactical and grammatical rules of a language is that they are the constructions of linguists and are not necessarily acquired by any language speaker. They are academic ways of describing language use rather than rules determining language use. Furthermore, this whole approach assumes that thoughts are somehow already there, waiting to be translated into words. But what are these thoughts before they are put into words? No answer is provided to this question and perhaps there is none because thoughts are already words.

These are conclusions of great significance in thinking about knowledge creation and knowledge management in organizations because mainstream views on these matters tend to be based on some kind of pre-existing rule-based account of how coherence in human communication is achieved. Reject this notion and you undermine mainstream views at their very foundation.

The global rule-based account, then, ascribes patterns of coherence to some kind of causal system of rules, a kind of blueprint shared by the individuals engaged in communication. The same kind of argument as that which employs the notion of grammatical systems of rules also assigns the cause of order in human action to impersonal social forces or institutional procedures as discussed in Chapter 3. Common to all forms of this approach is the idea that the cause of orderly action lies outside people in the form of global systems of rules that they internalize and then reproduce. Change in behavior can only occur if this global system of rules is changed and no satisfactory explanation, in my view, is provided of how this takes place.

As I have already mentioned, this particular explanation of how communication is coherently structured pays little attention to the content of communication. I turn now to an approach that does, but one that continues to locate the cause of coherence in a system of rules outside interaction between communicating people.

Narrative forms of communication

The previous chapter drew attention to the distinction some writers have drawn between propositional forms of knowledge of the "if-then" form expressed in theories and factual accounts, on the one hand, and narrative knowledge expressed in stories and narratives, on the other (Tsoukas, 1997). These writers point to how people cannot rely entirely on propositional knowledge in the form of procedures, manuals, and so on to do their jobs adequately. They also need to draw on narrative knowledge embodied in the informal stories they tell each other about their work (Brown and Duguid, 1991). A number of writers and researchers (for example, Boje, 1991, 1994, 1995; Grant *et al.*, 1998) in the area of organizations have taken this point up and explored the use of storytelling in organizational life.

As an example of this work, I take a paper by Gabriel (1999), who reviews definitions of narratives and stories in order to clarify how they constitute sense-making processes in organizations. He suggests that

stories are a sub-set of the category of narratives and points to three
different understandings of what a story is:

- From the perspective of folklore, storytelling is a traditional activity in
  which storytellers tell their stories to members of a community. The
  stories are fluid and evolving and their primary purpose is
  entertainment. Gabriel distinguishes stories from myths and fairy tales.
  The latter tend to be didactic and carry sacred meaning or some moral
  injunction and they explain, justify and console, while stories entertain.
  Legends might also be distinguished in that they have some historical
  basis even though this might be slim.

- From a modernist perspective, stories, and for that matter, myths, fairy
  tales and legends, are all seen either as fiction opposed to factual,
  objective information, or as highly subjective accounts of personal
  experience. Stories here are marginalized as sense-making processes,
  being rejected completely on the grounds of having no connection to
  fact, or subjected to some interpretivist approach on the grounds that
  they represent hidden subjective experience. The purpose of
  interpretation is to unmask the hidden meaning. The purpose of the
  story here is to provide people with a vehicle to evade the controls of
  society, even laugh at them. Stories, from a psychoanalytic perspective
  represent emotions, hidden desires and repressed wishes. They are
  distorted expressions of unconscious wishes. Interpretivists do not see
  stories as oppositional to facts but as hiding facts. They are taken as
  clues of social and psychological reality.

- For postmodernists, stories, not facts, make experience meaningful and
  are the privileged mode of sense-making. Here all human experience is
  a story of some kind and stories influence the way people talk. Boje
  (1991, 1994, 1995) sees storytelling as an institution's memory, which
  is continually recreating the past. For him stories are in continuous
  flux, taking the form of fragments of conversation.

Gabriel suggests that the term "story" be retained to describe an integrated
narrative with a plot having a beginning and an end, told by someone to
someone. For him, a story's purpose is that of entertaining, of stimulating
the imagination and reassuring people. It is not didactic or deep in the way
that a myth is. It is not at all factual in that its truth lies in the meaning of
the story itself. Stories are elements of symbolism and culture that may
express unconscious wishes. They are vehicles of communication,
expressions of political domination and opposition and occasions for
emotional discharge. This leads to concerns with whether stories are good
or bad stories, whether they generate meaning or destroy it.

As well as stories, myths, fairy tales and legends, Gabriel's definition of the category of narrative includes other forms of communication: factual and descriptive accounts of events that aspire to objectivity rather than emotional effect; opinions; interpretations; theories and arguments; numbers; logos; images; fantasies; daydreams; slogans; metaphors; fragments of story that he calls protostories; puns. Here, Gabriel distinguishes between narratives and experiences that have a factual basis and those that do not. He talks about discourse that has loyalty to facts, descriptions that are fact as information, and discourse owing its loyalty to story, that is, facts as personal, subjective experience. He regards stories as the folklore of the workplace, which may express hidden organizational realities. However, he sees organizations as dominated by other forms of discourse. Other forms of narrative are used to sustain and negotiate meaning.

Gabriel is among those writers who make sharp distinctions between forms of communication such as narratives, stories, theories and factual accounts. Others use story and narrative interchangeably. Whatever the definitions and the distinctions, however, all of these approaches see the account, whether factual or otherwise, as being about something other than itself. They are accounts about experience or about facts. They are accounts that people give and receive about a reality outside of the account itself. The concern, then, is with the definition of the kind of account and the reality it is pointing to, explaining or hiding. They are all expressing an already existing meaning and the question is how well they do this. Again, then, this is an approach that implicitly assumes Formative Teleology. The form of the account is unfolding meaning or experience that is already enfolded. The argument centers on which kind of account is superior. In mainstream thinking about knowledge in organizations, factual accounts and the theories constructed from them are thought to be superior conveyors of meaning. Critics of mainstream thinking argue for the superiority of narrative as a form for expressing meaning. For example, Lewin and Regine (2000) quote Bruner (1990) to argue that narrative, as opposed to factual accounts and theories, captures lived experience more fully. This is taken as a call to tell stories about life in organizations, using stories as a better research method, storytelling as a lost art that needs reviving. In effect, these critics suggest that people could learn more effectively if they told stories rather than constructed theories.

However, using Gabriel's analysis as an example, I argue that this view of narratives and stories as superior forms of discourse does not depart in an essential way from Sampson's suggestion of how communicative experience is structured. Communication in the form of narrative and story is still assumed to be structured by a system outside the act of telling the story. Stories are defined as having a particular structure and a particular purpose. When an individual follows these rules, he or she produces a story and when he or she fails to do so, then there is no story. The story is in effect a kind of artifact representing a reality outside of itself and this is particularly evident in the idea that stories conceal an unconscious reality. While the move to narrative and storytelling represents an important widening of our understanding of communication, certainly compared to Chomsky, it does not in itself lead to any change in assumptions about causality in that the duality of Rationalist and Formative Teleology continues. Nor does the move in itself have anything to say about the split between individual and social.

Now consider a third approach to the structuring of communication, this time one that draws on the complexity sciences to understand communication as self-organization based on local rules of interaction.

Local rules and the structuring of communication

A variation of the rule-based approach emphasizes the way in which sets of rules govern interaction between people at the local level of that interaction. The rules take the form of individual mental models or schemas, parts of which may be shared by many individuals. The rules are now inside people's heads rather than being located in some abstract global system outside of them. This way of thinking about human action as rule-driven is immediately compatible with the theory of complex adaptive systems. Notions of self-organization and emergence from that theory can then be used to provide an explanation of how coherent patterns of communication emerge in the interaction between humans governed by local rules. The emergent pattern, order or coherence is located at a level higher than the individual, in the form of an institution, organization, culture or society. This higher-level order is said to act back upon the individuals to affect their local rules of interaction. Change occurs when the individual rule sets change or when the patterns of connectedness between individuals alter, all closely analogous to complex adaptive system theory. In the global variations of rule-based accounts, coherence in communication is caused by an external blueprint, either as global rules of a language system and/or as the rules of narrative forms of communication. In the variant of rules-based accounts discussed in this section, coherence arises in a local rule-based, self-organizing process in the absence of an external blueprint.

An example is provided by Broekstra (1998) who argues that all behavior is communication (Watzlawick, 1976). By communication, he means the conversational exchange of messages, including stories, myths, fantasies and rituals. For him an organization is a conversational system in which communicative interaction constructs social realities: "The organizing process is continually reproduced and constituted in a loosely-coupled network of many micro-conversations and builds on local knowing" (Broekstra, 1998, p. 175). Consider how he thinks about this conversational system. For him, individuals are born or socialized into some tacit system of rules that govern their local interactions with each other. Drawing on one strand in complex adaptive system theory (Gell-Mann, 1994; Langton, 1993), he points to how rule-governed entities interacting with each other produce emergent patterns of order, or coherence, at a global level. The surface complexity of this global pattern of order arises in the deep simplicity of the rules of interaction between semi-autonomous individuals. He says that the conversational system, which produces coherent patterns of organization, has three levels. The first level is that of the rules, or grammar, taking an if-then form. The second level is the system of interaction between individuals who recursively apply the rules to their local interactions and individual behaviors. The third level is that of global pattern, which he describes as the level of cognition, that is, a description of the two lower levels by an observer embedded in a cultural, consensual language system. This global level of coherent pattern, the cognitive level, influences the level of rules by changing them and it influences the level of interaction by altering the degree of connectedness in the system. The rules are thus the dynamic outcome of the processes of cognition at the highest level: "This causal circularity of structuring and selecting exhibited in social systems can also be understood as the operation of unobservable rules governing the selection of (inter)actions and generating the observable behavior" (Broekstra, 1998, p. 163).

Thus when the individuals conversing at the level of interaction share these rules, they operate as an essential ingredient of the whole order-producing process. Broekstra describes the operation of this three-tiered system as social construction and argues that it is autopoietic (see the Appendix for a critique of autopoiesis), or self-producing, with a tendency to maintain its identity against outside disturbance:

> [T]he emerging social organization, produced and reproduced by the
> network of intended and unintended actions and interactions . . . in
> turn "selects," that is, constrains or enables, only those behaviors of
> participants that are compatible with their structure-determined
> constituents. . . .
>
> The selecting of behaviors and actions aids in explaining the
> conservative, organization-maintaining tendencies of social systems.
>
> (ibid., p. 162)

Transformation of the conversational system occurs through the
operation of the cognitive level on the first and second levels. He says
that change occurs when the rules are re-specified since they act like
genetic code, specifying individual behaviors and local interactions. It is
not clear to me, in this account, who re-specifies the rules, how they do
this, or how the changes come to be shared by others.

This variation relies just as much as the global rule-based account on the
operation of rules to produce coherence. However, it moves away from
the notion of a global blueprint to that of local rules sets and the
importance of local interactions. Order is then emergent in the sense that
it is a higher level that cannot simply be reduced to the rules. That higher,
or cognitive level, then acts upon both the interactive and rule set levels
in a constructive manner. Another difference from the global rule-based
account, then, is this circular nature of causality. Instead of a global rule
set directly producing coherence, there is local interaction according to
local rule sets that produce a higher level of coherence or cognition and
that higher level in turn constructs the local rules sets and patterns of
interaction, which in turn construct the higher level. This move, however,
does not seem to be one significant enough to produce a radically
different understanding of the nature of the coherence and how it is
brought about because Broekstra ends up with this statement, which he
suggests is an alternative to the current control-orientation of managers:
"Organizing the conversations founded on a value-based vision shared at
the individual level creates a coherent direction for the organization as a
whole, an internalized shared focus" (ibid., p. 176). I take this to mean
that what is now to be controlled is conversation itself and that such
control, based on shared constructs, produces the order of coherent
direction. Coherence and order continue to depend upon, presumably
individual, forms of globally aimed control. Change still comes from
intentional, cognitively directed changes to rule sets. But who does this
and how do they do it? The problems encountered by a global rule
approach continue to bedevil this kind of local rule-based approach.

There is no explanation of how individuals come to share rule sets nor any explanation of just how cognition changes them. In both cases, the recognizable human actually disappears from the picture. Broekstra clearly thinks in system terms, using insights from the complexity sciences as an extension of systems theory. What he is talking about is Formative Teleology in which the already enfolded order of visions and shared rules is unfolded in the conversational interaction between people.

In the end, rule-based accounts of whatever form fail to explain the emergence of novelty in communication between people because in relying on rules as the drivers of human action, they assume Formative Teleology. This emphasizes regularity in interaction, sidelining any interest in the irregularity and variability human beings actually experience from day to day. Rule-based accounts of human behavior remove the felt experience of being human. In such accounts, coherent, orderly patterns of behavior come about because people are behaving in accordance with shared systems of rules providing either long-lasting, universal and global blueprints, or more temporary, reproduced, local blueprints. All the focus is on sharing or agreement and the role of disagreement, the kind of conflict and mess that is part of everyday human experience, plays little part in coherent behavior. The shared systems may be taken as given or they may be taken as constructed by humans in their interaction. In both cases, however, the rules are assumed to be largely tacit, largely external to people to be internalized and shared by them, and then reproduced in both talking and other forms of action. Note how these explanations rely on a hidden model, or theory, in which the basic building blocks – the rules themselves – are largely tacit, unconscious and unobservable.

Adopting a fundamentally skeptical attitude to any rule-based account of how coherence and change arises in human communicative action involves more than simply taking a different theoretical position or making a move from formulating propositions to telling stories. It amounts to a serious questioning of the foundations upon which mainstream views of knowledge creation and management are built. The implications of this will be taken up in Chapter 10, but here I want to go on to consider an alternative to any rule-based account, one that draws on Mead's view of communication and the theory of symbols as the medium of communication outlined in the last two chapters. The alternative to rule-based accounts is action-based ones.

Communicative action as patterning process

In this section I will be arguing that communication between people is patterned in a process that does not rely on rules of any sort as the ultimate source of order in human action. Like the local rules variation discussed above, it makes a move from the global to the local. However, it understands coherent local interaction, not as the consequence of shared rules, but as arising in interaction itself. The central proposal is that human interaction is essentially a process in which people account to each other, negotiate with each other, in a collaborative process in order to "go on" together (Shotter, 1993). Coherence and order are reproduced and potentially transformed in a self-organizing process that is the meshing together of individual actions. This is an approach that does not distinguish between the level of the individual and the level of the social but sees them as different aspects of the same phenomenal level, as explained in Chapter 4. There is no split between theory and practice either because the theory, or explanation of action, is precisely what is being negotiated in that action.

This approach is built, not on surmises about tacit or unconscious rules driving behavior, but on direct observation of what people are actually doing as they interact with each other in the ongoing, day-to-day experience of living together. It provides an account drawn from ethnomethodology (Garfinkel, 1967; Goffman, 1981), conversational analysis (Jefferson, 1978; Shegloff, 1991; Sacks, 1992; Boden, 1994) and social constructionism (Shotter, 1993, 2000; Shotter and Katz, 1996). So, just what are the observable features of human communicative action of any kind that make it possible for such communicative action to coherently pattern itself? The features can be classified as follows:

- mutual expectations of associative response;
- turn-taking sequences;
- sequencing, segmenting and categorizing actions;
- rhetorical devices.

Consider each of these aspects of communicative action, bearing in mind that what is being described is not simply some exercise in purely verbal language because throughout their verbal exchanges with each other, people experience their interactions in their bodies, in the mode of feelings. People's symbolic exchange always has the multiple aspects of significant symbols and protosymbols, and sometimes also reified symbols. In their verbal exchanges people are also communicating directly in the form of resonating body rhythm.

Mutual expectations of associative response

Whenever people communicate with each other they quite clearly display, in the very act of that communication, some kind of expectation of each other. People expect those whom they are addressing to reply to what they are saying in some way that is associated with what they are saying. If people do not comply, more or less, with this expectation, there is no communication, and thus no meaning. Associative responding is the very basis of communicative action. Furthermore, people generally expect others to be more or less competent, compliant and reasonable in communicating, just as those others expect them to display those qualities too (Boden, 1994). People hold each other morally accountable for their communicative and other actions. Or, they may expect others to be incompetent, rebellious, unreasonable and immoral. These expectations have a profound impact on how people proceed together. They undertake very different kinds of communicative action depending upon the expectations they have and if they expect completely uncooperative responses from each other they will try to avoid communication altogether. Even if this is not possible, the meaning arising in the communicative action will be completely different in different contexts of expectation.

People do not refer to some set of rules, conscious or unconscious, in order to form those expectations. Instead, they form them in the very action of communication with each other. In that interaction, they may draw on, or point to, local or global sets of rules that have previously been formulated. However, they are not referring to those rules in order to form their expectations, but rather, as resources to be employed in their negotiations with each other. They point to external rules to justify their current actions or persuade others to change theirs. They are not simply applying the regularities of rules but referring to them in order to explain, justify or condemn their own, or others, deviations from them. They may refer to rules to guide their joint action together but since rules can never cover every contingency, what they will often be doing in their communication is negotiating how any rules are to be employed in the current context they find themselves in. Here action, rather than being rule-driven, is employing rules as tools, from time to time. This action-based approach emphasizes the social, or collaborative nature of the action of talking in which people make sense of their actions together, taking account of each other's sensibilities, spontaneously sustaining and repairing their unceasing flow of speech-entwined activity in an unreflective, unforced, unplanned and unintended way (Shotter and Katz, 1996).

Turn-taking sequences

The second, strikingly observable feature that imparts coherent pattern to communicative interaction is the turn-taking sequence that creates the rhythms of daily life (Garfinkel,1967; Goffman, 1981; Sacks, 1992; Shotter, 1993; Boden, 1994). The basis of this turn-taking sequence is the expectations people have of each other, as described above. People value turns to speak. They compete for them, abandon them and construct them, so making, as well as taking, turns to speak. People make turns for themselves and others by asking questions, soliciting advice, clarifying issues, expressing opinions, and so on. They negotiate rights and obligations in this turn-taking process and it is this negotiating that structures the action of talking and, therefore, most other human actions because they are accomplished in talking. Everyday turn-taking and turn-making in conversation are simultaneously stable and unstable, predictable and unpredictable. Here, talking, as a recursive and enactive process, structures itself from within itself.

Sequencing, segmenting and categorizing actions

Third, turn-taking and turn-making in communicative interaction impart structure to that communication by actions of sequencing, segmenting and categorizing. One of the most important of these categorization devices is that to do with membership (Boden, 1994): who may talk and who may not, who is "in" and who is "out." These are matters that I will return to in the next chapter. Another important aspect of the turn-taking/turn-making process is referred to as "adjacent pairs" (ibid.), which urge forward turns and topics. For example, turn-taking/turn-making exchanges tend to be organized in distinct matching pairs of question and answer, request and response, invitation and acceptance, announcement and acknowledgement, complaint and response, and so on.

Rhetorical devices

Fourth, people employ rhetorical devices such as "directive" and "instructive" forms of talk in which they are "arrested," "moved," "struck," and "feel called upon to respond" (Shotter, 1993; Shotter and Katz, 1996). In this way, people negotiate with each other, responding to each other's utterances in an attempt to link in their practical activities.

They notice and point to the content of each other's speech, including their references to the context; they agree and disagree with each other; they sympathize and fail to sympathize with each other. In doing this, they are constructing living social relationships as they connect, link and orient themselves to each other and to their surroundings in their turn-taking/turn-making communicative interaction.

The patterning effect of communicative action

Now consider the patterning effect of communicative action in which people take and make conversational turns, categorizing, using adjacent pairing and rhetorical devices, all influenced by expectations that arise as they do so. In this responsive process people gesture and respond in the form of utterances of one kind or another. Incomplete sentences, stories, propositions, and so on, mutually shape the evolution of their exchanges. The local, situated use of words by one produces responses in others, making momentary, practical differences. People resonate with each other and they may grasp something new, unseen but sensed in the emerging interaction. They are not transmitting information about things but, rather, they are going on with each other in a responsive expression and potential understanding that grows from their very interaction. If they share anything, it is certainly not rules, but sensibilities and responses that are refined and elaborated (Shotter, 1993). It is the very features of the process of interaction, namely, taking turns, using rhetorical devices, categorizing, and so on, in the context of mutual expectations, that impart coherence and pattern to people's ongoing communicative interactions.

However, while this patterning produces coherence and stability, it also has within it the possibility of change. That possibility exists because the beginnings of understanding arise in the moments that strike people and these are often small details that may seem at first to be trivial, but which may amplify into new patterns of relating (Shotter, 2000). It is in the unique variations in each other's expressions, as opposed to the exact regularities of rules, that people have their living understanding of each other. Living moments of the unique variations strike people and so arrest the ongoing routine flow of spontaneously responsive activity. As these variations are articulated, elaborated and refined, people change. Complex mixtures of unique influences occurring both within and around people shape their actions in this way, as reciprocally responsive movement between them points beyond the present moment to other possible connections. These movements of dialogue are both repetitive and potentially transformative and it is in the minute variations that the possibility of the novel arises. Given the local unrepeatable nature of context, these moments are inevitably unique, where thought, feeling, perception, memory, impulse and imagination are so tightly interwoven that they cannot be separated (Shotter, 2000). As a result people's actions are never fully orderly nor fully disorderly.

Public and private patterning of communication

However, just how do people do all this if their actions are not governed by rules of some kind, either conscious or unconscious? This question takes the argument back to Mead and the relationship, explored in Chapter 4, between the private role play that is individual, self-conscious mind and the public interaction that is group or social. As individual bodies act communicatively with each other, each simultaneously acts communicatively toward him or herself. In other words, as individuals engage in public, vocal conversation with each other, they simultaneously engage in private, silent conversations with themselves.

These silent private conversations that are an individual mind have exactly the same features as the public vocal conversations described above: they mirror each other. Minds are associative, with one thought or voice silently triggering another thought or voice. One "voice" seeks to persuade or negotiate with some other "voice," in a silent role play, always involving the bodily rhythms of feelings just as in the public vocal conversations. One has expectations of oneself as one has of others, namely, that one should be competent and reasonable and morally accountable to oneself as well as to others. One seeks to justify oneself to oneself, to account for oneself to oneself for both one's public and private communicative and other actions. The same sequencing of turn-taking is evident as first one aspect of oneself and then another takes turns, makes turns, to participate in the role play. The same kind of membership categorization occurs in which some thoughts have a voice and others are denied or repressed. An individual asks questions of him or herself and gives replies, complains and responds, compliments and denigrates oneself, and so on. Furthermore, the same kinds of rhetorical device are in evidence in one's silent conversation with oneself. One is struck by some aspects of this conversation with oneself and such striking moments call forth responses from oneself.

What I am arguing, then, is that the private role play and the public interaction proceed simultaneously in the same modes and the one makes the other possible.

The importance of history

However, there is more to it than this and the more is "history." Although a beginning and an end might be ascribed to a particular sequence of communicative interactions, that description is purely arbitrary, for even before a particular episode begins, even between total strangers, each has a history of experience. That history has patterned the private role playing of each individual in particular ways that enact, that is selectively enable and constrain, what that individual responds to both privately and publicly. That history establishes what aspects of the gesturing of the other will be striking, will call forth, or evoke, a response and what kind of response it will evoke. This dance of enactment and evocation is made possible, and at the same time limited, by previous history. And when they are not strangers, the history of their own personal relating to each other, and the histories of the groups they are part of, also become relevant. However, this history is not some kind of "true" factual account but a reproduction in the living present that always leaves room for potential transformation.

Furthermore, those collective and individual histories reproduced in the living present of communicative action are extending those histories into the future. This points to the narrative-like structuring of human experience. It is not simply that people are telling each other stories or that narrative is simply an alternative type of knowledge. The turn-taking, responsive relating of people may be thought of as forming narrative at the same time as that narrative patterns moral responsibility and turn-taking. In other words, the experience of the living present, like the past, is structured in narrative-like ways.

Notice two important points about the process I have been describing. The notion of causality underlying these processes of communicative action is clearly that of Transformative Teleology (see Box 3.1, p. 60). It is in the micro-interaction of their turn-taking conversation that people are perpetually constructing the living present and thus the future. This perpetual construction has the paradoxical characteristics of repetition and transformation at the same time. And what is being constructed is nothing less than the individual and collective identities of those involved, identities always open to potential transformation.

I use the term narrative-like, rather than narrative, in order to make an important distinction. A narrative or story is normally thought of in its "told" sense. A narrative is normally someone's narrative, told from the perspective of a narrator. It normally has a beginning, an end and a plot that moves the listener/reader from the beginning to the end in a more or less linear sequence. This kind of "narrative told" must be distinguished from the narrative-like process that is narrative in its making. Interaction in the manner described above evolves as narrative-like themes that normally have no single narrator's perspective. Beginnings and endings are rather arbitrary and there are many plots emerging simultaneously. The narrative told is retrospective while narrative-in-its-making is currently emerging in the living present. The former is inevitably linear while the latter is intrinsically nonlinear. Despite these differences, there is a connection and it is, I think, useful to think of experience as being patterned in a narrative-like way. This idea is explored in the following section, which looks at how one might think about the pattern, both private and public, that people spin together as they interact communicatively in the manner described in this section.

The narrative-like patterning of experience

The neuroscientist, Damasio (1999) suggests that human bodies construct consciousness and knowledge in interaction with each other in a process in which the biological correlates of this activity take a narrative-like form. Damasio says that consciousness:

> consists of constructing an account of what happens within the organism when the organism interacts with an object, be it actually perceived or recalled, be it within the body boundaries (e.g., pain) or outside of them (e.g., a landscape). This account is a simple narrative without words. It does have characters (the organism, the object). It unfolds in time. And it has a beginning, a middle, and an end. The beginning corresponds to the initial state of the organism. The middle is the arrival of the object. The end is made up of reactions that result in a modified state of the organism.
>
> (ibid., p. 168)

Damasio is suggesting that humans become conscious, they develop a feeling of knowing, when their bodies construct and present a "specific kind of wordless knowledge" to do with being changed by contact with others and he describes in detail how this might happen.

As far as the brain is concerned, the organism in the hypothesis is . . . the state of the internal milieu, viscera, vestibular system, and musculoskeletal frame. The account describes the relationship between the changing . . . [state] . . . and the sensorimotor maps of the object that causes those changes . . . As the brain forms images of an object – such as a face, a melody, a toothache, the memory of an event – and as images of the object *affect* the state of the organism, yet another level of brain structure creates a swift nonverbal account of events that are taking place in the varied brain regions activated as a consequence of the object-organism interaction . . . Looking back, with the license of metaphor, one might say that the swift, second order non-verbal account narrates a story: that of the organism caught in the act of representing its own changing state as it goes about representing something else. But the astonishing fact is that the knowable entity of the catcher has just been created in the narrative of the catching process.

(ibid., p. 170)

The resonance with Mead's description of the "I–me" dialogue described in Chapter 4 is striking. Mead talks about interactions between organisms while Damasio focuses on the biological correlates, that is, interactions between neural patterns in different brain regions. In doing so, he in effect provides an explanation of Mead's contention that the mind and self arise in interaction and that the central nervous system is such as to enable this to happen.

Detailed studies of the early development of the infant mind also point to a basic narrative-like structuring of experience. For example, Stern (1985, 1995) describes the interactive, social relationship between infant and mother in which an infant's crying, fretting, smiling and gazing are responsively interwoven with rocking, touching, soothing, making noises and so on, amounting to what Mead called a conversation of gestures. Mutual touching, looking and vocalizing between infant and caregivers, therefore, amount to what might be called a protoconversation, where the communication is concerned not only with meeting the infant's physiological needs but also the need to be met and understood at a feeling level, in the realm of sensuous lived experience. Caregivers who intuitively respond to an infant with gestures that, in their rhythm, recognize the bodily rhythms of the infant in effect confirm a felt sense of reality. Participants in this protoconversation are mirroring, echoing and resonating with each other's temporal feeling dynamic in a process of attunement. Stern argues that it is in these protoconversations that an infant's sense of self and other emerges. If the mother is sufficiently attuned to the feeling dynamic, in a way affirming the validity of what the infant feels, he or she experiences a growing sense of his or her own agency. He or she develops a sense of being able to evoke a needed response in the other as well as experiencing an ability to have evoked a response that affects the other.

Stern points out that episodes in such protoconversations have a rhythm, a beginning and an end as well as some motive. He gives the example of a hungry baby crying for his mother to come and feed him and suggests that this baby's subjective experience takes a narrative-like form which he calls a protonarrative – the enactment of a local motive with its attendant affects which has a beginning and an end.

Both Damasio's hypothesis about brains organizing experience and Stern's studies of how infant experience is organized, how selves evolve, point to forms of protoconversation forming narrative-like structures of experience. Both are consistent with Mead's view of how experience is organized, discussed in Chapter 4, and with the conversational processes described in this chapter. They are focusing on episodes with a beginning and an end but it is not difficult to see how such episodes combine with others to form seamless narrative-like experience stretching continuously over time.

Bruner (1990) presents very similar views on the narrative structuring of adult experience. He suggests that humans are born with a predisposition to organize experience in narrative form and that the self is an autobiographical narrative that is continually retold, with variations. He is concerned with the manner in which narrative organizes experience.

First, the sequential order of narrative provides structure, one that is internal to itself. It is this internal structure, or plot, that gives the narrative its meaning, one that has nothing to do with a reality, true or false, outside of itself. The meaning of the narrative lies in its overall configuration or plot and each event, happening or mental state takes its meaning from the overall configuration. In order to make sense of the constituent parts of the narrative, one must grasp the overall plot. Narratives are inextricably interwoven truth and possibility.

Second, narratives display sensitivity to what is ordinary and what is exceptional in human interaction. The negotiation of meaning between people is made possible by this feature of narrative. Narrative achieves its meaning by identifying deviations from the ordinary in a comprehensible form. As they interact with each other in a group, each person takes it for granted that others will behave appropriately in a given situation, the norms for such appropriateness having been established by their history of interacting with each other. In other words, the habits, or practices, developed in the past create expectations for current and future action. When people behave in what is taken to be the normal, ordinary way, there is no need for further explanation. It is simply taken for granted and if pressed for an explanation, people normally reply that such actions are what everybody does or is supposed to do. However, deviations from these expected actions or ways of speaking, trigger a search for meaning that is usually provided by a story giving an account of an alternative world in which the unexpected action makes sense, that is, provides reasons for the behavior. Narrative, therefore, mediates between the norms of culture and unique individual beliefs, desires, and hopes. It renders the exceptional comprehensible. It provides a means of constructing a world and identifying its flow as well as regulating the affects of people.

The point I am making is that throughout life, the interactive communication between people forms narrative-like sequences and it seems that there are biological correlates for this. It is not just that people tell each other stories but that their very experience together is organized in story-like patterns that emerge in their turn-taking going on together. Experience is narrative-like in its formation and patterning in the living present and afterwards that experience may also be recounted in the form of the narrative "told," but only ever partially. And such "narratives told" feature prominently, as a tool, in the ongoing process of communicative negotiation between people in the living present.

The thematic patterning of experience

I am arguing, then, that human relating is human communicating and that human communicating is the action of human bodies in the medium of symbols. Through communicative interaction with each other, and with themselves, humans are able to cooperate in sophisticated ways in joint action using tools to operate within their human and non-human surroundings. It is communicative interaction that enables people to construct significant features of the nonhuman environment they live in: they breed cattle; they build physical structures; they design equipment that extends the range of communication, for example. However, communicative action in the medium of symbols does much more than this in that it constructs both individual mental and social realities.

In communicative interaction, people actively respond to each other and in so doing their experiences are patterned in narrative-like forms. Human experience is story-like. In their relational communication people are constructing intricate narratives and abstract-systematic frameworks. When they reflect on what they have been doing, on what they are doing, and on what they hope to do, they select aspects of these dense narratives/abstract frameworks to tell stories or extend their abstract-systematic frameworks of propositions in order to account for what they are doing and make sense of their worlds. In the process their very identities, individually and collectively, emerge.

Life, on this view, is an ongoing, richly connected multiplicity of stories and propositional frameworks. In this sense the process is nonlinear, although stories told select a theme in all of this and give it a linear structure. My proposition, then, is that all human relationships, including the communicative action of a body with itself, that is mind, and the communicative actions between bodies, that is the social, are story lines and propositions constructed by those relationships at the same time as those story lines and propositions construct the relationships. They are all complex responsive processes of relating that can be thought of as themes and variations that recursively form themselves.

The private role play, the silent conversation, of each individual and their public interactions can be thought of as themes and variations reproducing history that enactively melds with evocations triggered by the gestures of others in the transformative process of the living present. It is these themes and variations that organize an individual's experience in the living present. However, what those particular themes are at a particular moment will depend just as much on the cues being presented by others as upon the personal history of a particular individual. Each individual is simultaneously evoking and provoking responses from others so that the particular personal organizing themes emerging for any one of them will depend as much on the others as on the individual concerned. Put like this, it becomes clear that no one individual can be organizing his or her experience in isolation because they are all simultaneously evoking and provoking responses in each other. Together they immediately constitute complex responsive processes of a recursive, reflexive, self-referential kind. And as they do so themes emerge that organize their experience of being together out of which further themes continuously emerge.

The social can then be thought of as continuously replicating patterns of themes and variations that organize the experience of being together

(Stern, 1985, 1995; Stolorow *et al.*, 1994). These themes emerge, in variant and invariant forms, in the interaction between people as those themes organize those very interactions. The themes organizing the experience of being together emerge in the interaction. In that sense they are between people and therefore cannot be located "inside" any individual. However, the experience that is being so organized is always a bodily experience. I am suggesting, then, that both individual and group themes always arise between people, while always, at the same time, being experienced in individual bodies as fluctuations, marked or subtle, in the feeling rhythms of those bodies. Furthermore, this notion of themes organizing the experience of being together, does not mean that all interacting individuals share the same theme. Each member is responding differently to emerging themes. There is no need to postulate the sharing of any kind of mental content. Nothing is being shared at all as people resonate individually around common themes to do with being together. They are responding to each other in a meaningful way, not sharing something.

Analogies from the complexity sciences

The essence of a complex adaptive system is the interaction between agents, which consist of arrangements of digital symbols. In the explanation I have been developing in previous sections, the essence of human action is the communicative interaction between people in the medium of reified, significant and proto symbols. They are clearly very different kinds of interaction in very different kinds of symbols. However, I argue that there is an analogy in that both forms of interaction can be thought of as self-organizing processes with the property of emergent coherence. When the interaction takes place between different arrangements in these symbols it has the potential for transformation and repetition at the same time. Why bother with this kind of analogy? The answer is that the simulations of complex adaptive systems clarify and point to the possibility of self-organizing interaction in the medium of symbols organizing itself into coherent patterns. The power of this insight is the suggestion that there is no need to look for some kind of hidden reality or mechanism other than interaction itself to explain coherence in human action with its characteristics of continuity and potential transformation. By demonstrating the possibility of self-organizing processes and the emergent coherence they produce, complexity theories offer a way out of having to postulate some designer, or program, or set of rules, to explain how the coherence comes about. In the absence of a serious, convincing demonstration of the power of self-organization and emergence, the only alternative to rules and blueprints as an explanation of coherence, seems to be some form of mystery, such as group mind, deep structures, the collective unconscious, and so on.

Now consider further analogies between the simulations and human complex responsive processes. In the simulations of complex adaptive systems, an attractor is a pattern of interaction between groups of agents, that is, between algorithmic rules. One of the examples of this is a pattern of fluctuating increase and decrease in bit strings of different lengths in the Tierra simulation (see pp. 73–75). The analogue in human interaction is recognizable patterns in themes in conversational life. For example, the announcement, or even the rumor that two organizations are to merge, or that one is to take another over, immediately becomes a very powerful theme patterning conversations throughout both organizations. Another example is the imminent retirement of the head of an organization. The analogy of an attractor is then the theme around who the new boss will be. Or, in the case of an individual mind, one's silent conversation may be powerfully attracted to a theme of separation or loss, for example. However, this is an analogy and there is nothing to be gained, in my view, in applying the term "attractor" to the themes organizing conversation. In fact, it is rather misleading to do so. The term "attractor" has a mathematical meaning that is not applicable to conversational patterns and the word in ordinary conversation has the connotation of a force pulling something toward itself. This is not what I mean by conversational themes that are not being pulled anywhere but are perpetually constructing the future.

Analogous with attractors, themes organizing the experience of conversational life between people may display the properties of simultaneous stability and instability typical of the edge of chaos in computer simulations of complex adaptive systems. In the dynamics of the edge of chaos, stability is preserved by the properties of redundancy, loose coupling and the power law. Redundancy means that the same pattern can be produced in a number of different ways. In other words, there is a repetition of effort, which is unnecessary if one thinks entirely in terms of efficiency, but which impart stability because more than one kind of interaction can produce the same result. Parts of the process can be damaged or not succeed in producing a repetition of a particular behavior but others will survive and succeed in doing so. Loose coupling has much the same result. Here, one interaction does not depend in a very exact way on the successful completion of a number of other interactions. Once again, behavior can be stably repeated in the presence of failure in parts of its functioning. There is an analogy with ordinary, everyday conversation. People repeat what they say to each other in a number of different ways that could not be judged as efficient. However, this repetition increases the chances of sustaining a stable sense of meaning and thus of action. One does not need to understand every single word or concept another uses in a conversation to get some idea of what it means, a form of loose coupling.

The power law leads to controlled change in that there are small numbers of large extinction events, or system failures and large numbers of small ones. Conversations exhibit this property too. As people converse with each other there are many small misunderstandings and few large ones. Stability of meaning is thereby preserved. However, this kind of stability is always in tension with instability. In other words, as they converse, people never fully understand each other and no one knows what has been well understood and what has been misunderstood. For this reason, conversational themes trigger others along unexpected and unpredictable routes. Small misunderstandings may escalate and major ones suddenly occur with important consequences for joint action. Once again, this property of paradoxical stability and instability applies as much to the silent conversation of mind as to the vocal conversation of interaction between people.

There are further analogies. In the computer simulations, diversity and thus the capacity to spontaneously evolve are provided by random mutation and cross-over replication. These processes generate variety and diversity. The analogue in human interaction is imperfect communication between people, misunderstanding, and the partial taking into silent conversation by one person of ways of conversing acquired from others in the course of public conversations. Diversity arises in misunderstanding and in the cross-fertilization of concepts through interaction between different patterns of conversation. The dynamics of fluid conversation within constraints, the analogue of edge of chaos dynamics in computer simulations, are associated with critical levels of misunderstanding and cross-fertilization. If there is little misunderstanding between people forming a group with well-established concepts and ways of talking to each other, their conversations are likely to be repetitive. If there is too much misunderstanding between people drawn from very many disparate groups, then there is the disintegration of communication, a "tower of Babel." This is where the tension between conformity and deviance becomes important. It is this deviance that imparts the internal capacity to spontaneously evolve new patterns of conversation, that is, new conversational attractors. The conditions for creative, fluid conversations lie in some critical range between these extremes.

Finally, in computer simulations it is the pattern of digital symbols that is organizing itself, simultaneously as patterns in individual bit strings and as patterns of interaction across the system. The analogue of this in the case of human interaction is the manner in which themes patterning experience are patterning themselves as both pattern of individual mind and as pattern of group relating at the same time. Human experience is these themes. So, to say that the themes pattern experience is to say that they pattern themselves. The primary medium for this self-organization is conversation. Conversation patterns itself. It is self-referential and sustains identity while promoting difference.

Conclusion

The action-based approach I have been describing moves away from the notion of systems of rules operating to cause coherence in human communication and looks for ordering properties in the nature of communicative action itself. It focuses attention on the negotiated nature of turn-taking and turn-making in conversation and on the intrinsic properties of responsive communicative action to produce coherence and novelty that arises in the variations. It explains that production of coherence in terms of self-organizing themes and variations around them that pattern experience, the private experience of mind and the social experience of being together. Organization, coherence and structure are realized as action, which is an essentially local, self-organizing process of turn-taking in conversation in the living present. The very constitution of organizations depends on the production of local knowledge through local language practices.

Making a conceptual move of this kind has dramatic implications for how one thinks of knowledge creation and management in organizations. It suggests that the whole idea of locating organizational knowledge in explicit rules simply misses the point. Organizational knowledge lies instead in the themes continuously reproduced that pattern the experience of being together. Any explicit, procedural or narrative knowledge can be no more than a resource called upon in the thematic patterning of experience, a tool used in communicative interaction. What then would be the nature of knowledge management? What could any manager hope to do about knowledge creation? These are the questions raised and they will be returned to in Chapter 10. However, before that, it is necessary to take this chapter's argument about communicative action a step further. Communicative action cannot be understood without addressing the question of power and it is to this that the next chapter turns.

7 The emergence of enabling constraints: power relations and unconscious processes

- Turn-taking, power and ideology
- The dynamics of inclusion–exclusion and anxiety
- Fantasy and unconscious processes
- Conclusion

The last three chapters have outlined an argument in which the starting position is that humans are fundamentally social animals. In other words, the distinctive feature of humanity is the sophisticated manner in which individual human bodies undertake joint action, that is, cooperate with each other, in order to survive and develop. This joint action, which they undertake to transform their environment in the interest of their survival and development, is accomplished by the use of tools and this requires continuous communicative interaction between them. That communicative interaction is accomplished in the medium of proto, significant and reified symbols and in that interaction emerges the very identity of humans, both individual and collective.

There are observable ways in which human bodies communicate in the medium of symbols:

- Symbols are associative in that they are gestures (vocal or any other kind) by one body calling forth an associated responding gesture from another body. Gestures fit in with one another in a responsive, relational manner that constitutes symbol, that is, meaning. In other words, the very possibility of communication rests upon mutual expectations of accountability, without which it would be impossible to negotiate ongoing cooperation.
- This associative use of symbols is accomplished in turn-taking and turn-making interactions. If people did not take turns it would not be possible for them to jointly link their symbolic gestures to indicate the

further evolution of their actions in their accounting for those actions to each other.

- Turns are made and taken through the use of general linking devices such as adjacent pairs, for example, question and answer. The turn-taking/turn-making process also arises in the manner in which symbols are sequenced, segmented and categorized. One of the principal processes of categorization is that which establishes membership categories, identifying who is to take a turn, as well as how and when they are to do so.
- In their turn-taking, humans act in rhetorical ways to persuade each other and thus negotiate an evolving pattern of action.

The communicative activity outlined above patterns interaction, or experience, into narrative-like themes patterning that communicative interaction in the living present. The narrative-like themes form, and are formed by, the process of communicative interaction at the same time. In other words, communicative interaction patterns itself in a self-organizing way in which patterns emerge from patterns, constituting the history of interaction. The organizing themes, however, do not take only narrative forms. Another form is that of propositions, or rules, and these also pattern communicative interaction in much the same way, this time producing emergent abstract-systematic frameworks, such as the law, organizational procedures and scientific theories. These too constitute the history of interaction, or experience. This history, with its simultaneous narrative and propositional themes is what patterns people's relating to each other. Indeed, it is in this history, narratively and propositionally patterned, that individual and collective identities emerge at the same time. History constructs thematic patterns that select or enact bodily gestures in the living present at the same time as those gestures evoke and provoke responses in others, similarly selected or enacted by their history of experience, all in circular processes that reproduce and potentially transform the historical thematic patterns. Agency is patterning process forming while being formed.

The term I use to describe this entire process is that of complex responsive processes. It is these complex responsive processes that enable sophisticated collaboration, or joint action, and that also enable the emergence of the individual selves/minds/identities, as well as the collective identities, without which human collaboration is not possible. So far, then, I have presented a rather edifying picture of cooperative human beings acting collaboratively together in their joint interests. As we all know only too well, this is only part of the picture. What of competition, aggression and downright refusal to cooperate? What about unscrupulous acts of communication to secure individual interests at the expense of the collective? What about joint destruction and the incredible cruelty humans are capable of? What about abusive relating? *Any explanation that does not encompass these widely experienced destructive aspects of human action is, I think, of little use.* What I find fascinating about the action-based, social explanation of human communicating is this: the very features that account for the stability that enables collaboration also account for its disruption. Even more fascinating is the way in which this disruption is essential to the emergence of novelty in human communicative action. This chapter will explore how *communicative interaction simultaneously produces both emergent collaboration and novelty, as well as sterile repetition, disruption and destruction at the same time.*

Turn-taking, power and ideology

I have suggested that patterns of communicative interaction between human bodies take the form of narrative and propositional themes and variations. These themes emerge in processes of associative turn-taking/turn-making that are communicative interaction in the living present. At the same time, however, these emerging themes and variations pattern the associative turn-taking/turn-making. These themes and their variations, however, do not emerge out of nowhere. They are reproduced and potentially transformed in the very actions of communication and what are being reproduced, each time with unique variations, are themes that have emerged in the previous history of each individual, in the previous history of the grouping they currently find themselves in, and in the wider communities and societies they are part of. The process is the same for individual minds and interactions between bodies, the social.

Of particular importance to the whole process is the emergent reproduction of themes and variations that organize communicative actions into what were referred to in the last chapter as membership categories. These tend to be themes of an ideological kind that establish who may take a turn, as well as when and how they may do so. It is the ideological thematic patterning of turn-taking/turn-making that enables some to take a turn while constraining others from doing so. There is another aspect. To go on together, people have to account to each other for what they do. In other words, the maintenance of relationship imposes constraint. Power is constraint that excludes some communicative actions and includes others. However, at the same time, power enables. The process of turn-taking/turn-making is both enabling and constraining at the same time and it therefore immediately establishes power differences in which some people are "in" and others are "out." This process of power relating, with its dynamic of inclusion and exclusion, is ubiquitous in all human communicative interaction, that is, in all human relating. The very process of turn-taking/turn-making makes the dynamic of inclusion and exclusion an inevitable and irremovable property of human communicative interaction quite simply because when one person takes a turn, others are at that moment excluded from doing so. And this inevitable dynamic has very important consequences. If communicative interaction is essential, not only for the survival of every individual, but also for the continued reproduction and transformation of their very selves, or identities, then any exclusion must be felt as very threatening. For a being for whom the social is essential to life itself, the deepest existential anxiety must be aroused by any threat of separation or exclusion since it means the potential loss or fragmentation of identity, even death. Also, categorizing people into this or that kind, with this or that kind of view, may also be experienced as threatening. This is because it creates potential misrepresentation of identity and potential exclusion from communication.

I am suggesting then, that the process of turn-taking/turn-making that reproduces and transforms themes of emergent patterns of collaboration, at the same time reproduces and transforms themes to do with inclusion and exclusion, or power, and these arouse feelings of existential anxiety, which trigger themes to deal with that anxiety in some way. The themes triggered by anxiety may well have to do with re-patterning the dynamic of inclusion and exclusion, with shifting the relations of power. These and other themes triggered by anxiety may well disrupt collaboration and they may also be highly destructive. However, without such disruptions to current patterns of collaboration and power relations there could be no emergent novelty in communicative interaction and hence no novelty in any form of human action. The reason for saying this is that disruptions generate diversity. One of the central insights of the complexity sciences is how the spontaneous emergence of novelty depends upon diversity (Allen, 1998a, 1998b).

Furthermore, there is a link between anxiety and the use of fantasy to cope with it. By this I mean that an individual who experiences, not necessarily consciously, the anxiety aroused by exclusion, may well elaborate on his or her own actions and those of others in the private role play/silent conversation of mind, in a way that has little to do with what they are actually doing. The result can be fantasy and misunderstanding to varying degrees, even serious breakdown in the whole process of communicative interaction. Again, however, there is a close relationship between fantasy and misunderstanding, on the one hand, and the emergence of novelty, on the other. Fantasy is close to imaginative elaboration and misunderstanding triggers a search for understanding thereby provoking continued imaginative elaboration and communication. It is in such continued struggles for meaning, and the imaginative elaboration going with it, that the novel emerges. I will return to this in a later section of this chapter.

These inter-related matters of power and anxiety, fantasy, imagination and misunderstanding, therefore, are central to an understanding of the communicative action that is human relating and the rest of this chapter explores them further.

The associative nature of turn-taking

A key feature of communicative interaction, one upon which the whole patterning effect of turn-taking/turn-making depends, is that of association. Expectations emerge from past experience that people will link their communicative actions together in an associative manner. Communicative cooperation arises in the process of people holding each other accountable for their actions in some way. They act toward each other in a manner that recognizes their interdependence and so negotiate their actions with each other. Without this, relating breaks down.

The immediate consequence of such interdependence is that the behavior of every individual is both enabled and constrained by the expectations and demands of both others and themselves. To carry on participating in the communicative interaction upon which an individual's very life depends, that individual has to rely on the enabling cooperation of others. At the same time that individual has to respect the wishes of others and those wishes will frequently conflict with his or her own. Communicative interaction is, thus, the patterning of enabling and conflicting constraints, a central feature of any complex process. Broadly defined, power describes interpersonal relationships of just this kind.

Power enables one to do what one could not otherwise have done and it also constrains one from doing what one might autonomously like to do.

Communicative interaction is a process in which people account for their actions and negotiate their next actions. This is a political process, the exercise of power. Because all relationships have these characteristics, all relationships are simultaneously power relations (Elias, 1970, 1989) and communicative interaction. If one accepts that an individual mind is the private role play of communicative interaction, taking the same form as the public, it follows that an individual mind is also a role play in power, a private political process. What is being suggested, then, is a self-referential, reflexive process in which individual minds are formed by power relationships while they are, at the same time, forming those power relationships in both private relations with themselves and public forms of power relations with others.

These private and public processes are self-organizing, or emergent, in that they pattern themselves as continuity and change. In other words, processes of communicative action, that is, processes of power relating, are such that they both preserve continuity, or identity, and promote transformative change at the same time. Power relations are both stabilized and changed by particular uses of symbols, that is, particular ways of talking (Elias, 1970, 1989) that have to do with the membership categorization that is part of the pattern forming process of communication. It is in this categorization that the dynamics of inclusion and exclusion emerge and those dynamics have the characteristics of stability and change at the same time. Consider how this happens.

The dynamics of inclusion–exclusion and anxiety

Elias and Scotson (1994) studied events following the influx of a working-class group into a new housing estate in the UK, adjacent to an older estate that was also occupied by working-class people. Although there was no recognizable difference between the two groups, hostility soon appeared in which the older inhabitants denigrated the newer ones. Elias and Scotson explained this in terms of the cohesion that had emerged over time in the already-established group of inhabitants. They had come to think of themselves as a "we," a group with common attachments, likes, dislikes and attributes that had emerged simply because of their being together over a period of time. They had developed an identity. The new arrivals lacked this cohesive identity because they had no history of being together and this made them more vulnerable. The more cohesive group therefore found it easy to "name" the newcomers and ascribe to them hateful attributes such as being dirty or liable to commit crimes. So, although there was no obvious difference between the two groups, one group used the fact that the other was newly arrived to generate hate and so maintain a power difference. This was, in a sense, "accepted" by the newcomers who took up the role of the disadvantaged. I would describe what happened here as follows. Organizing themes of an ideological nature had emerged in the communicative interaction within and between both the established and the newcomer groups. That ideology established, and continued to reinforce, membership categories and differences between those categories.

One of the principal ways that power differentials are preserved, then, is the use of even trivial differences to establish different membership categories (Elias and Scotson, 1994). This suggests that it is not that a racial or religious difference generates hatred of itself, but rather that such differences are given an ideological form and then used to stir up hatred in the interests of sustaining power positions in a dynamic of inclusion and exclusion. Dalal (1998) points out how this is an unconscious social process in that the hatred between the groups emerges in an essentially self-organizing process that no one is really aware of or actually intends. Note how the very differences that are essential to the emergence of the new are, at the same time, generators of destructive processes of hatred. It should also be noted that what I have been describing is an everyday occurrence in less dramatic ways. For example when we debate differences in our theories, or when we talk in particular ways in ordinary, everyday life we are often using differences to sustain power relations. This view of communicative action and human relating is very different from the more idealistic view presented by social constructionists, described in Chapter 3. They call for relational responsibility, for responsibility located in "we," in a manner that ignores the kind of dynamic I have been describing, one that *makes purely caring relationships impossible* for humans, it seems to me.

There are other aspects of ideological themes that also serve to preserve power differentials in essentially unconscious, self-organizing ways. A key aspect of ideology is the binary oppositions that characterize it and the most basic of these is the distinction between "them" and "us." Ideology is thus a form of communication that preserves the current order by making that current order seem natural. In this way, ideological themes organize the communicative interactions of individuals and groups. As a form of communication, as an aspect of the power relations in the group, ideology is taken up in that private role play, that silent conversation, which is mind in individuals. Note that ideology here is thought of as mutually reproduced in ongoing communicative action rather than anything shared or stored. Here, ideology is not some fundamental hidden cause located somewhere. It is not stored anywhere, transmitted and then shared. Rather, it is a patterning process, that is, narrative themes of inclusion and exclusion organizing themselves in perpetual reproduction and potential transformation. Ideology exists only in the speaking and acting of it.

Elias and Scotson point to how ideology emerges in a self-organizing process of gossip. Streams of gossip stigmatize and blame the outsider group while similar streams of gossip praise the insider group. The gossip builds layer upon layer of value-laden binary pairs such as clean–dirty, good–bad, honest–dishonest, energetic–lazy, and so on. In less obvious form, the same point applies to the "in-out" dynamic created by particular ways of talking, for example, talking in terms of complexity, in terms of psychoanalysis, in terms of management control, and so on. Such gossip and other ways of talking attribute "charisma" to the powerful and "stigma" to the weak, so reinforcing power differences. In established, cohesive groups, streams of gossip flow along well-established channels that are lacking for newly arrived groups. The stigmatization, however, only sticks where there is already a sufficiently large power difference. Again these are social relations that are reflected in the private role play of individual minds, conferring feelings of superiority on the powerful and feelings of inferiority on the weak. Eventually, however, the weak or marginalized groups will probably retaliate with what may be thought by others to be unreasonable vigor. In the next chapter I will refer back to this process of gossip as "shadow" themes organizing the experience of being together.

Categorizing and unconscious processes

The inclusion–exclusion dynamic I have been describing is not some aspect of power relations and communicative interaction that humans could somehow decide to do without. The very process of categorizing itself makes the dynamic inevitable. The act of naming or categorizing an experience is an act of breaking that experience up into different parts, and relating those parts to each other. To categorize is to place experience in one category rather than another, thereby identifying a difference from other experiences not placed in that category. The effect is to locate similarity within the category, so obliterating differences between experiences in that category in what Matte-Blanco (1975, 1988) has called symmetric logic. However, between categories it is the difference that is emphasized and similarity between them that is obliterated in what Matte-Blanco calls asymmetric logic.

In this way, experience is polarized into similarity and difference and the paradox of simultaneous similarity and difference within and between categories is lost sight of. Matte-Blanco suggests that humans do this unconsciously. Conscious thinking tends to focus attention on difference at the category border while obliterating similarity between the categories. In other words, conscious thinking is heterogeneous and asymmetrical. Unconsciously, however, experience is organized in homogeneous, symmetrical patterns in which differences within a category are obliterated. So, when some in a group are named "British," the others all become "not-British" and symmetrical thinking is immediately applied to both "British" and "not-British" in that homogeneity is imposed on each group. Within each group the differences between members are obliterated and the fact that this is being done is unconscious. At the same time there is asymmetrical thinking in that a difference is being drawn between the two groups and the similarity between them, the fact that both are human, say, tends to be obliterated.

Dalal (1998) develops Matte-Blanco's thought to make an important point about identity and difference. At the center of identity there is symmetry, an unconscious symmetry that cannot be tested without destroying that identity. He sees this as an aspect of the social unconscious and links it with discourse. Within each discourse there are certain categories taken to be natural, the equivalent of identities, and these are homogenized and so hidden from questioning. It is these categories that constitute the social unconscious and what is being made unconscious is the power differential. People cluster around their similarity – the symmetrical – to hide the difference of power: "every sentence contains globules of homogeneity, which are connected by heterogeneity . . . *Thus all thought could be said to consist of a weaving together of islands of unconsciousness*" (Dalal, 1998, pp. 190–191). Dalal draws on Elias and Matte-Blanco to develop Foulkes' (1964) notion of the social unconscious, key elements of which are the collective:

- use of talk about differences between one group and other groups to stir up hatred against others in order to preserve unconsciously sensed power differences;

- categorization of experience into binary opposites that become entrenched as ideologies, which make behavior seem right and natural;
- use of the logics of symmetry and asymmetry to obliterate some differences and highlight others, so polarizing experience.

These socially unconscious processes are self-organizing and they produce emergent patterns of communicative action and power relations. Furthermore, they are taken into the private role play of individual minds to constitute individual unconscious processes. This is a very different notion of the unconscious to either Freud or Jung, for what is unconscious here is woven into what is conscious, rather than lying beneath the conscious, or being more primitive than it. It is not repressed wishes of an aggressive or sexual nature. What is unconscious is basically the themes sustaining identity and defending against its fragmentation or destruction. I will take this argument up again in the next chapter when I come to talk about "shadow" themes organizing the experience of being together.

The examples I have been using to illustrate the way in which ideologies, themes and other aspects of the process of communicative interaction sustain power relations have been of the more dramatic and obvious type. However, they are not confined to the obvious and the dramatic. They occur continuously in ordinary everyday life, including in organizations.

The dynamics of inclusion and exclusion in organizational life

I am arguing that communicative interaction between human bodies patterns human experience in two opposing ways at the same time: as stability, continuity and identity, on the one hand, and as potential transformation, on the other. However, the transformation is potential and there is no guarantee that it will emerge. Furthermore, there is no guarantee that the transformation which does emerge will be judged to be creative as opposed to destructive, or ethical as opposed to unethical. My reasons for this assertion follow.

The turn-taking sequencing of communicative action patterns that communicative action in stable, coherent themes as identity, always with the potential for transformation. That turn-taking process depends for its functioning on the history-based expectations people have of each other that they will link in their actions, that they will associate. In other words, people hold each other accountable for their actions and they expect to be held accountable. Turns are made and taken through adjacent pairing of actions, such as question and answer, that in effect segment and categorize experience. Furthermore, in negotiating their accountability to each other people employ a range of rhetorical devices to move and persuade each other. Communicative action of this kind immediately spins power relations and the process of categorizing itself patterns ideological themes of inclusion and exclusion that unconsciously sustain the stable pattern of power relations and, thus, identity. Simultaneously, these ideological themes arouse opposition and thus the potential for change in power relations. It is these features of communicative interaction, particularly categorization and the dynamics of inclusion and exclusion, that both enable and constrain ongoing communication, which reproduce patterns as identity with the potential for transformation.

However, the effect of these processes of communication is also, simultaneously disabling, in the following way. The processes of categorizing, which sustain ideologically based patterns of power relations, immediately create the dynamics of inclusion and exclusion through particular ways of talking. People who adhere to those ways are unconsciously included, they are the "in crowd," and those that do not, or cannot, are excluded, the "out crowd." Any change in the process of communicative interaction must at the same time constitute a shift in power relations and, therefore, a change in the pattern of who is "in" and who is "out." Such shifts generate intense anxiety and communicative interaction is recruited in some way to deal with this existential anxiety. These ways may be highly destructive of effective joint action and may even completely disrupt the reproduction and creative transformation of coherent communication.

Any organizational change, any new knowledge creation, is by definition a shift in patterns of communicative interaction, hence a shift in power relations and, therefore, a change in the patterns of inclusion and exclusion. *Anxiety is thus an inevitable companion of change and creativity and so, it follows, are destructive interruptions in communication.* Furthermore, it is the very difference this whole process generates between the ways people talk that is essential for changes in what people do and the new knowledge they together develop. When one ignores the shifts in power relations and insider/outsider dynamics generating and generated by change, one is taken by surprise at the unexpected turns that change takes. When one expects the unexpected generated by these processes, it all makes more sense and anxiety levels drop as one accepts that change cannot be controlled by anyone.

An example: the health care trust

Let me give an example of what I mean. I was recently asked to take part in an exercise to be undertaken by a healthcare trust that faced drastic reorganization. The intention was to split the large trust into four smaller ones in line with changes in government policy. No one yet knew who was to fill what management position in the new organization, or even where they would be located, and the change was only some months away. There was no doubt that everyone was carrying on with their day-to-day tasks in an atmosphere of great confusion and increasing levels of frustration, stress and anxiety. The need to do something to prepare for the change was indeed pressing.

One course of action proposed by senior management was that an exercise be undertaken to identify the existing qualities of good leadership that should be taken into these new organizations, whatever they turned out to be. A number of focus groups of management and staff were to be set up to identify what these qualities were and they would then be used as criteria for selecting people to fill the management positions in the new organizations and then also used as criteria against which management performance was to be judged. I was asked to attend a planning meeting to decide just what these focus groups should do and then facilitate the work of one of those groups. Some of the themes emerging in that planning meeting, themes organizing the experience of being together at that meeting, seem to be as follows: designing criteria that must be established in advance; setting measures for performance so that people knew what they had to do; judging performance and giving rewards according to the criteria; setting action plans and ensuring that targets were met; focusing the discussion of the groups so that they talked only about leadership and did not "open the can of worms" that constituted the current situation, and so on. Another theme that ran through the meeting had to do with an exercise mounted two years previously called a "Better Future." It was very difficult to raise critical questions about the benefits of this program over the past two years.

There were two people at this meeting who expressed some skepticism and wondered what the proposed focus groups could hope to achieve. However, they were not being taken seriously. There was clearly a particular pattern of talking structured by and structuring the particular themes I have just mentioned. Those who talked in this way were the "in" group and those who did not were clearly being excluded. I joined the "out" group in their skepticism and began to suggest other ways we might proceed, perhaps, by focusing attention on what was going on now and what the next step might be, as an alternative to some abstract exercise about a future about which none of us knew much.

This caused great irritation for some and a debate ensued. Why the irritation? The person most irritated was a member representing senior management and in charge of Organization Development. The themes structuring the talk and making it "in" were themes from the language of OD professionals. Any attempt to shift the language and talk about self-organizing processes and emergence would clearly shift the figuration of power and in so doing create a new figuration of who was "in" and who was "out." The ideology of OD, therefore, had to be defended because it was the basis of the current power structure, certainly at that meeting and, I am sure, more widely. In the end, the dominant pattern of talking held out and the focus group proposal went ahead. However, the meetings themselves never took place and when I asked why, I was told that it was a long story. The reorganization is not over yet and there will no doubt be other attempts to shift the pattern of talk.

I am suggesting, then, that it is only when the themes organizing and organized by communicative interaction shift that there will be any change in this organization and I am pointing to just how difficult this will be because any such shift immediately alters power relations and insider/outsider dynamics. If the ensuing anxiety cannot be borne, then great efforts will be undertaken to reproduce that particular pattern of communicative interaction with as little variation as possible. Living with this anxiety is going to be very difficult, perhaps impossible, in a situation in which people's complete work situation is undergoing such massive and uncertain change. Faced with the death of their existing organization, they may be trying to save something to do with good leaders. Perhaps the whole idea of focus groups and the criteria they must design, which all sounds so rational, is part of a fantasy of salvation, the pursuit of which makes it unnecessary to confront the truly distressing situation they find themselves in. Such fantasy has an advantage of a defensive kind but it disrupts communicative action directed at the current source of difficulties and as such may be a disruption of communication, one that blocks change.

This brings us to the role of fantasy in communicative interaction, power relations and insider/outsider dynamics.

Fantasy and unconscious processes

The previous section described how the process of vocal gesture and response, that is, language, patterns itself as categories of "in" and "out." Themes to do with inclusion and exclusion are basically what ideology is about. Ideological themes are consciously expressed as gossip, that is, themes organizing conversations that sustain patterns of inclusion and exclusion that are not objectively "there in reality" but are constructed in communicative action. Gossip, rumors and the like amount to a kind of public, social fantasy, or if you will, imaginative elaborations of similarities and differences between people. Rumors and gossip are not confined to matters of inclusion or exclusion, however. They may be organizing themes that construct other kinds of social reality.

For example, on one of my consultancy assignments senior executives in a major multinational conglomerate spoke about edicts from their chief executive threatening to fire them if they did not achieve all performance targets, including those over which they had no control. Their experience of being together was powerfully organized by this theme over a two-day meeting. Later the chief executive expressed his astonishment at how they all came to believe this. It was not what he said. This then is a social fantasy unconsciously elaborated from a few chance remarks.

Much the same process of fantasy or imaginative elaboration is evident in the silent conversation of mind. There is the same process of categorization, evidenced in extreme form by splitting in which themes organizing the private role play of mind take the form of "this person is all bad" and "that person is all good," for example. This is the private form of the dynamics of inclusion and exclusion. Another example of fantasy in the private role play of mind is provided by the phenomenon of transference. This is the reproduction in the living present of responses to one's own and others' gestures that are repetitions of themes acquired early in childhood and frequently repeated thereafter, that have to do with relating to family members. These themes pattern responses to others even though they are not family members and, therefore, amount to a form of fantasy. A further example is the process of projection. From the perspective I am suggesting this might be thought of as the calling forth in oneself of a response to one's own or another's gesture, that is largely imagined in one's private role play and ascribed to the other.

However, it is important not to focus attention solely on fantasy as the distortion of reality because the same process can also amount to imaginative elaboration that constructs creative social realities and new meanings. Fantasies and imaginative elaborations, in both their public (social) and private (mind) forms, are continuously reproduced as themes organizing communicative action/power relations. Since they are reproductions, almost always with variations, they are open to transformation. Indeed, the differences created by fantasy and imagination can be amplified into novelty. Elias was one who saw this link when he stressed the use of language and symbols of all kinds in the elaboration of fantasies:

> The capacity for producing fantasy knowledge is as fundamental and distinct a human gift as the capacity for producing reality-congruent or, in other words, rational knowledge and thought. The failure to find in one's theoretical models of humankind a place for fantasies is one of the factors responsible for the failure to link theories of culture, and thus also of religion, to theories of other aspects of human beings and their various manifestations.
>
> (1989, p. 77)

The points I am making about the unconscious private process of fantasy and related public processes of ideologically-based action link directly to the creative process and to what constitutes health, both social and mental. Where themes organizing experience, particularly those of gossip and fantasy, are reproduced in sparse, highly repetitive, habitual form with little variation, then there is very little possibility of creative transformation in either social or individual terms. However, when the themes organizing experience are rich in variety, reproduced with high levels of spontaneous variations, through imaginative elaboration, then the prospects for creative transformation are high. The connection with social and individual health is this. Mental ill health takes the form of highly repetitive private role plays and many social ills also take the form of highly repetitive themes of gossip. When complexity is high enough so that individual private roles plays are rich and varied, then the possibility of personal transformation, of the evolution of personal identity are much higher (Foulkes, 1964). The same applies to communities.

This way of thinking about what is unconscious in human interaction is very different to other approaches. In the mainstream literature on learning and knowledge creation in organizations, the cognitivist perspective, what is unconscious is labeled as "tacit" and it is transmitted from one individual to another largely through processes of mimicry. Just what tacit actually is, however, is not elaborated on. It is simply said to be reflected in skilled behavior and others acquire it by copying that behavior. In complex responsive processes, it is themes and variations that are unconscious in both public and private communicative action. Since this is an action-based understanding there is nothing to transmit and no need to rely on mimicry.

Psychoanalytic perspectives on organizations understand what is unconscious as "the unconscious." This is an individual-centered perspective in which it is defenses against unacceptable wishes to discharge drives that are unconscious. Or, from an object relations perspective, "the unconscious" consists of inherited fantasies elaborated by experience of relationship with others. Individuals are assumed to unconsciously put individual mental contents into each other. In group terms, it is assumed that individuals anonymously donate mental contents to group unconscious processes (Bion, 1961a). From the perspective of complex responsive processes, themes organizing experience may be unconscious, as well as the way in which they are elaborated in fantasy. Looked at like this, there is no notion of individuals moving mental contents from on to another. Unconscious processes are forms of communication that are elaborations of social processes rather than primitive processes, present at birth, arising originally in individuals. Both individual mental and social change is change in the themes organizing communicative action and power relating and that change emerges in the interaction of organizing themes.

Conclusion

This chapter has argued that ideological themes organize people's experience of being together as power relations. Power relations are an essential feature of the communicative interaction in which knowledge arises. To manage knowledge, therefore, would be to manage ideology and power relations. This chapter has also argued that fantasy, or imaginative elaboration, in the private form and in the public form of gossip, is an essential feature of communicative interaction. To manage knowledge creation would also, therefore, be to manage private fantasies and public streams of gossip. The notion of managing knowledge becomes more and more implausible.

The next chapter explores how the patterning of communicative interaction, with its features of ideology, power relating, fantasy, imaginative elaboration and gossip, constitutes the complex responsive processes in which organizational knowledge emerges.

8 Organization as communicating in the living present: how knowledge emerges in complex responsive processes of relating

- Identity and difference
- Complex responsive processes of relating in the living present
- Conclusion

At a general level, organizations exist in order to enable people to accomplish the joint action required for human living. The essence of organization is purposeful joint action and the last four chapters have been suggesting a way of understanding human action in terms of particular assumptions about its purpose. In other words, the foundations of the explanation I am suggesting are teleological. Teleology is concerned with why a particular phenomenon becomes what it becomes, that is, with the purpose that causes it to do what it does. To put it another way, teleology has to do with the kind of movement into the future that is being assumed. For example, the movement could be toward a known state, or it could be toward the unknown. In the former case the future is already given in some way and in the latter it is under perpetual construction. Teleology also has to do with the reason for the movement into the future. For example, the reason a phenomenon is moving toward the future could be: to achieve some optimal arrangement; to realize a chosen goal; to actualize a mature form of itself; or to sustain and transform its identity.

The assumptions I have been making about teleology in the last four chapters are summarized by the term Transformative Teleology. Here, the movement of human action is toward an unknown future, that is, a future which is under perpetual construction by the movement of human action itself. The reason for the movement of human action is to express continuity and transformation of individual and collective identity and difference at the same time. The movement of human action is, therefore, fundamentally paradoxical in that it both sustains identity (the known, sameness, continuity) and, at the same time, it creates the novel, that is, variations that have never been there before (the unknown, difference, discontinuity). The process of human action is that of perpetual reproduction of identity, with the potential for transformation. There is no optimal, mature or final state, only the perpetual construction of the known and the unknown, at the same time. The future is unknowable but yet recognizable.

From this perspective, the process of perpetual construction is one of communicative interaction, in the living present, between human bodies and the context they find themselves in. In other words the cause of the movement toward a known-unknown future is the detailed, self-organizing process of bodily communicative interaction as it forms and is formed by itself at the same time. This is circular, reflexive, self-referential causality in which human interaction forms and is formed by interaction. What is organizing itself here is the patterning of communicative interaction between people as narrative and propositional themes, in which variations arise when those interacting are diverse. In other words, themes pattern interaction having the characteristics of habit and of spontaneity. Interaction itself amplifies small differences in communication into discontinuous, novel change, so operating as transformative cause. With regard to the individuals interacting, fantasy and imagination may elaborate and amplify small fluctuations in individual experience into unique, different forms of private role play/silent conversation. These unique differences between individual persons may be further amplified in their public interaction with each other. Meaning, or knowledge, emerges in this local communicative process in the living present, as does freedom of choice and intention within the conflicting constraints of power relations. Knowing is, therefore, the process of communicative interaction.

The perspective of Transformative Teleology, consistent with some of the thinking coming from the complexity sciences, suggests that making sense of organizational life requires attending to the ordinary, everyday communicative interacting between people at their own local level of interaction in the living present. This is because it is in this process that the future is being perpetually constructed as identity and difference. The last four chapters have been suggesting a way of understanding this as a continuous process of gesture-response by human bodies, that is, one of turn-taking/turn-making action in the medium of symbols (proto, significant and reified), patterning itself as narrative and propositional themes that organize the human experience of being together. These themes take many forms, including the conflicting constraints of power relations characterized by the dynamics of inclusion and exclusion, and the ideologies that sustain and shift such power relations.

This whole process is what I mean by complex responsive processes of relating in which meaning and, thus, knowledge emerges. Knowledge itself cannot be stored, although reified symbols can be stored as artifacts, that is, "abstracted" themes describing past interactions and the qualities that emerged in those interactions. Such "knowledge" artifacts, symbolizing identities past, may be used as tools in local communicative interaction in the living present. I am arguing that complex responsive processes of relating are the basis of all forms of human joint action using tools no matter how sophisticated those tools might be. I am also arguing that it is not just joint action that is made possible by complex responsive processes of relating. The very identities of individual persons and the collective identities of their groups, organizations and societies emerge in these processes too.

This chapter will explore how the perspective summarized above might help to make sense of life in organizations. By "life in organizations" I do not mean what people should be doing according to a "new" perspective called complex responsive processes but, rather, how that perspective might illuminate what people are already doing in organizations. The exploration begins by considering the patterning of group and organizational identities by making three distinctions between identity and difference.

Identity and difference: boundaries around a system or movements of process?

As soon as one talks about a particular group or organization, one is making a distinction between "it" and other groups and organizations. In other words "it" is being ascribed an identity that makes it different to other groups and organizations. A boundary is being delineated between "it" and others. On what basis is an organization to be ascribed an identity and a boundary distinguishing "it" from others?

I take an organization to be biological individuals relating to each other in the medium of symbols, thereby forming, while simultaneously being formed by, figurations of power relations between them, and between their group or organization and others in a community. The ongoing processes of relating always have a history: the history of each individual and of the group, organization, community and wider society, all of which are processes of relating. The processes of relating also encompass a particular physical place, particular resource availabilities and particular tools and technologies. Furthermore, people are members of more than one group, organization and community and membership of one affects functioning in another. On what basis would one draw boundaries, given this high degree of interconnection?

Task boundaries

An organization could be identified in terms of its purpose, its mode of fulfilling its purpose, that is, its tasks, and the individuals who are formally assigned roles in carrying out the tasks. Its identity then depends upon the tasks it undertakes within its larger community, and its boundary separates those with formal, task-related roles from others. Identity here is defined by formal propositions as to roles and relationships between roles, tasks and purposes. When identity is understood in these formal terms, difference is of two kinds.

First, those who do not have formally defined roles in carrying out the tasks of the organization fall outside its boundary so that difference is the lack of formal roles. However, tasks change as redefinitions and new tasks emerge, so that the definition of tasks is not as easy as at first it sounds. There is also the problem of just how closely connected someone has to be to the task, just how formal the role definition has to be, to justify inclusion in the organization. For example, are subcontractors essential to carrying out the tasks, or consultants, to be considered within the boundary of an organization?

Second, all informal relationships between members of the organization will constitute difference. However, although many relationships between people are not formally defined by their roles or clearly related to their tasks, it is well known that no organization can function without them. Also, some having no formal role in an organization may nevertheless play an important part through informal links, for example, the husbands or wives of chief executives.

So, when one defines the identity of an organization in formal task-related terms alone, one excludes many interactions that are clearly vital to its continuity, that is, its identity. The difficulty is that when one defines identity in terms of tasks and formal roles, one is in effect defining communicative interaction as almost entirely taking place in the medium of reified symbols patterned as propositional themes, that is, procedures and systems referring to abstract-systematic frameworks. However, as Chapter 5 argued, communicative acts always involve bodies and are, therefore, always also simultaneously conducted in the medium of protosymbols and significant symbols, self-organizing as protonarrative and narrative themes. In other words, the formal and the informal are inseparable aspects of processes of communicative interaction. It is, therefore, inadequate to define identity in purely formal terms. However, if one then says that organizational identity encompasses the formal and the informal, the notion of a boundary around the organization becomes problematic because informal relationships and practices extend in so many directions. Also, would all informal relationships and practices of any kind fall within the boundary of an organization? Most would not want to say that their group is defined by illegal or unethical practices. Identity and boundary defined along this formal–informal distinction is therefore problematic. So, what other distinction might one use?

The conscious–unconscious distinction

The identity of an organization, that which gives it continuity, could be defined in terms of the distinction between what people do consciously and what they do unconsciously as they act jointly in a purposeful manner. For example, Chapter 7 explored the notion of a social, group or dialogic unconscious, arguing that people are usually conscious of the formal propositional themes patterning their communicative interaction and reasonably reflective people are also often aware of many of the narrative and protonarrative themes. However, most of the latter are likely to be unconscious and may well be linked to others protecting them from exposure to consciousness.

In Chapter 7, for example, reference was made to ideological themes that unconsciously preserve power relations and the dynamic of inclusion and exclusion. While people are usually aware of who is "in" and who is "out," they tend to be unaware of the purpose this categorization is serving, namely, that of sustaining existing power relations. Here, the ideology itself may be conscious but its dubious basis is unconsciously excluded from reflection. In fact, the very categorizing and logical procedures of language may work to highlight certain differences and obliterate others in what is ultimately an arbitrary way. The difference is conscious but what it obliterates becomes unconscious. It seems that the very act of defining identity obliterates any difference within that identity and highlights the difference from what is outside. This is what makes it ultimately problematic to distinguish between identity and difference and why boundaries in human groups are so fuzzy and indistinct.

The formal identity of an organization is likely to be conscious and the same applies to many informal relationships. Moving to a definition of identity as conscious communicative interaction, therefore, widens the scope of identity because it now includes informal relationships and practices that are conscious. However, this is still problematic because processes of great importance in sustaining identity are excluded simply because they are unconscious. Both conscious and unconscious themes are important when trying to understand what an organization is. So, what other distinction might be used to draw boundaries around an organization?

The legitimate–shadow distinction

Another possibility is to define the identity of an organization in terms of relationships and practices that are collectively considered to be legitimate. Here, legitimate means those communicative interactions that it is acceptable to conduct openly in public. The difference can then take two forms. The first is themes that are illegitimate or illegal. The second is themes that are not illegitimate or illegal but nevertheless are felt, either consciously or unconsciously, inappropriate to conduct openly in public. I have called the latter shadow themes patterning communicative interaction (Stacey, 1993, 2000). Shadow themes take the form of, for example, gossip (Elias and Scotson, 1994), or the grotesque, that is, the humor of parody and the mockery of "carnival" (Bhaktin, 1986), usually only freely expressed in small trusted groups.

Identity defined in terms of legitimate themes patterning communicative interaction includes both formal and informal themes, for example, to do with the constraints of power relations and the ideology making those constraints feel natural. Such themes are likely to be conscious. However, the arbitrariness of ideology and the means being employed to sustain power differentials are likely to be unconscious. Some of these themes may be legitimate, that is, openly expressed, but many are likely to be shadow themes, expressed only privately in small groupings. This is much the same notion as Bhaktin's (1986) unofficial ideologies.

However, if identity is that which is legitimate and difference is that which is shadow, then the identity of an organization is being defined in terms that exclude shadow relationships and activities that may have a major impact on how organizational identity is sustained.

The problem with boundaries

It seems that every move to make the distinction between identity and difference with regard to an organization in terms of boundaries founders because it ends up excluding as difference what turn out to be important processes in sustaining organizational identity. This difficulty suggests that it might not be appropriate to think about human action in terms of boundaries. The concept of a boundary is central to systems thinking because if one is to identify a system, then it is essential to identify the boundary separating that system from others and from the environment. Here, the concept of boundary is essentially a spatial metaphor that has no temporal aspect. If one shifts from systems thinking to the kind of process thinking outlined in the last four chapters, then the concept of "boundary" has no place. This is because process is essentially about movement, which is both spatial and temporal at the same time but not boundaried. Process as living movement has fractal temporal pattern where it is meaningless to talk about what is inside and what is outside (see Chapter 3).

The question then becomes how one might think about identity and difference in process terms. As process, identity is elusive and fundamentally paradoxical movement of the known-unknown, so that "it" is impossible to pin down or grasp, but is nevertheless deeply important. Societies, organizations, groups and individuals are always reaching for identity but they can never possess it, simply because by its very nature it is not a thing but a process, continuously reproduced and potentially transformed in the living present. It follows that it is impossible to draw clear boundaries around a society, a group or an individual. Instead of thinking about the formal–informal, conscious–unconscious and legitimate–shadow distinctions in terms of boundaries, I argue that they are helpful distinctions when it comes to reflecting upon the multiple currents of communicative processes in organizations. Instead of standing outside an organization as a thing and drawing boundaries according to particular distinctions, I am suggesting that the distinctions relate to ways of articulating or interpreting the movement of organization as process, that is, the movement of the communicative interaction that one is participating in. The distinctions are simply ways of directing one's attention to aspects of fractal processes of identity (continuity) and difference (spontaneous variety) in their emergence, not things that can be grasped inside or outside boundaries that can be drawn. When one draws a boundary, it becomes something definite that has a tendency to close down further thought. However, when one pays attention to the movement of communicative action in different ways, then thought keeps moving.

I am going to distinguish five different ways of paying attention to the movement of the same process of communicative action as themes patterning the experience of being together:

- formal–conscious–legitimate;
- informal–conscious–legitimate;
- informal–unconscious–legitimate;
- informal–conscious–shadow;
- informal–unconscious–shadow.

I want to stress that I am not suggesting that these are five boxes that one might use to categorize communicative acts. I am suggesting that for the purposes of discussing communicative interaction in a reflective way, these five categories direct attention to different aspects of what is one process.

Some examples

Take a meeting I recently attended of the managing directors of the subsidiaries of a large multinational company. We assembled at the invitation of the chief executive with the purpose of identifying and exploring key strategic issues facing the company. The chief executive and his planning staff had met before the meeting and its design reflected the hierarchy and the bureaucracy, which are also designs, that is, implementations of prior decisions taken by those in formal positions of power.

They start talking about recent market developments and sales and profit performance in different market segments. As I listen to them, I pay attention to the propositions they are communicating to each other, interspersed with narrative anecdotes. I am paying attention to the procedures they follow and the kinds of hierarchical deference, they pay when, for example, they frequently glance at the chief executive to gauge his reaction. I notice how their conversational turn-taking/turn-making, at least initially, tends to be prescribed by formal power relations. As I now recount this experience to you I would say that communicative interaction here has formal–conscious–legitimate aspects. I do not sit at such a meeting putting what people are saying to each other into a box called formal–conscious–legitimate. As I pay attention in order to participate usefully, I do not normally have time to put communicative interactions into abstract categories. However, in making sense of the whole process now, for example, it might be useful to talk about these particular kinds of theme.

Let me continue with the experience of this meeting. I could pay attention to what is going on in a different way to that just described. For example, I notice that one of the more junior managing directors is taking a dominant role, but one that in no way threatens the overt power structure or the official ideology. I notice that when he does this, conversational turn-taking is patterned by informal, but perfectly conscious and legitimate differences in the personal power and persuasiveness of those present. Here, then, I am paying attention to informal–unconscious–legitimate themes patterning our experience of being together, at the same time as our experience is being patterned by the formal–conscious–legitimate themes already referred to.

At the same time, I notice how this young managing director seems to dismiss any interventions made by his one female colleague and I begin to conjecture that, although he may not be all that aware of it, his taking the lead could have something to do with an unconscious attitude around male superiority that his other male colleagues also seem to share. Here, then, our experience of being together is being patterned by informal–unconscious–legitimate themes, at the same time as it is being patterned by the other themes I have already referred to.

I also find myself paying attention to what the others are doing while the young managing director is taking the lead. Three of his colleagues exchange glances in what seems to me a kind of complicitous way and I wonder whether this indicates some collusive intention to undermine what he is proposing and their collusive agreement to say nothing about this. So, while communicative interaction is being patterned by

formal–conscious–legitimate propositions and by informal–conscious/
unconscious–legitimate themes, it is also being patterned by
informal–conscious–shadow themes. They are shadow themes in the
sense that they are not being publicly disclosed , indeed it would not be
legitimate to do so. The fact that they are shadow themes opens up the
possibility of subversive undermining of the legitimate themes.

I begin to wonder whether the acts of the three signaling their silent
disagreement to each other, and the possible collusion of some of their
colleagues in ignoring this, may have something to do with their fear of
the chief executive and their knowledge, or "fantasy" that the young
managing director is his favorite. If there is anything in my conjecture it
would mean that our experience of being together was also, at the same
time, being patterned by themes that are informal–unconscious–shadow.
There seems to me to be an unconscious distinguishing of sub-groups into
"them" and "us" and as I pay attention to this I begin to understand more
about the communicative interaction I am participating in. I hope that the
way I am paying attention will assist me to participate more usefully.

Again, I want to stress that I am not proposing another set of categories
for people to put their experience into. I do not do this, as I have said, and
I am not recommending that anyone else should. I am simply using this
categorization in this book to assist me to explain, in general terms, how
I think communicative interaction patterns communicative interaction.
When I work with people I do not think in terms of abstract categories
but, rather, I pay attention in different ways to what I am participating in
and how others and I are doing this. Later I might try to explain the
experience using abstract categories.

Complex responsive processes of relating in the living present

Figure 8.1 presents a graphical summary of the aspects of complex
responsive processes of relating that I have been describing. They are
temporal processes of interaction between human bodies in the medium
of symbols patterning themselves as themes in communicative action.
These themes, with all their multiple aspects, are continuously
reproducing and potentially transforming themselves in the process of
bodily interaction itself. These themes are the emergent enabling
constraints within which individual and collective identity and difference
are perpetually constructed as continuity and potential transformation.

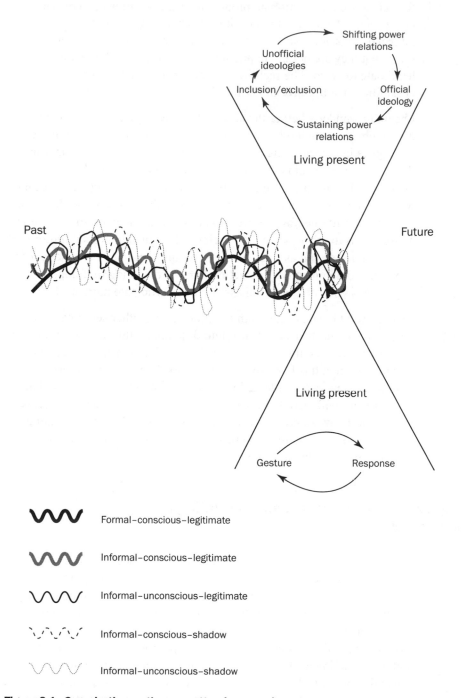

Figure 8.1 *Organization as themes patterning experience*

Figure 8.1 depicts the variations of the temporal process of themes flowing from the past to the present, with all their many aspects depicted as different lines. This is an attempt to point to the fractal process nature of communicative interaction, meaning that all the aspects of communicative interaction are simultaneously present in the flow. The present is described as living, which means that instead of just being a point that separates the past from the future, the present has the temporal structure of communicative interaction. This temporal structure takes the form of gesture-response between living bodies in the medium of symbols in which meaning arises in the whole social act, not just in the gesture on its own. Chapters 4 and 5 explored this turn-taking/turn-making process in some detail and Chapter 6 described how the process patterns itself as narrative and propositional themes, forming while being formed by bodily interactive communication at the same time, leaving behind the traces of history. The figure indicates an opening up of the present in another, closely connected way. This is the way in which communicative action, patterned as official ideological themes, sustains current power relations, thereby giving rise to the dynamics of inclusion and exclusion, which are associated with the evolution of unofficial ideologies that challenge official ideology. These matters were dealt with in Chapter 7.

It is in this living present that the future is perpetually being constructed. Mead (1938) used the term "specious present," that is, the forming present, to signify the time structure of forming while being formed at the same time as the inclusion of the past and the future in the experience of the present. Husserl (1960) pointed to the same temporal structure when he used the terms "living present" as ongoing potential and "life world" as the context. Wittgenstein (1980) referred to a similar notion as "the background" or "the hurly burly" of everyday life and the same thought is to be found in Shotter's (1993) emphasis on ordinary, everyday conversation. Focusing attention in this way on the living present places the constructive role of ordinary, everyday communicative interaction between people at the center of one's understanding of how organizations evolve. Figure 8.1 depicts a process in which people negotiate and account for their immediate actions to each other in ordinary conversation with its turn-taking/turn-making, gesture-response structure. Figure 8.1 also points to how this is simultaneously a process of sustaining and shifting ordinary, everyday power relations.

There are two further important points to be made about communicative interaction in the living present. First, it is action of a local nature. Communicative interaction consists of acts of one body directed to others in a particular situation at a particular time. The themes patterning interaction are themes local to those who are interacting and attention is therefore directed to themes emerging in local interaction between people rather than thinking in terms of themes across global situations. Whatever the global themes one might want to articulate for an organization or a society, *they have reality only insofar as they are expressed in local situations in the living present.* Themes do not "exist" outside of bodily interaction and bodily interaction has to be local. Second, in their local interaction in the living present people may use highly sophisticated communicative tools, some taking the form of global systems, which have a powerful impact on that local interaction. I will return to these matters of local situation and tools of communication later on in this chapter, but first I want to make a number of points about the nature of the themes referred to in Figure 8.1.

Themes patterning communicative interaction

The most obvious themes are, not surprisingly, those that reflect the official ideology as formal–conscious–legitimate themes. These are the publicly proclaimed visions, values and cultures of an organization, as well as its hierarchically defined roles, policies, procedures, plans and ways of using its tools, that is, its information and control systems and its technologies. They all sustain current power relations, indeed that is usually their purpose, although official ideology may from time to time include policies aimed at shifting power relations, for example, by positive discrimination. Furthermore, it is well known that these formal–conscious–legitimate themes are not sufficient on their own for an organization to function and it is widely recognized that informal–conscious–legitimate themes pattern communicative interaction. Many of the cultural themes that pattern interaction are below the level of awareness so that informal–unconscious–legitimate themes also play a part. The aspects of communicative interaction so far mentioned are shown as heavy lines in Figure 8.1. These themes are continuously reproduced with minimal variation as habits, customs and traditions. This is what institutionalization means in the way of thinking that I am suggesting.

However, this largely institutionalized configuration of patterning themes, the official ideology they express, and the current power relations they sustain, must all have arisen at some point in the past as changes from other configurations. Furthermore, current configurations may well change, or they may remain the same despite efforts at change. In other words, power relations shift, or fail to shift, as changes emerge in the thematic patterning of communicative interaction. Organizational change is change in power relations, is change in the conflicting constraints of relating, is change in communicative interaction, is change in the communicative themes patterning the experience of being together. But how does this change occur? It is in relation to change that the other configurations of patterning themes shown in Figure 8.1 are most important.

People in organizations interact with each other in the living present in ways that are patterned by informal–conscious/unconscious–shadow themes at the same time as that experience is patterned by the legitimate themes already referred to. These themes may have qualities of spontaneity and many will reflect unofficial ideologies, conscious and unconscious, that may well undermine official ideology and so shift power relations. As such shifts emerge they are reflected in emergent changes in formal–conscious–legitimate themes. It must be remembered that none of these themes are stored anywhere, but rather, they are continually reproduced and potentially transformed in the ongoing relating between people in the living present. It is not that formal–conscious–legitimate themes are of one kind, say, intentional and designed, and informal–unconscious shadow themes are self-organizing/emergent. All are aspects of self-organizing processes of continually reproduced and potentially transformed communicative interaction, where intentions and designs are themselves themes. They differ in their public visibility and in their fluidity but they are not different in kind and they are never separated from each other. They are dynamically interlinked processes of evolution. Why, then, am I making distinctions between them?

Conflict

I think it is important to make distinctions between different aspects of themes patterning experience because although they are simultaneous and inextricably interlinked aspects of the same process of symbolic interaction, they are often contradictory and conflicting. In effect, they often serve completely different purposes. Legitimate themes, whether they are formal or informal, conscious or unconscious, are largely habitual. They have arisen in previous communicative interaction and are being reproduced in communicative interaction in the living present with relatively little variation. It follows that they are stabilizing and largely constructive of continuity. They are constraining in a particular way, namely, one that, in reflecting official ideology, sustains current power relations. In their constraint, legitimate themes enable repetitive joint action. Whether conscious or unconscious, shadow themes (always informal) are much more spontaneous and reflect unofficial ideologies, which may either sustain or threaten current power relations. For example the official ideology may espouse equal opportunity policies while unofficial ideologies, making it feel natural to continue discriminating against women and minorities, sustain current power relations. On the other hand, shadow themes may express unofficial ideologies that covertly undermine official ideology and so threaten current power relations. It is in this potential for conflict between shadow and legitimate themes that the potential for transformation arises because transformation always involves some shift in power relations, some shift in current identity.

The currents of communicative interaction, therefore, do not constitute some harmonious whole and the living present is as much about conflict and competition as it is about harmony and cooperation. Indeed, without this paradox there could be no transformation. Figure 8.1 intentionally depicts the evolution of the inseparable aspects of communicative interaction in a messy way. Looking backward or forward, no one is able to fully articulate what the themes were or how they linked into each other in reinforcing and contradictory ways. Each articulation is an act of interpretation in the living present as part of communicative interaction in the living present. Each act of interpretation in the living present reconstructs the past, potentially changing its meaning. Furthermore, no one can articulate all the themes in the process of communicative interaction in the living present of a particular local situation, each interpretation being yet another gesture in the ongoing flow of gesture-response. It is even less possible for anyone to articulate all the interacting themes across an organization, an industry or a society. Again, any attempt is simply a localized interpretation in the living present.

Nevertheless, coherence emerges in the vast complexity of communicative interactions across enormous numbers of local situations because of the intrinsic capacity of self-organizing interaction to pattern itself coherently. That this is possible is demonstrated by the work of some complexity scientists referred to in Chapter 4. However, the pattern of this coherence is not predictable in advance and it involves both destruction and creation, both stability and instability. Analogies from the complexity sciences may provide some further insight into the stabilizing features of communicative interaction.

The stabilizing effect of clustering: an analogy from the complexity sciences

Kauffman's (1995) simulations of complex systems provide a demonstration of a possibility that, I argue, provides an analogy with human interaction. His simulations show that the number of connections between agents comprising a complex system determines the dynamics of the system. When the number of connections between agents is small, the dynamics take the form of stability, that is, highly repetitive patterns of behavior. This happens because small numbers of connections mean that the constraints agents impose on each other will be few. When the number of connections is very high, the dynamics are highly unstable because the conflicting constraints agents impose on each other are numerous. But at a critical number of connections, neither too few nor too many, the dynamic "at the edge of chaos" arises, which is neither stable enough to obstruct the potential for change nor so unstable as to destroy pattern. Kauffman suggests that living "systems" evolve to "the edge of chaos" because it is in this dynamic that they are changeable, neither stuck in repetition nor destroyed by instability.

He also suggests that "patching" plays a part in this evolution. "Patching" is the organization of agents into sub-groups or clusters, where the number of connections between agents within a "patch" may be high but the number of connections with agents in other patches is low. In other words, "patching" reduces the number of connections across the whole system and so tends to stabilize it enough to avoid the destructiveness of highly unstable dynamics. The system is stabilized by its capacity to organize itself into clusters and so reduce the overall number of conflicting constraints.

Although Kauffman sometimes talks about patching as an approach to the design of solutions to difficult highly interconnected problems, he also talks about patching as a spontaneous process in which clusters of connections form, being strongly connected within the cluster and weakly connected to other clusters, as systems self-organize to the "edge of chaos." It is in this latter sense that I want to use patching as an analogy for human organization. Here, patching means that each cluster of agents pursues its own activities, largely ignoring the effect on other clusters and only weakly affected by activities in other clusters, even though they are all part of wider interaction upon which their survival depends. What is interesting in Kauffman's work is how he demonstrates the possibility that this kind of arrangement can produce reasonably coherent, viable patterns in the absence of any blueprint. Interactions that cluster in this way are more likely to produce reasonably stable patterns than those that sustain the high number of connections reflecting the impact all agents have on each other. I argue that what Kauffman has to say about abstract systems self-organizing into patches offers an analogy for human interaction.

Clustering in organizations

From the perspective of mainstream thinking, the conclusion reached above is highly counter-intuitive. It is normally thought that groupings of people in an organization who attend primarily to their own ends, ignoring their impact on the whole organization will damage it. An organization consisting of groups all doing their "own thing" and only weakly taking account of their impact on the whole organization is normally thought to be a recipe for disaster. Systems thinking encourages people to take account of the whole and design systems tools to help them do this. This, in effect, increases the number of connections, which Kauffman's work suggests is actually destabilizing. It seems that an organization consisting of groups doing their "own thing" while paying some attention to the rest but not too much, is more stable than everyone being so connected that they always try to take account of the impact of their actions on the whole (Bentley, 2000). The patching arrangement is more stable and has the potential for emergent order while highly interconnected arrangements are destabilizing with the potential for disorder.

This has important implications for thinking about organizations. It is normally thought that policies and plans must be devised to cover whole systems. Systems thinking encourages people to take account of the impact of their actions across the whole system (Senge, 1990). Whole system consulting tries to "get the whole system in the room" (Owen, 1992; Weisbord and Janoff, 1995; Pratt, *et al.*, 1999). There is concern with whether the right people are being invited to get involved in change initiatives. To be at all worthwhile, interventions must aim at behavioral change across a whole organization. Programs must be rolled out and rolled down an organization if they are to have any effect. The notion that policies and interventions are not much good if they do not cover the whole organization is thus widespread. The "patching" analogy suggests that this "whole system" approach may not only be unnecessary for the production of coherent action but might actually be destabilizing and produce incoherence instead.

I argue that the institutionalization of the process of human communicative interaction between people amounts to a form of patching or clustering and serves much the same purpose as patching in the abstract models of the complexity scientists. The institutional themes organizing the experience of being together, taking the formal–conscious–legitimate form, limit the connections between people and so move the process toward stability. Hierarchical reporting structures in an organization may be thought of as patches because they are a form of clustering in which the numbers of connections between people are reduced. In a hierarchical structure, people mainly interact with their immediate superior, who in turn interacts with a person higher up in the hierarchy. This clearly cuts down on the number of connections. The accomplishment of hierarchy, habits, customs and traditions is to replace many potentially conflicting constraints with a few in the interests of ongoing joint action. When current power relations are sustained by this means, stability emerges. I am suggesting here that one might think of social structures, cultures, bureaucratic procedures and hierarchical arrangements as forms of patching that emerge, often as intentions and designs, in the self-organizing process of communicative interaction. This is a way of thinking about, say, hierarchy that is more encompassing than the usual way of simply identifying it as a designed structure. What is more encompassing about the way of thinking I am suggesting is the inclusion of hierarchy and decisions about hierarchy in the wider process of communicative interaction. Unlike Kauffman, then, I am not saying that organizations need to be designed as patches. Instead I am saying that human organization spontaneously produces emergent patching, which we call social structure, hierarchy, habit, and so on.

While patching reduces connection through institutionalizing the themes that organize the experience of being together, other aspects of the process of communicative interaction have the opposite effect. For example, communicative interaction organized by informal–conscious/ unconscious–shadow themes tends to increase the connections across sub-groups in a much faster moving manner. When both are conflicting currents in the same process of communicative interaction and neither is too dominant, then communicative interaction in the living present is more likely to have properties *analogous to those of "the edge of chaos."* The greater public visibility and lower volatility of formal–conscious–legitimate themes serves an important purpose to do with sustaining enough stability in the process of change and they do so through their clustering effect on the process. This argument has implications for prescriptions to do with designing organizations as webs and networks so as to reduce or even remove hierarchies. These prescriptions may well destabilize organizations in unhelpful ways.

The patching analogy suggests that the social process may be one that patterns communicative interaction as clusters of strong connections linked to other clusters by much weaker connections. Such clusters of strong connections would constitute institutions and organizations, in turn patterned as clusters of strong connections with weaker links to others, for example, as departments and project teams within an organization. This could be understood as an intrinsically stabilizing process in that it reduces numbers of connections and hence the numbers of conflicting constraints. In doing so, closely linked clusters establish power differences both within and between clusters, so constraining both those within the cluster and those in other clusters, but in a less destabilizing manner than closer connections between clusters. The strong connections take the form of habits. In this way powerful institutions and organizations emerge that constrain the choices open to people but in a way that is actually less constraining than always trying to take account of connections across very large groupings of people.

However, institutionalization as formal–conscious–legitimate themes organizing the experience of being together is only one aspect of the process. At the same time experience is also being patterned by, for example, informal–unconscious–shadow themes. These too display the patching process as people organize themselves into shadow pressure groups in organizations, sometimes displaying the kind of fluid communication between people that tends to be stifled by institutionalized themes. These pressure groups and their shadow themes will frequently be antagonistic to institutionalized themes and it is in the tension and the conflict between them that change in institutionalized themes emerges. This analogy from complex adaptive system theory, I think, helps one to understand the dynamics of the processes of communicative interaction in the living present required for the emergent unstable-stability in the perpetual construction of novel futures in the living present. I want to develop these points in relation to what is probably the most important form of communication in organizations, namely, conversation.

The conversational life of an organization

Conversation in organizations is that form of communicative interaction conducted in the medium of vocal symbols, language, having the same aspects (formal–informal, conscious–unconscious, legitimate–shadow) as any other communication. From the perspective I have been suggesting, the future of an organization is perpetually constructed in the conversational exchanges of its members as they carry out their tasks. How those conversations pattern, while being patterned by, communication in the course of task performance is thus a matter of great importance. I argue that an analogy from the complexity sciences, that of stable, unstable and "edge of chaos" dynamics, illuminates the dynamics of conversation in the living present.

Some conversational processes display the dynamics of stability when patterned by habitual, highly repetitive themes. In this dynamic, people are "stuck" and their conversation loses the potential for transformation. Identity arising in "stuck" conversation is continuity with little variation. One might characterize such conversational dynamics as neurotic. The quality is lifeless, depressing, even obsessive and compulsive. Other conversational processes display the dynamics of instability in which coherent pattern is lost as fragments of conversation trigger other fragments with little thematic structure. One might characterize such conversation as disintegrative, approaching the psychotic. The quality is manic confusion and distress with a fragmenting of identity. Yet other conversational processes display the dynamic analogous to the "edge of chaos," where patterning themes have the paradoxical characteristics of continuity and spontaneity at the same time. The felt qualities of such conversations are liveliness, fluidity and energy but also a feeling of grasping at meaning and coherence. There is excitement but also, at the same time, tension and anxiety. When conversational processes are characterized by this kind of dynamic, they have the potential for transformation.

Although they may not have used the analogy from the complexity sciences, others have pointed to the kind of distinction I am making. For example, in describing the quality of therapeutic conversation, Foulkes (1948, 1964) referred to "free flowing conversation" and he contrasted this with the location of neurotic symptoms in individual members of a group which lead to stereotypical patterns of conversation that have no therapeutic, that is, transformational potential.

I argue that organizational change, learning and the creation of knowledge in organizations are transformations in the thematic patterning of its communicative interaction, particularly its conversational life. The characteristics of fluid conversation with transformative potential are thus of great importance. A further analogy from the complexity sciences is helpful here. Allen (1998a, 1998b) has used abstract models to demonstrate a possibility, namely, that it is only interaction between diverse entities that gives rise to the potential for transformation. With regard to human conversation, this analogy suggests that transformative potential arises in conversations when participants are diverse, that is, sufficiently different to each other. In these conditions interaction may amplify small differences into major discontinuous changes in understanding. This is not all that surprising. It is well known that cross-discipline and cross-functional conversations stimulate new insights. It is in their struggling to understand each other in fluid, spontaneous conversational exchanges that people create new knowledge. Such conversations are characterized by ambiguity and equivocality (Weick, 1979) and by tension between inquiry and advocacy, positivity and negativity, focus on self and focus on other (Losada, 1998).

However, this is by no means an easy communicative process. First, it entails misunderstanding, which is usually experienced as frustrating, even distressing, as well as stimulating and exciting. However, the pressure to relieve the frustration may well lead to the closing down of conversational exploration, making knowledge creation a highly precarious process. This connection between misunderstanding and the creation of knowledge is, it seems to me, an important and provoking insight.

Second, conversational processes, having transformative potential, by their very nature threaten the continuity of identity. If a group of people have spent the past decades thinking and talking in terms of systems, for example, their individual and collective identities are inevitably closely tied up with that way of thinking. Conversations that challenge it hold out the potential for transformation but at the same time they threaten identity. If we do not talk and think in systems terms, then how will we think and talk? If we do not build models of systems then who are we? If we have spent decades publishing books and the Internet is more than just a faster way to distribute them, then what kind of company will we be? In other words, conversations with transformative potential inevitably arouse anxiety at a deep existential level. When we experience anxiety, we seek to defend ourselves against it through processes of denial, repression, splitting, and so on. In other words, themes emerge in conversations that counter themes with transformational potential and so shut down further exploratory conversation. The questions of how people in an organization deal with the anxiety, almost always unconsciously, and how they might find ways of living with it, are therefore central to an understanding of the knowledge creation process.

Third, conversation with transformative potential inevitably threatens current power relations, which are also an important aspect of organizational identity. The analogy of patching was used above to understand the emergence of institutionalizing themes in communicative interaction but it is also relevant to the more fluid facets of conversational life in organizations. As issues emerge in an evolving organization, people find themselves clustering around particular issues. Some of these clusters will interact communicatively in ways patterned by themes forming unofficial ideologies, which may threaten the official ideology. So, conversations patterned by informal–conscious/unconscious–shadow themes are interspersed within and around conversations patterned by institutionalized themes. The sensed undermining of existing power relations provokes reactions that once again seek to shut down exploratory shadow conversations with their transformative, knowledge creating potential. Conversations that threaten current power relations raise the real fear of exclusion or amplified inclusion and so also prompt moves to shut them down.

I am suggesting, then, that the conversational life of an organization is a potentially transformative, knowledge-creating process, when through the diversity of participation it has the dynamics of fluid spontaneity, liveliness and excitement, inevitably accompanied by misunderstanding, anxiety-provoking threats to identity and challenges to official ideology and current power relations. If one is to make sense of the process as one participates in it, then all of these aspects require some attention.

I now want to return to two points I flagged earlier on, namely, the use of tools in communicative interaction and its local situatedness.

The tools of communicative interaction

Communicative interaction between people in organizations involves the use of highly sophisticated tools. Obvious examples are telephones, the Internet, email, documents of all kinds and the wider media of television and newspapers. Less obvious, perhaps, are those tools that are usually mistaken for communication itself, indeed for the organization itself. I am referring here to management systems of information and control, including budgets, plans of all kinds, monitoring, evaluation and appraisal systems, databases, and so on. Even less obviously, perhaps, tools of communicative interaction include statements of visions, missions, values, policies, and so on.

When people interact with each other in the living present of their local situations in an organization they talk to each other in ways that have reference to all of the kinds of systems and procedural tools referred to in the previous paragraph. Meaning does not lie in the tools but in the gestures-responses made with the tools.

For example, a decision whether to make an investment or not emerges in the communicative interaction between a number of senior managers. Their communication around this issue is patterned in an emergent way by a great many themes forming while being formed in their conversations with each other. Many of those conversations take place between small groups of two or three managers and the kinds of theme patterning their interaction will have all the aspects, legitimate and shadow, conscious and unconscious, formal and informal, discussed earlier on in this chapter. Their conversations with each other may refer to documents setting out discounted cash flow analyses, risk factor appraisals, mission statements and other communicative tools. In other words, they will be using documents that set out specific abstract-systematic frameworks as tools in their communicative interaction. They will refer to the documents as rhetorical tools to persuade others of their opinion. The documents are tools in the process of negotiating with each other and accounting to each other for the positions they take. The constraints provided by an organization's budget and financial policies are used in similar ways, as are the procedures laid down for obtaining investment approval. All of these tools are essentially aspects of the process of institutionalization and the constraints it imposes on action.

However, *it is important not to mistake the tools for communicative interaction itself* because this leads to obscuring the nature of the themes patterning the decision-making process, creating the illusion that the decision is largely a calculation. This then acts as a defense against taking into account the underlying ideological processes and the ways they are sustaining or shifting power relations, as well as any anxiety provoked by the potential for transformation of organizational, subgroup and individual

identities. Most significant investment decisions shift power relations to
some extent and also potentially transform identities of one kind or
another. The debate around such decisions has as much to do with such
shifts in power relations and identities as it does with monetary aspects.

From the perspective I am suggesting, national and international financial
systems can be thought of as tools in, as enabling constraints on,
communicative interaction within organizations, so entering into the
patterning of the themes of communicative interaction. In fact, these tools
shape the themes of communicative interaction, both enabling and
exercising powerful constraints on that communication. One cannot take
part in a discussion about an investment project in a particular
organization, for example, if one does not talk in the prescribed language
of discounted cash flows, risk factor analyses, budget constraints and
investment approval procedures. This language can create a kind of
myopia in which participants no longer "see" other aspects of the wider
process of communicative interaction they are participating in around,
say, an investment proposal. The very magnitude of the tools may also
lead those using them to lose sight of the local situatedness of their
participation.

The local nature of communicative interaction

Earlier in this chapter, I made the point that communicative interaction
always takes place in specific local situations in the living present. The
local nature of these situations is often not hard to see, but particularly
when it comes to managers and leaders at the top of an organizational
hierarchy, the local nature of interaction might require some explanation.
After all, it is supposed to be the role of the chief executive, for example,
to act in relation to the whole of an organization. However, I suggest that
closer examination of what a chief executive actually does, points to
another interpretation. A competent chief executive will indeed be
thinking and talking about the organization as a whole but to whom does
he or she talk in this way? A chief executive, like anyone else in an
organization talks most frequently about matters of greatest concern to a
relatively small group of trusted others. The chief executive's important
communicative interactions take place, therefore, in the local situation of
other senior executives. Their communicative interaction is patterned by
the processes of themes shaping themes, formal and informal, conscious
and unconscious, legitimate and shadow, just as anyone else's is.

There are, of course, differences as well as similarities between the processes of communicative interaction involving a powerful chief executive and those involving the much less powerful. When a chief executive makes a public gesture it potentially calls forth responses in much larger numbers of others than is the case with the less powerful. However, just what those responses will be cannot be arranged by the chief executive, as anyone in that position knows only too well.

For example, suppose the chief executive of a major multinational corporation announces his new vision of the "corporation as global leader in network solutions." Perhaps 100,000 people around the globe hear the gesture and a great many feel called upon to respond in some way. However, the meaning of the vision, like the meaning of all gestures, does not lie in the gesture. What it means will be created in the responses. Will most just pay lip service to it and carry on doing what there were doing before? If they do not, just what will they do? The gesture may call forth the response of many meetings around the globe as people discuss what it means and what they are supposed to do about it. The meaning of the chief executive's gesture and its impact on the organization will emerge in many local situations, including his or her own, in the living present of conversations around the globe.

Take another possibility. Again, after discussion in his own local situation with his closest colleagues, a chief executive might announce that a new investment appraisal procedure is to be installed and he may set out its general features. Others will develop the outline and a new tool in communicative interaction across the organization will be created. However, again, just how it will be used and what impact it will have will depend upon the communicative interaction between a great many people in many local situations.

By analogy with some work in the complexity sciences (Kauffman, 1995), and its use in relation to organizations (Marion, 1999) discussed in the first volume of this series (Stacey et al., 2000), I argue that no one can determine the dynamic of interaction within an organization because that dynamic depends upon what others both within that organization and in other organizations are doing. In other words, an individual, or a group of individuals, powerful or otherwise, can make gestures of great importance but the responses called forth will emerge in local situations in the living present where an organization's future is perpetually being constructed.

Note that I am not saying that powerful managers, such as chief executives have no effect on the "whole" organization. Clearly, they often have major, widespread effects. I am arguing that what a chief executive does emerges in his or her local communicative interaction and that the nature of the impact on the organization emerges in many other local situations, all in the living present. The focus of attention, in trying to make sense of what happens, shifts from the chief executive's statement or new tool to the processes in which the statement or tool arises and to the widespread local situations in which they have their effects. Instead of taking it for granted that powerful chief executives actually individually change organizations directly through their intended actions, the perspective I am suggesting invites one to explore the communicative processes in which the mere presence of, the images of, and the fantasies about leaders all affect local processes of communicative interaction in the living present.

Knowledge creation and complex responsive processes of interaction

The perspective I am suggesting immediately focuses attention on the importance of local communicative interaction in the living present, particularly its thematic patterning, its gesture-response structure and its reflection in ideologies and power relations as depicted in Figure 8.1. This represents a way of understanding the emergence of knowledge in complex responsive processes of relating in which people use both the tools of communication and the tools and technologies with which they transform their material environment. This view of knowing as process counters the widespread tendency to focus attention on knowledge as artifact or systems tool used in the active process of communicative interaction. Instead of focusing attention on the tool, the perspective I am suggesting focuses attention on how the tools are used.

The tools are used in wider processes of communicative interaction in which particular ways of talking are "in" and others are "out." A concern with the knowledge-creation process would, therefore, involve an exploration of this dynamic as it manifests in local situations in the living present. What kind of exclusion is operating? What impact does this have in terms of obstructing or encouraging the emergence of new knowledge? Such questions soon lead to reflection on the manner in which ideologically based power relations are being sustained and challenged.

What impact does this have on communicative interaction and the emergence of knowledge? A concern with the knowledge-creating process also involves an exploration of the identity-threatening and anxiety-provoking aspects of the process, so focusing attention on these and other aspects of the conversational life of an organization and its transformative potential.

This refocusing of attention raises important questions with regard to mainstream thinking about knowledge creation in organizations. What can it mean to talk about managing knowledge creation in organizations when knowing is action in local situations in the living present? What can it mean to create a learning organization? What can it mean to talk about measuring and managing the intellectual capital of an organization? What are governments and educational establishments doing when they operate quality assurance systems to ensure quality learning?

In practical terms, taking the perspective I am suggesting focuses one's attention in a particular way when one engages in communicative interaction in an organization. It leads me to pay attention to the themes that seem to me to be organizing the experience of communicative interaction in a particular grouping in a particular organization at a particular time. Instead of trying to get the whole system in the room, or trying to get a picture of the whole system, I am asking what themes seem to be evident in the way people are relating to each other in a local situation in the living present in which I am participating. For example, what important informal–unconscious–shadow themes seem to be evident and how are they engaging with the institutionalized themes? What power relations are being sustained and undermined? How is anxiety being dealt with? My participation is then influenced by my conjectures as I ask questions and draw attention to this or that theme. Participating in this way has a different impact on the conversational life of an organization to participation that focuses simply on the tools of communication.

Conclusion

I am suggesting, then, that human organizations are processes of complex responsive relating between bodies in human and non-human contexts. These are processes of communicative interaction in the medium of symbols, patterned as organizing themes. Only one kind of symbol can be stored, namely, reified symbols stored in written and other artifacts but they have no meaning until they are used as tools in the process of communicative interaction. The other kinds of symbol, protosymbols and significant symbols are continuously reproduced in bodily interaction and so cannot be stored. It is in the ordinary, everyday detail of such interaction in the living present that people are constructing the future of their organization, enabled and constrained by the communication tools they and others have constructed. In their communicative interaction with each other people use the tools of technology, artifacts and systems, all being some form of extension of their bodies. But these are only tools, not knowledge itself. This perspective places power relations, or the emergence of enabling and conflicting constraints, at the center of the explanation. It views change as the evolution of the thematic patterns organizing the experience of being together, with all its excitement and anxiety. That evolution is processes of reproduction and potential transformation as intrinsic properties of relating itself. Such evolution is possible only when the dynamics of communicative interaction are fluid enough, when there is diversity, tension and conflict in the thematic patterning of communicative interaction, analogous to the "edge of chaos."

From this perspective knowledge is meaning and it can only emerge in the communicative interaction between people. It emerges as meaning in the ongoing relating between people in the living present. This is an evolutionary concept of knowledge as meaning continuously reproduced and potentially transformed in action. Knowledge is, therefore, the thematic patterns organizing the experience of being together. The process of learning is much the same and there does not seem to be much point in trying to distinguish the one from the other. Identity, both individual and collective, evolves and communicative interaction, learning and knowledge creation are essentially the same processes as the evolution of identity. From this perspective, it is meaningless to ask whether organizations learn or whether people in organizations learn. It is the same process. It is meaningless to ask how tacit knowledge is transformed into explicit knowledge since unconscious and conscious themes organizing experience are inseparable aspects of the same process. Organizational change, learning and knowledge creation are the same as change in communicative interaction, whether people are conscious of it or not. This perspective suggests that the conversational life of people in an organization is of primary importance.

Part III
Systems thinking and the perspective of complex responsive processes:
comparisons and implications

Part III has two purposes. The first, undertaken in Chapter 9, is to compare the theory of organizations as complex responsive processes of relating with the theoretical frameworks of mainstream thinking and its critics. The comparison is essentially with systems thinking. Chapter 9 will argue that the perspective of complex responsive processes leads to a significantly different conceptualization of organizational knowledge to that found in systems thinking. In the latter, knowledge tends to be thought of as something stored, shared and diffused around an organization. The concern is with how this might be accomplished for different categories of knowledge, particularly tacit and explicit. From a complex responsive process perspective, however, knowledge is meaning that emerges in relating between human bodies. Knowledge is themes organizing the experience of communicative interaction and power relating. Knowledge is thus continuously reproduced and transformed as a process of perpetual construction of identity and difference. Here knowledge is action and so cannot be stored, shared or diffused only practiced in local situations in the living present in a participative way.

Chapter 10 then goes on to point to the implications of this difference between systems thinking and a complex responsive process perspective on knowledge. If knowledge is thought of as something stored and shared, then it may make sense to talk about measuring and managing it. If knowledge is process, if it is emergent themes patterning the experience of being together in the living present, if it is ordinary, everyday human relating in conversation and other kinds of communication in local situations, then it makes no sense to talk about measuring and managing it. The implication is that much of what is done in the name of knowledge management must be serving some other purpose. What does make sense from a complex responsive process perspective is the joint exploration of, and reflection on, patterns of participation in the ongoing flow of communicative interaction in which knowledge emerges.

9 Comparing systems thinking and the perspective of complex responsive processes

- From sender–receiver to responsive relating
- From storing to perpetually constructing memory
- From the individual–social split to individuals in social relationships
- From the individual tacit/unconscious to unconscious processes of relating
- From systems of language to the action of language
- Institutions, communication and power
- Dialogue and ordinary conversation in the living present
- Conclusion

This chapter draws out the differences between mainstream, that is, systems thinking about knowledge creation in organizations (see Figure 2.1) and the complex responsive process perspective presented in the chapters of Part II (see Figure 4.5). In Chapter 2, I argued that mainstream thinking is built on assumptions about causality that amount to Formative Teleology and on cognitivist psychological assumptions (Rationalist Teleology) about human acting and knowing. The alternative I have been arguing for in Part II is built on assumptions about causality that amount to Transformative Teleology and action-based assumptions about human knowing. The change in fundamental assumptions becomes particularly evident in differences between the two explanations in relation to the following matters:

- the process of relating between people;
- the nature of memory;
- how new knowledge is created;
- the meaning of tacit knowledge and unconscious process;

- the role of power and communication;
- the nature of dialogue.

Each of these differences will now be explored.

From sender–receiver to responsive relating

In systems thinking about knowledge creation and human relating (see Figure 2.1), an individual's mind is thought of as a mental model, an inner world, inside his or her head. It is thought that this inner world has been structured in past experience into personal values and beliefs, as well as assumptions about and expectation of others and the world in which people are together operating. It is on this basis that an individual A chooses an action in relation to another individual B and then acts, in so doing transmitting to B what is in his or her mind. For example, individual A might translate an idea in his or her mind into language and then act by saying this to B, thereby transmitting the idea in his or her mind to the mind of B. In this way knowledge developed in the head of A is transmitted as information to B, who then processes that information through his or her mental model and chooses a reaction to A. Then, knowledge in the head of B is transmitted to A in the form of information. Individual A then processes it in the same way. If they interact in this way without any change to their mental models, then single loop learning is said to have occurred but if in the course of the interaction one or the other changes mental models, that is, values, beliefs and assumptions, then double loop learning is said to have taken place.

According to this way of thinking, relating is a process in which one party thinks first, translating an idea into language, then chooses an action, and then acts, thereby transmitting mental contents from one mind to another. This cognitivist perspective on relating is similar to that of psychoanalytic theory in some respects in that the latter uses the concepts of introjection, projection, identification and projective identification as processes in which people are said to unconsciously take into their minds feelings from and representations of others and in turn put feelings into them. In the course of these sender–receiver processes of relating, both cognitivist and psychoanalytic, people are said to develop habits and traditions of one kind or another, that is, social structure, which in turn acts back on them, influencing the development of their habits of thought or mental states. Here social structure emerges from individual interaction and constitutes a separate reality above individuals, a reality with its own governing principles. Individual minds and social structure are therefore taken to be at separate ontological levels. For organizations this means that a distinction must be drawn between individual knowledge located in individual heads and organizational knowledge located in some kind of social structure, such as information systems, procedures, cultural norms and so on.

In the alternative perspective (see Figure 4.5) developed in Part II, individuals A and B are not posited to have mental models or inner worlds as the basis of their actions. Instead, each individual is thought of as a biological organism that acts toward others, the social, and toward itself, mind. There are biological correlates of the action of mind as well as biological correlates of social actions. These biological correlates may be thought of as cascading variations in body rhythms, where body rhythms are feelings and emotions. Biological organisms in communication interact with each other. They are not putting anything into each other nor are they transmitting anything to each other. Rather, they are resonating bodily with each other as they link their actions in order to "go on" together. In this "going on together," they are interacting cooperatively and competitively in joint activities, usually employing tools of some kind, in order to express identities and "earn a living." The processes of cooperative and competitive interaction being described here are essentially responsive in that each individual responds to others so as to fit their actions into the actions of those others. This ongoing flow of relating is at one and the same time private, as an individual biological organism relates to itself in private role play, and public, as that biological organism interacts with others. Self-organizing patterns emerge at the same time in both the private role play of mind and the public role play of the social.

Experience, both that of the social and that of individual mind, is being organized by themes around which there are always unique variations, and themes and variations emerge in, and at the same time pattern, relating between people. This is an explanation in which A's "chosen" gesture is emerging in the private role play of mind, calling forth a "chosen" response from B, who is also engaged in the private role play of mind, which is calling forth the "chosen" gesture of A, in a simultaneous and endless flow of relating. What is organizing itself here are the themes and variations that are patterning the gesture-response action of individual mental and social relating while being patterned by it. As they "go on" together, interweaving their actions with each other, people in relationship develop habits, customs, traditions, cultures, and the like. In other words, themes organizing the experience of being together become institutionalized where this means that the themes are repeated with less variation as habits. The social is not a "structure" existing above people, rather, it is regularities, a high degree of repetitiveness, in the themes that organize the experience of being together. However, as they "go on" together, small variations around themes may be amplified into shifts that simultaneously emerge in patterns of private role plays and public "plays" of social interaction. Change is at one and the same time change in the thematic patterning of individual mind and social interaction. Although people may copy or mimic each other, mimicry is not required to explain how mental contents move from one individual to another because no such movement takes place. Instead, people act in relation to each other and in their interaction change in minds and in the social emerges.

From this perspective, public patterns of relating between people, that is, the social, and private patterns of each individual organism relating to itself, that is, individual minds, are self-similar processes. In other words, they are fractal in that no matter how closely one examines social interaction or mental activity, there is the same rhythmic, responsive process. Cooperative social activity could not take place without the individual capacity for largely private role play, nor could that private role play take place without social interaction. Mind and the social are thus at the same ontological level. One might think of the biological as a lower ontological level from which mind and society emerge together. Mind and society in turn influence the biological activity from which they emerge in that body rhythms, and all other bodily activities, are affected by, and affect, mental and social activity.

Comparing the two perspectives

The two perspectives, then, present very different notions of relationship. In the systems perspective, those relating to each other act on each other on the basis of models inside them and put something from these mental models into each other, thereby potentially influencing and changing each other. In doing this they create institutions and other social structures quite outside themselves, which follow their own causal principles and act back upon the individuals, potentially altering their mental models or inner worlds. In this scheme organizational knowledge is outside individual heads and located in social structures and technology.

In the complex responsive process perspective, individual minds and the more repetitive themes organizing social experience arise together in the interaction between people. Knowledge, or meaning is in the interaction, not in people's heads. Meaning, or knowledge, emerges in the public interaction between people and simultaneously in the private role play each individual conducts with himself or herself. From this perspective, knowledge does not exist outside relationships. Whatever it is that is embodied in tools and artifacts such as procedural manuals, it is not knowledge until someone uses the tools and artifacts. Organizational knowledge here is not located anywhere but arises continually in the relationships between people within organizations. This perspective poses very different questions about the management of knowledge in organizations to those posed by systems thinking.

To summarize, consider some of the fundamental differences between the two views of relating between people:

- In the systems perspective, individual minds are thought of as already existing processors of data and information, while social structure is thought of as already existing habits and traditions, some of which are embodied in artifacts, tools and technologies. New knowledge could change these already existing processors and structures. In the complex responsive process perspective, there is a move from thinking in terms of something already existing to thinking in terms of patterns that are continually reproduced and potentially transformed. The organizing themes of the individual, private role play of mind are being reproduced with variations and potentially transformed in the living present. At the same time, the public display of habitual and traditional themes organizing experience is also being reproduced with variations and potentially transformed in the living present. This is knowledge as process of continual reproduction and potential transformation of relational themes.
- The systems perspective pays little attention to the constitutive role of feelings and emotions in the process of relating. Feelings are, rather, treated as motivational factors. In the complex responsive process perspective, feelings and emotions are never split off from thought and action because that perspective focuses on the responsive interaction between human bodies and living bodies are never without feelings. People cannot relate other than as bodies and all relating is fundamentally, therefore, a temporal process of variations in feelings, that is, variation around themes expressed in body rhythms. Emotions and feelings are not phenomena that can be distinguished from thought

and action but are always aspects of the same process. Knowledge is therefore not some cognitive framework but a continually reproduced and potentially transformed pattern of intertwined feeling (body rhythms), thinking (private role play) and acting (social relating).

- The systems perspective not only splits feelings and emotions off from thought and action, it also splits thought from action. First, the individual thinks, that is, processes data and information through a mental model. Then, the individual acts. Action here is an individual choice or intention made on the basis of reason and knowledge is transmitted from one to another. From the complex responsive process perspective, there is an ongoing flow of action. In gesturing, one is calling forth responses in others, as each engages in ongoing private role play with himself or herself, that is, thinks. Public acting and the private action of thinking are aspects of the same bodily interactions. From this perspective, choice or intention emerges in the interaction with others as a theme organizing their interaction. Each is still selecting or choosing what to respond to in a gesture and intending how to respond to it but such selection, choice and intention is also being called forth by the other, embedded in the ongoing flow of interaction, making it impossible to locate it in the individual in any simple fashion. So, in the systems perspective, choice and intention are designs produced by individual cognitive processing while in the alternative perspective they emerge in an ongoing flow of individual interactions.

I turn now to how the two different perspectives being discussed deal with the question of memory.

From storing to perpetually constructing memory

The cognitivist psychological foundation of systems thinking takes human memory to be a store of past experience located in mental models, or inner worlds, at the individual level. Additionally, at the social level, the collective memory is a store of shared values and beliefs located in the culture (myths and rituals, for example), as well as a store of existing knowledge located in artifacts, systems and technologies. When an individual is presented with data or information, the relevant mental model is said to be retrieved from long-term memory banks and used to process the data or information to produce appropriate meaning, or knowledge. Collectively, people process data and information through cultural memories to produce meaning. The metaphor of a computer is frequently used to illustrate the proposed procedure of memory retrieval and data processing.

Both individual and cultural memories must be stored in individual human brains and some neuroscientists in the cognitivist tradition present explanations of how this is done. At its simplest, the explanation runs as follows. The brain represents a stimulus in the form of a pattern of neural connections formed and stored in one location in the brain. Subsequent experience of that stimulus triggers the reproduction of that pattern to produce an accurate re-presentation of the stimulus and in this way, memory is retrieved. Some neuroscientists (Barrie *et al.*, 1994; Freeman, 1994, 1995; Freeman and Schneider, 1982; Freeman and Barrie, 1994; Kelso, 1995; Skarda and Freeman, 1990) question this possibility, at least in the rather simple form often assumed. Their research indicates that:

- It is no longer tenable to identify a particular memory with a particular brain locale because patterns resulting from a stimulus tend to be spread across large sections of the brain.
- Initial neural patterns formed by attention to a stimulus are rapidly washed away and replaced by constructions of the brain itself meaning that the stimulus is not simply represented in the brain. Changes in brain chemistry following exposure to a stimulus have so far been shown to persist for no more than a few hours (Rose, 1995), leaving unexplained how the brain can store anything for years. Instead of storing in any simple fashion, it seems that the brain perpetually constructs patterns as biological correlates of bodily actions rather than straightforward representations.
- When the context of a stimulus is altered, the pattern of corresponding brain activity also changes. This means that the same stimulus does not always trigger the same neural pattern.
- Patterns of neural activity associated with one stimulus change when other stimuli are subsequently learned.

These findings suggest that the brain does not represent stimuli or store them in any straightforward way or process them in the manner assumed by the cognitivist model. What some neuroscientists (Freeman,1994) are suggesting instead is as follows:

- The biological correlates of long-term memories are neural patterns widely distributed across many brain regions.
- Experience of stimuli permanently alters the highly plastic structure of

the brain which forms and reforms connections throughout life to produce emergent patterns of neural activity.

● Memory is not a representation but a reconstruction, an emergent pattern, that is always changing. The biological correlates of memory are neural patterns that are continually reproduced and potentially transformed rather than stored anywhere in a simple way.

This points to the idea that the biological correlates of memory are associative processes of reproduction and potential transformation, just as individual mind and social interaction are, according to the argument presented in Part II. Freeman (1994) has suggested that the brain correlates of memory might work in the following manner. A particular nerve cell assembly is triggered by a particular stimulus but this does not provide the memory of the stimulus, rather, it is the first step in the process of triggering the reproduction of a global pattern, an attractor. This global pattern would be the brain correlate of a memory. This correlate, however, is reproduced anew each time it is triggered, not retrieved from a store where it is waiting to be called upon. The reproduced pattern correlating with a memory is different to some extent each time it is reproduced because in the meantime other experiences have altered the brain. This is not an accurately stored record awaiting retrieval and processing but a dynamical, associative process of reproduction and potential transformation. This view of the brain is consistent with Transformative Teleology in that the brain perpetually constructs memory as continuity and transformation.

The complex responsive process view of mind and the social is consistent with these findings and suggested interpretations of brain functioning. When a person encounters a salient stimulus, the response called forth involves a shift in the private role play, organized by themes formed in past experience but now reproduced and transformed by changes in context and what has been learned since the last time the stimulus was encountered, just as in the above account of brain correlates. The stimulus becomes, as it were, an active image, voice, or rhythm in the private role play and its participation is organized by that continuously reproduced role play, potentially transforming it. The response is not one retrieved from a store and processed but one of current reproduction organized by themes made habitual by past experience and variations on those themes. Memory is thus a dynamical associative process of reproduction and transformation rather than retrieval and processing in both the mind and its brain correlates. What has been "stored" in the form of a change in the brain and the body is a strengthened connection (Hebb, 1949) that operates not as a store but as a trigger of patterns of role play, themed in ways formed by experience. Previous experience has shaped brain–body functioning in a particular way and ongoing experience reshapes it in a way that affects memories of the past. The same dynamical process applies to the role play of a body with itself. This account is near to experience, I suggest, because memories are, in my opinion, rarely recalled in the same way twice.

The shift here is from a notion of some past experience being more or less accurately recorded and placed in storage to be retrieved from a specific location in the same state in which it was laid down, to the notion of past experience shaping biological correlates of the themes that are later reproduced in private role play and public interaction when a person encounters a similar stimulus. The memory of past experience is thus registered and later altered to some extent in new situations. The memory here is not something already specified that is called out and elaborated but the trigger to a pattern that could come forth in not already specified, novel ways.

In systems thinking, history is a store of memories that can be more or less accurately retrieved as the basis of current actions. From the perspective of complex processes of relating, history is an account that is reproduced in interaction between people in the living present. The accounts of history are always affected by the current context of interaction and are, therefore, rarely exactly the same. Historical accounts are communicative actions playing the same kind of role as other communicative actions in the ongoing process of people fitting their actions into those of others. It is important to note that the emphasis on the living present in the complex processes of relating does not mean that patterns of interaction arise completely anew each moment, from nothing as it were. Rather, patterns of interaction arise in reproduction with the potential for transformation.

From the individual–social split to individuals in social relationships

Systems thinking locates the cause of human action and the creation of new knowledge primarily in the individual. At its simplest this may be causality of the efficient type in which a stimulus, say, the act of another, causes an individual to have a particular thought which is the origin of that individual's action. In more sophisticated arguments causality may be of the formative kind in which the context of relationships with others and the features of the physical environment may specify a situation in which the individual thinks certain thoughts that lead to certain actions. Here the actions are formatively caused by the individual interacting in an already specified context. Individuals in context constitute systems and environments and it is the systemic process that causes the action. This brings the social level into the formatively causal process in that social structures and institutions are acting upon the individual and action flows from individual motivations within a social context. This motivational process immediately brings in teleological causality in the sense that the individual has a purpose, intention or motive, affected by social structure and institutions, which drives the choice of action. As already discussed in Chapter 3, some critiques of the simpler cognitivist approaches, such as critical realism, institutionalism and structuration theory, all ultimately locate causality, or agency, in the individual with the social acting in some way upon individual motivation.

When agency is ultimately located in the individual in this way, then the question of how novelty, that is, the creative or destructive new, comes about also has to be answered in terms of the individual. Novelty has to arise in the head of an individual but there is little explanation of just how this is supposed to occur. If social structure is the repeated, enduring habits of action that influence the development of an individual, then it becomes difficult to identify just how social structures and institutions change. Once again the answer has to be found in the heads of individuals and their intentions to change social structures. New knowledge has to arise in individuals, motivated by the social, and then spread to others so that is becomes institutionally embedded. Just what is being spread and just how this spreading and embedding occur is problematic. In Chapter 3, I argued that these views, which split the individual and the social, implicitly assume some mixture of Formative and Rationalist Teleology. The social constructionist approach points to Transformative Teleology but ultimately locates agency in the social, the "we."

The notions of causality and the explanations of novelty are radically different in the complex responsive process perspective where patterns of relationship cause themselves in a circular, recursive type of causality. Those patterns of relationship, arising in patterns of relationship in a never-ending flow of relating, include, at the same time, both the patterns of each individual's body relating to itself in the private role play of mind and the patterns of relating of those bodies with each other in the public "play" between them as they go about their ordinary everyday lives in groups and institutions, that is, the social. The process of relating is expressing identity in both individual minds and the social at the same time and the expression of identity is, of course, at the same time, the expression of difference. This is Transformative Teleology in which there is no fundamental distinction between the individual and the social.

It is important to hold in mind that these complex responsive human processes are processes of relating between uniquely different individuals. Each individual participating in the interaction with others is uniquely different because each has experienced a uniquely different life history expressed in a uniquely different identity, that is, a private role play that is uniquely different from all other largely private role plays. How has this uniqueness come about?

First, there is the property general to all complex processes in nature, namely the capacity to amplify minute differences in context and history into qualitatively different historical patterns. This is, of course, the property known in chaos theory as sensitive dependence on initial conditions, or the butterfly effect, and in the theory of dissipative structures as fluctuations from which order emerges. No two human beings have the same body rhythms and as they go through life, no two bodies experience exactly the same context of family, school, place, and so on. Even twins brought up in the same family will experience slight differences in context, but these are enough to be amplified into qualitative differences in the patterns of private role play each engages in. In other words tiny differences can escalate into significantly different role plays.

In addition, and just as important, I suggest, is what may be a peculiarly human capacity for imaginative elaboration and fantasy. An individual brain does not accurately represent external reality and store those representations in a form that is reliably retrievable. It seems that brains construct biological correlates of experience that are later triggered into reproducing patterns easily transformed by intervening experience and changes in current context. There is a similarity here with the private role play that is the individual mind. That role play is not an accurate reflection of the "actual" experience, whatever "actual" might mean. Instead, the role play is a private construction that is greatly elaborated in an imaginative and fantastical way. When early patterns, or more accurately, themes organizing that role play, are later recalled, they are not retrieved in pristine form from a memory store, but rather, reproduced and potentially transformed in the course of further fantasy and imaginative elaboration. What I have been describing is, I suggest, near to experience. In my own exploration with others of my own and their ways of making sense of what we are doing together, we frequently become aware of how we have elaborated what the others have been saying. We transform the communications of others through processes of private role play that may have more to do with our own past patterns of relating than with the current situation.

This emergence of unique identity through the capacity for imaginative and fantastical elaboration in the private role play of mind is of the greatest importance. It means that the interactive complex processes of group/social life involve the participation of individuals who are uniquely different from each other while also being similar to each other. These complex processes are then characterized by what Allen (1998a, 1998b) has referred to as micro-diversity. In the complexity sciences, systems with the property of micro-diversity have been shown to have the inherent capacity to produce true novelty of a kind that has never existed before. This is not novelty already specified, one enfolded, and then elaborated or unfolded, but true novelty. By analogy, I argue that the difference between individuals interacting with each other also imparts to their interaction the intrinsic capacity for spontaneously producing emergent novelty. If individual uniqueness were to be the result of fluctuations in context alone, then the self-organizing process of relating could only elaborate on what was somehow already specified; it could only unfold what was somehow already enfolded. However, where uniqueness arises because of the internal dynamic of the individual itself, then micro-diversity arises and interaction between such diverse individuals has the intrinsic capacity to produce true novelty.

The point of this discussion is as follows. It is because humans have the capacity to imaginatively elaborate on reality in their private role play, because they embellish that role play in fantasy, that they are uniquely different. Since their communication with each other is the public expression of the private role play called forth by the public expression of others, in turn an expression of their private role play, it follows that they will often fail to understand each other. Now all of this is usually regarded as a problem. After all, the aim is to understand each other and much effort is expended on improving communication between people. In psychoanalysis, fantasy is a distortion of reality and maturity is equated with the reduction of fantasizing in the interests of behaving according to the reality principle. From a complex responsive process perspective, however, fantasizing and consequent misunderstanding is the very source of potential novelty, both creative and destructive. By analogy with the complexity sciences, I would argue that minimal fantasy and high levels of understanding between people produce the dynamics of repetition (boredom and depression) with very little transformation indeed, while very high levels of fantasizing and subsequent misunderstanding would produce the dynamics of fragmentation (paranoia and schizophrenia). However, at some critical level of fantasy and misunderstanding one would expect the dynamics of potential transformation in the reproduction of patterns of relating, that is of potential novelty.

It may be necessary to counter any impression created by the above discussion that the potential for novelty lies in uniqueness located in the individual. In complex responsive process this cannot be so because the uniqueness of the individual is not a property arising in the individual in isolation. It is the consequence of a history of relating and furthermore, the uniqueness expressed in any current participation with others is as much called forth by them as it is selected in the individual private role play. It must be borne in mind that it is not simply uniqueness in private role plays that is emerging but also uniqueness in the public pattern of interaction, that is uniqueness of a collective or social kind. One is never possible without the other. Fantasy and misunderstanding are never simply a property of one person but a property of their participation with each other. Uniqueness only has any meaning in relation to difference from another.

This brings me to the matter of power relations once again. Since all relating is a process of enabling constraint that both moves people and holds them back, power relations must always be a feature of the public sphere of interaction. Since the private role play of mind is the same relational or communicative process it too must have the characteristics of power relations displayed by the way in which different "voices" in the private role play both enable and constrain each other. This is most evident when one cannot "make up one's mind." *Identity and difference in both its individual and group senses is, therefore, also an emergent quality of power relations.* Micro-diversity in human relating is therefore also a consequence of power relations. Power relations are thus also essential sources of novelty in its radical sense. This too is not part of conventional thinking in which power tends to be ignored because bringing power differences into the open causes so much discomfort. Where it is discussed, the tendency seems to be to regard it as "a bad thing" and the easily assumed prescription becomes that of reducing power differences and conflict. The complex responsive process perspective suggests that critical degrees of power difference impart the capacity for emergent novelty.

From cognitivist and many other perspectives, it seems reasonable to talk about the organization's knowledge as distinct from the individual's knowledge and to talk about managing the process of knowledge creation and novelty production. From a complex responsive process perspective there is no essential distinction between individual and organizational knowledge since both are reproduced patterns of relating between bodies. Knowledge here may be embedded in artifacts, but only in a dead sense. The use of artifacts can only take place in relationships. The emergence of novelty relies on micro-diversity, on capacities for fantasizing, on power differences and misunderstanding. So does it make any sense at all to talk about managing such processes?

From the individual tacit/unconscious to unconscious processes of relating

An important distinction to be found in the mainstream literature on organizational knowledge creation and management is that between explicit and tacit knowledge (see Chapter 2). Explicit knowledge is that knowledge which an individual is aware of and can articulate. It is an easily expressible cause of individual action and because it can be expressed, it can be codified in the form of propositions, procedures and rules. It can be systematized and so easily become widely available to others. It can easily be transmitted from one individual to another. Implicit knowledge, on the other hand, is knowledge possessed by an individual, which that individual cannot articulate but which nevertheless causes behavior. It is recognized that most skilled behavior cannot be reduced to rules and procedures, or explicit knowledge and so the cause of skilled behavior is said to lie in tacit knowledge, which is hidden even from the individual possessing it. It can only be witnessed in the exercise of skilled action. The field of knowledge management is therefore very much exercised with the issue of how tacit knowledge can be transmitted from the one possessing it to others so that the organization's knowledge of how to carry out its tasks is not subjected to individual idiosyncratic behavior, including that of leaving the organization. It is suggested that tacit knowledge is transmitted by imitation or that it is conveyed by the stories members of a community of practice tell each other.

This notion of a hidden cause of human behavior, a reality lying behind the appearance of action, is also central to psychoanalytic perspectives on organizations. This is the notion of the unconscious, which is not so much the hidden cause of effective action but the hidden cause of obstacles to contact with reality. In the classical Freudian view, the motivation for behavior comes from inherited instincts of sexuality and aggression expressed in the id as drives. These drives seek release in accordance with the pleasure principle. Society constrains people from expressing every wish arising in the id and that constraint leads to the formation of the ego, which mediates between the id and society by repressing inappropriate wishes. The ego forms defenses against wishes originating in the id, defenses such as denial, projection, idealization and identification. The wishes do not disappear, however. Instead they go underground as it were, as do most of the defenses against them. Both the wishes and the defenses against them become unconscious and continue to cause behavior but now in ways the actor is no longer aware of. These unconscious causes are not in touch with reality and so people take action that is not in accordance with reality. More effective action ensues when people understand the nature of their repressed wishes and their defenses against them and so act more in line with the reality principle.

Or, in later object relations psychoanalytic theory, people frequently do what they do because of universal inherited fantasies of aggression and persecution of a paranoid-schizoid kind against which they defend themselves using processes of splitting objects into the good and the bad and projective identification in which they put unwanted feelings onto each other. More effective action follows when people understand the nature of their fantasies and the defenses they adopt against them. When they are in touch with their fantasies, they move to the depressive position when they find it possible to hold the ambiguity of an object being both bad and good at the same time. This approach has been developed into a theory of group behavior in which groups of people succumb to unconscious process of splitting, scapegoating and other defenses against anxiety such as dependency and fight–flight behavior. Again, when they become aware of the unconscious group processes driving them, or when they are adequately contained by clarity of role and task they are able to operate together more effectively.

From the perspective of complex responsive processes, there is no ultimate reality underlying the appearance of interactions between people. There is no tacit or unconscious cause of what they are doing. Instead, patterns of relating, both those of the private role play of minds and those of the public play of social interaction, are mutually causing themselves. This, however, does not mean that those who are interacting are aware of, or can articulate the patterning of their private and public play. Indeed, they are unaware of a great deal of it. So, there is something that is tacit, or unconscious but it is not of the kind suggested in the theories pointed to above. What those participating in the ongoing flow of responsively relating to each other cannot be fully aware of is all the narrative themes in their own and others' private role play, or of the narrative themes that are patterning public interaction. In this sense many of the themes are tacit or unconscious. Those participating are not always likely to be aware of their own, or others', changing body/feeling rhythms. Since much of their responsive relating to each other is very rapid and spontaneous, they are likely to be unaware of its patterning. A great many themes organizing the experience of being together are thus inevitably unconscious.

Furthermore, when these tacit or unconscious themes are articulated they are not exposing some hidden reality but constitute further gestures and responses into the ongoing flow. Any articulation by anyone of what they imagine might be unconscious or tacit is simply a further contribution to the ongoing patterning of the relational process, a communicational construction just like any other, with its own implications for power relations. There is then nothing fundamentally special about articulating or interpreting what is unconscious. Such activities may turn out to be helpful or they may turn out to be harmful, just as with any other action into the ongoing flow. From this perspective, then, there is no ultimate or hidden reality, exposure of which improves effectiveness. Instead there is the reality of patterns of relating and any comment on them is a further action into that ongoing reality. What makes action more effective is the quality of the contribution into the ongoing flow of relationship. What contains the anxiety of facing the unknown is the quality of the relationships and the historically shaped qualities of the private role plays of the participants in those relationships. What enables one to live with anxiety is qualities of relating, such as trust, maturity and self-confidence.

What I am suggesting is an approach to understanding what is tacit or unconscious that focuses on relationship, and since human relationships are importantly conducted in language and always have implications for power relations, their implications for thinking about what is unconscious are central. In commenting on the Elias and Scotson (1994) analysis of the connection between power relations and ideology, Dalal (1998) points to how ideology, which of course is a relational theme organizing pattern in relational themes, unconsciously maintains power relations. People subscribe to an ideology of, say, racism, in order to sustain their power by unconsciously making a distinction between insiders and outsiders. The outsiders respond by trying to stigmatize the insiders but

> the attempt of outsiders to stigmatize the established is not effective as they do not have the power with which to drive the stigma in. What the marginalized groups are then forced to do, *as a strategic necessity*, is use the same weapon, and assert a new essentialism at the margins, effectively trying to establish a new centre at the margins. These groups insist that there is something essentialist about being black, or being a woman, or working class, or Freudian, or whatever, and use it to cohere around this identity. Elias has demonstrated that cohesion is a necessary prerequisite for the formation of political strength. The name, the identity, is the ensign around which the resistance is organized. The margins of this identity are patrolled as ferociously as any other . . . they assert their difference from the dominant group – in order to cohere themselves and so challenge the dominant order, in order, eventually, to participate at the centre. The paradox is that they form in order to eventually dissolve. It is important that the knowledge of this eventual fact is kept hidden, that is, unconscious.
>
> (Dalal, 1998, pp. 206–207)

Dalal further develops the notion of the unconscious as a social phenomenon in relation to the structure of language. Humans categorize or partition experience in order to deal with it and this act of naming is intrinsically binarizing: the deep structure of language is a binary logic – things are categorized as "A" or "not-A." There seems to be an inevitable tendency, as humans frame their experience, to binarize and polarize it. The next point is that there seem to be two different forms of logic used by humans to frame their experience, forms that Matte-Blanco (1975, 1988) called asymmetrical and symmetrical logic (see Chapter 7). Asymmetrical logic establishes difference in that it distinguishes things from each other and locates them in time and space. Symmetrical logic, on the other hand, treats all objects as the same. Symmetrical logic homogenizes everything and recognizes no contradictions, no negation and no degrees of certainty or uncertainty. There is no difference, no space, no time. Matte-Blanco argued that both forms of logic are applied in all forms of thought at the same time.

Thus, what is unconscious from a complex responsive process point of view is neither knowledge hidden entirely in individual heads, nor inherited wishes or fantasies that are defended against, but much of the patterning of interaction between people expressed primarily in the way they gesture in language and employ ideology to cover over their power relations and attempts to sustain them. More effective performance is then more effective participation in relating, which is continuing dialogue around emerging pattern, both those labeled conscious and those labeled unconscious. The source of skilled behavior is not tacit knowledge locked in an individual's head but the ongoing participation in patterns of relating.

From systems of language to the action of language

From the cognitivist viewpoint, language is a system of signs or symbols, in which those symbols are manipulated according to a set of rules, grammar and syntax (see Chapter 6). The symbols represent a reality already there and the syntax enables the system of signs to be processed in a logical manner to produce meaning. First, there is the conscious individual with at least a sense of self, and then there is the use of language to extract meaning from what the conscious self encounters. An example of this kind of argument is that presented by Damasio (1999) in his study of the functioning of the brain. He holds that language is a translation of non-linguistic images that stand for entities, events, relationships and inferences. In other words, the mind first forms ideas or concepts in its encounter with an external reality and then translates that ongoing mental process into words. Consciousness and a self exist before the use of language. Language simply gives a person names for things and these include an "I" and a "me." This leads to the conclusion that language essentially alienates humans from their real experience, namely, that of non-linguistic forms, of emotions and feelings. Mainstream psychoanalytic reasoning adopts much the same view of the nature of language and its connection with mind (Wright, 1991).

The complex responsive process view draws on Mead (1934), Vygotsky (1962), Elias (1970) and Bhaktin (1986), among others, in holding that concepts and ideas are already words. There is nothing behind or more fundamental than the word that refers to an object in the process of thinking. The word and the idea are one and the same. Thinking takes place in linguistic symbols and individual minds, as we know them, are not possible without language. Indeed, language is a vocal gesture that calls forth a vocal response and together they constitute a social act that is meaning. The private role play that is the individual mind is conducted to a significant extent in language and the self is a dialogue between the "I" and the "me." Here then there can be no sophisticated individual mind without language and language is the main medium in which the private dialogue of mind is conducted. This view does not remove or ignore the importance of other modes of communication or gestures such as facial movement, pictorial images and so on. The private role play of mind includes responsive interaction in the form of feelings triggering feelings, that is, body rhythms triggering body rhythms. However, this view does stress the importance of language in the development of a self and of the capacity to call forth the same response in oneself as in the other. Language is essential for the public interactions between bodies that form the social and the private interaction of a body with itself that constitutes mind. Both are social processes whose current form could not exist in the absence of language.

Damasio objects to this argument on the close connection between language, self and mind on the ground that people with damage to particular brain regions lose the capacity for using language but still demonstrate consciousness and the capacity to think. They are still awake, attentive and can still act purposively in a manner appropriate to their situation. They communicate with facial and hand signals and they display emotion. One might make a similar point about people who are both deaf and mute. The argument is that these are people who cannot use language and yet no one would argue that they do not have minds or selves. What these people are doing, however, is communicating in the medium of significant symbols in the Mead sense. For Mead, a significant symbol is a gesture capable of calling forth in oneself the same response as in the other. This possibility does not reside in the vocal symbol alone but in any bodily gesture. It is just that the vocal symbol enables the development of greater sophistication in such responsive gesturing because the one making it can hear it in the same way as those to whom it is directed. The brain-damaged, the deaf mute and other language-impaired people are still conscious, they have minds and selves because they are still able to communicate in the medium of significant symbols. Mind is still a private role play in the medium of symbols. However, they clearly have difficulties in a society where others have language abilities. Furthermore, their abilities to communicate publicly, and therefore, presumably their private communications with themselves, have been and are being formed in a web of relationships within which others can and do speak. A society in which no one spoke and all communicated in non-vocal significant symbols would be completely different to the one we know and so then would individual minds. Damasio's example seems to me to leave Mead's argument intact.

There are, for me, further difficulties with Damasio's presentation of the notion that ideas are translated into language. He suggests that ideas are non-linguistic images, where those images are registered in the body in response to sensory stimulation:

> The words I am using to bring these ideas to you are first formed, however briefly and sketchily, as auditory, visual and somatosensory images of phonemes and morphemes, before I implement them on the page in their written version. Likewise, those written words now printed before your eyes are first processed by you as verbal images before they promote the activation of yet other images, this time nonverbal, with which the "concepts" that correspond to my words can be displayed mentally. In this perspective, any symbol you can think of is an image . . . Even the feelings that make up the backdrop of each mental instant are images in the sense articulated above, somatosensory images, that is, which mostly signal aspects of the body state.
>
> (1999, p. 319)

He clearly adopts the sender–receiver model of communication. He has non-verbal images in his mind (brain/body) that correspond to a "concept." He translates these into words that the reader then processes as visual stimuli, which form an image in the reader's mind (brain/body), the same image of the concept that was in the writer's mind (brain/body). But what kind of an image can this "concept" be? Is it another visual image? Or an auditory one? Or a somatosensory one? Why is the first visual image not enough? Note that he is not saying that one word is triggering associations with other words. He is saying that the meaning of the word is a "concept" in his head that is conveyed in translated form to the reader's head, where it must be re-translated. Note how the meaning is there in the "concept" in separate heads, not in the context of the relationship between writer and reader. If instead of saying or writing a word, one person makes a hand gesture to another, which conveys an idea to that other, then does the hand gesture have to be translated? Does every gesture of one to another have to be translated? But if so, into what? If your hand gesture provokes a feeling of fear in me and my feeling rhythms register this, is that not enough for meaning to have been created between us? Does my body state have to be translated into something else to denote the "concept" of fear? But what could that be other than another body rhythm?

The explanatory framework of complex responsive processes drawn from Mead avoids all these convoluted problems of translation by locating meaning in the social act carried out in a context. The medium of sophisticated social acts as we know them is above all that of language and human thinking as we know it is conducted, above all in language. However, whether talking to oneself silently or to another vocally, one is always a body and bodies always have feeling rhythms. Language is thus always interwoven with feeling. When I say, therefore, that mind and society arise in language, I mean in the ongoing flow of feeling-laden human interrelating expressed to a significant degree in language.

Institutions, communication and power

As Chapter 3 pointed out, cognitivist approaches to knowledge creation and management in organizations take institutions, including organizations, as a separate level emerging from interaction between people. The basis of institutional life is taken to be habit and routine, shared values and beliefs, missions and visions, that is, culture, and the rules and procedures carried out in accordance with hierarchical levels of authority. With regard to that form of institution known as an organization, the emphasis is on the prior design of hierarchical structures, procedures and rules as part of information and control systems, as well as the prior design of supportive cultures. Power is largely an aspect of the hierarchical structure. Indeed, power not exercised in accordance with hierarchical structure tends to be regarded as illegitimate. Power here is external to communication, being a coercive force applied by one person to another and it is not usual to see it as essential to, and inevitable in, any form of human relating. From this perspective, organizational knowledge is located in designed, systematic procedures and organizational change is an intentional change in that design. The identity of an organization, that is, its purpose and essential characteristics, is thought of as chosen, or designed, by those with power in hierarchical terms.

When organizations are understood as complex responsive processes of relating, however, institutions are patterns of relating between people characterized by a high degree of repetitiveness. Patterns of relating are communicational themes that organize the experience of being together and this experience is itself communicational themes. The themes and variations in them cause themselves and they can be spoken of as relations of communication or relations of power. Here power and communication are one and the same in that patterns of power relating are

at the same time patterns of communicating, in that they both enable and
constrain the participants in a relationship. Ideologies, or patterns of
belief, are themes in communication that make a pattern of power
relations feel natural and thus justify their maintenance. Institutions,
including organizations are thus habitual, or highly repetitive patterns of
communication and power relations.

The complex responsive process framework places power relations, and
the ideological themes unconsciously sustaining them, at the center of the
organizational knowledge creation process. Power relations in
organizations arise in ideologically patterned talking, creating the
dynamics of who is "in" and who is "out." This is reflected in an
unconscious process that distinguishes ways of talking that are to prevail.
For example, in most organizations nowadays the privileged language is
that of rules and procedures. Those who can talk effectively in these terms
can silence others and in so doing affect what it is possible to do. Those
who use the language of spontaneity and intuitive response to
opportunities will not prevail in such a context and to have an effect they
will find it necessary to translate their proposals into the dominant
language. Those who do not do this will find themselves "out." Similarly,
where the most persuasive members of a group of people have developed
the facility of talking about concepts such as self-organization and
emergence, it is they who will constitute the "in" sub-group, while those
with less facility in this way of talking will find themselves at the fringes.

I am suggesting that the communicational/power relational dynamic in
which "in" and "out" sub-groups emerge is ubiquitous and inevitable. The
consequent feelings of inclusion and exclusion then have significant
effects on the further evolution of joint cooperation, tending to disrupt it
through competition and rivalry. Those who experience exclusion become
frustrated and in more extreme situations come to feel abused or
victimized. There is then an ever-present possibility of abuser–abused,
victimizing–victimized dynamics in organizational life.

From this perspective, organizational knowledge is a process of continual
reproduction and potential transformation in patterns of communication
and power, in patterns of inclusion and exclusion. Organizational change
is a shift in patterns of communicating and power relating, a shift in
patterns of inclusion and exclusion. It is in this process that organizational
identity emerges, that is, the purposes and inspirations for carrying on
being together are continually reproduced and potentially transformed,
causing themselves.

Dialogue and ordinary conversation in the living present

The literature on the learning organization (Senge, 1990) has brought the importance of dialogue to the attention of management practitioners. This discussion of dialogue is primarily based on the views of Bohm (1965, 1983; Bohm and Peat, 1989) and takes place in language that is similar in many ways to that which I have been using to develop a view of organization as complex responsive processes of relating. However, this similarity covers fundamental differences, which I now go on to point to in briefly summarizing the way in which Senge takes up Bohm's ideas.

According to Bohm, dialogue means the free flow of meaning through a group of people, allowing them to discover insights not attainable individually. This is a collective phenomenon that occurs when a group of people becomes open to the flow of a larger intelligence. Bohm talks about a new kind of mind that comes into existence. People are said to participate in this pool of common meaning, which is not accessible individually. He talks about the whole organizing the parts. The whole here is this common pool of meaning, a kind of transcendental mind analogous to the idea in quantum physics that the universe is an indistinguishable whole. This is Bohm's idea of an implicate order that is unfolded by experience. The parts in this way of thinking are individual mental maps that guide and shape individual perceptions.

The differences between this perspective and that which I have been developing relate to what is being assumed about causality and what is being assumed about the relationship between the individual and the group. First, I have been suggesting an explanation of communicative interaction that assumes Transformative Teleology in which the future is under perpetual construction. Bohm's thought differs in that he clearly assumes Formative Teleology, in which the future is the unfolding of what is already enfolded as implicate order, rendering any true novelty impossible. This idea of an already enfolded implicate order is expressed in the notion of a common pool of meaning, a kind of transcendent whole or group mind which people access when they interact with each other in dialogue.

Second, for Bohm, individual and group are separate levels of being, with group being a mystical kind of collective mind. But where and what could this common pool and this larger intelligence be? The complex responsive process of relating perspective that I have been developing sees individual mind and group interactions forming and being formed by each other at the same time. Individual and group are the same phenomenon and there is no transcendent whole, or group mind, or common pool of meaning outside of them. Instead, meaning is emerging in the communicative interaction between people in their local situation in the present. Bohm takes a perspective in which there is *both* a collective pool of meaning *and* an individual mind that is shaped by the common pool, quite outside individuals, in dialogue. This is completely lacking the kind of *paradoxical movement* to be found in Mead's way of thinking, on whom I have been drawing.

For Bohm and Senge, dialogue is a special kind of collaborative conversation, quite distinct from discussion, which is primarily competitive. Dialogue, as special conversation with a life of its own, is said to be rare nowadays and the call is for a return to ancient wisdom, to ways characteristic of so called "more primitive" people who used to practice it. North American Indians are often given as an example of the few people who still practice it today. Senge says that when we do rarely experience dialogue nowadays, it is a chance product of circumstance. Thus, he calls for systematic effort and disciplined practice of the art of dialogue, which we need to rediscover to satisfy a deep longing. If we do it right we will all win. In order to do it right, people have to participate in a particular way: they must suspend, that is, be aware of their assumptions; they must regard each other as colleagues and friends; and there should be a facilitator present who holds the context. Resistance and defensive routines are then reduced and dialogue can take place. Bohm claims that in these circumstances people can become observers of their own thinking and that once they see the participative nature of their thought they separate themselves from it. Conflict then becomes conflict between thoughts and not conflict between people. Dialogue, therefore, offers a safe environment in which it can be balanced with discussion. Dialogue becomes a new tool and a prescription for management behavior (Isaacs, 1999), although Bohm himself thought dialogue was virtually impossible in hierarchical organizations.

The approach I have been developing stands in stark contrast to this. First, there is no Romantic notion of having lost the Eden of dialogue and a deep longing to rediscover what we have lost. Instead, I have been pointing to the spontaneous and paradoxically creative and destructive nature of ordinary, everyday conversation in local situations in the living present. I have been suggesting how we might understand the highly complex communicative, relational process in which we accomplish joint action in the living present. This is interaction between people that is competitive and cooperative at the same time (hence the paradox) and cannot be artificially made safe. I have not been presenting new conversational tools of an idealized kind but suggesting how we might understand the communicative interaction we currently engage in within hierarchical organizations, with all its conflict and its collaboration. Ordinary communicative interaction is not necessarily safe at all and the interesting question is how we understand the nature and impact of inevitable resistance and defensive routines, and how we cope with any lack of safety. If it were true that we had lost the art of dialogue in which creative change is possible, it is difficult to understand how the rapid change we currently experience is occurring.

Conclusion

The complex responsive process view of organizational knowledge creation leads to completely different conclusions to those of the perspectives with which I have compared it in this chapter. Knowledge is the themes and variations in them that organize the experience of being together and they can be "found" only in the actions of relating between people. Knowledge is not designed, nor does it exist in a transcendent common pool, but emerges in a process in which it causes itself in the interaction between bodies in local situations in the living present. From this perspective, it becomes impossible to think of designing such a process and it makes no sense to think of managing it. The next chapter considers these implications in more detail.

10 **The organizational implications of complex responsive processes of knowledge creation**

- The limitations of mainstream prescriptions on knowledge management
- Focusing attention on the evolution of knowledge as participative self-organization

In Chapter 2, I briefly mentioned mainstream prescriptions for learning and knowledge creation in organizations. In this chapter I want to point to how one would think about these prescriptions, essentially to do with managing knowledge, from a complex responsive process perspective. After that I will suggest how thinking in complex responsive process terms focuses attention in a way that is different to mainstream thinking.

The limitations of mainstream prescriptions on knowledge management

The first of the prescriptions to be considered is that of measuring the intellectual capital of an organization.

Measuring intellectual capital and managing knowledge

Those arguing for the need to measure and manage an organization's intellectual capital (for example, Roos *et al.*, 1997; Sveiby, 1997) point to the gap between measures of many corporations' capital bases on their balance sheets and much higher capital market valuations. The differences are ascribed to organizations' intellectual capital, which they are said to own. A number of writers think it strange to manage financial and physical capital, while ignoring the much more valuable intellectual capital, and so they call for steps to measure the latter on the grounds that what is measured can be managed. The aim of measuring intellectual capital is that of managing its contribution to shareholder value. Roos *et al.* (1997) draw on the experience of measuring intellectual capital at Skandia to suggest that it consists of human capital and structural capital.

The first of these categories is the knowledge embodied in the employees of the corporation, its "thinking" capital, consisting of the competence, skills and education of its members. Human capital, referred to as the "soul of the company," is in turn divided into three categories and indicative measurements for each are suggested:

1 Competence, where suggested indicators are: percentage of employees with advanced degrees; IT literacy; hours training per employee; average duration of employment.
2 Attitude, where suggested indicators are: hours spent in debriefing; hours spent by senior staff in explaining strategy and actions; a leadership index; a motivation index.
3 Intellectual agility, where indicators are: savings from implemented employee suggestions; new solutions suggested; a variety index; a company diversification index.

The second category of intellectual capital is invisible assets and processes, "non-thinking" capital, consisting of routines, procedures and systems, as well as relationships with customers, suppliers and partners. Three sub-categories are suggested here:

1 Relationships, where the indicators are: percentage of supplier/customer business the corporation accounts for; length of relationship; partner satisfaction index; customer retention.
2 Internal efficiency, where indicators are: the ratio of administrative expenses to revenues; revenues from patents; processes completed without error; cycle/process time.
3 Renewal and development, where indicators are: percentage of business from new products; training cost/hours per employee; ratio of renewal to operating expenses; new patents filed.

Finally, the indicators outlined above are to be combined into a weighted index of Intellectual Capital (the IC index). The purpose of all this measuring is to enable managers to monitor and control the flows of intellectual capital through their organization in the interests of managing shareholder value. Knowledge is thought of as an asset to be managed like any other asset, and to the extent that conversation has anything to do with knowledge generation, it too is to be managed. The justification for prescriptions like these is to be found in mainstream thinking outlined in Chapter 2. But how would one make sense of them from the perspective of complex responsive processes of relating?

From that perspective, meaning and therefore knowledge arise in the local, detailed, ordinary communicative interaction of people in organizations in the living present. Knowledge creation is an evolutionary process of reproduction and potential transformation at the same time. In other words knowledge is neither stored nor shared because it is not an "it" at all but a process. It is communicative action, particularly in the form of conversation. Knowledge is the themes organizing the experience of being together and knowledge evolves as active experience. Knowledge is created as changes in the thematic patterning of bodies relating to each other and that thematic patterning organizes itself. The thematic patterning of communication is the same process as the thematic patterning of conflicting constraints emerging in relationships, that is, power relations. Knowledge cannot be grasped, owned by anyone or traded in any market and its creation is a process of communicating and power relating that is both stimulating and anxiety provoking at the same time.

If one takes a view of knowledge creation along these lines, then it is not only impossible to manage knowledge, even asking the question makes no sense. Furthermore, it is quite impossible to measure "intellectual capital" simply because it does not exist in measurable, or any other reified form. If knowledge itself is a continuously reproduced and transformed process of acting, if it is not stored anywhere, if people do not "share" it because one cannot share actions, only perform them, then putting the words "intellectual" and "capital" together makes no sense. Indeed, the whole notion that an organization can own this "intellectual capital," that is, can own the attitudes, competence and intellectual agility of individuals is not only dubious but, for me anyway, deeply repugnant. Some of the suggested indicators measure relationships and organizations are said to own them. How can anyone or anything own a relationship? Organizations are said to "have a soul," which by implication they own, and by further implication they "own" the souls of their employees. The more one reflects on what is being said, the more absurd and repugnant it becomes. It also becomes particularly clear how the move to measure

capital and manage knowledge reflects a particular ideology of
instrumental control that makes it feel natural to sustain particular kinds
of power relations. Clearly, the perspective I am suggesting reflects a
completely different ideology and implies some kind of shift in power
relations.

If the suggested ways of measuring intellectual capital do not measure
what they are supposed to, then what do they measure? Some of them
simply measure what they say they are measuring without any necessary
link to anything else. For example, if the hours spent on training per
employee go up, this simply means that employees on average spent more
time at training courses. It does not say anything about whether they
learned anything relevant to their interactions at work. From the
perspective I am suggesting, other measures, such as numbers of patents,
refer to tools that people use in their communicative interaction. Patents,
or "intellectual property" are abstract-systematic statements in the form
of what I have called reified symbols (see Chapter 5). They are mistaken
for knowledge itself but knowledge only arises when it is employed as
tools in communicative interaction between people.

Capturing knowledge in explicit form

A central feature of mainstream thinking about knowledge creation in
organizations is the split it makes between tacit and explicit knowledge.
Tacit knowledge is assumed to arise in individual minds and this is
thought to create a problem for organizations. The assumption is that
humans are reluctant to share their individual tacit knowledge with others.
To the extent that they do, it is in informal exchanges. Mainstream
literature tends to express a profound mistrust of these informal
exchanges and is greatly concerned with people leaving an organization
and taking their implicit knowledge with them. This leads to the major
emphasis mainstream literature places on the conversion of individual
tacit knowledge into explicit form and the storing of that explicit
knowledge in either centralized or distributed systems. Linked to this are
the prescriptions to do with developing Information Technology. It all has
to do with capturing the knowledge held by individuals so that it can be
owned and controlled by organizations.

The complex responsive process perspective, on the other hand, holds that
tacit and explicit knowing are facets of the same communicative process
and, therefore, that it makes no sense to talk about them separately or to

believe that one is converted into the other. Furthermore, knowledge is not simply located in individual minds, nor is it stored in any straightforward sense. Instead, knowledge is continuously replicated and potentially transformed in the communicative interaction between people. Communicative interaction is human relationship and that is a living process, which cannot be captured, stored or owned by anyone. People participate in relationships as mutually constructed and none of them can individually own their processes of mutual construction. Again, the prescriptions to do with converting tacit into explicit knowledge, capturing and storing it, all reveal a particular ideology to do with control. Although mainstream thinking places so much emphasis on ultimately locating knowledge in individual heads, it ends up downgrading the importance of the individual. This reflects an ethical position in which the collective is elevated above the individual in the concern with knowledge as the property of the organization. The alternative perspective I am suggesting does not locate mind/self, meaning and knowledge simply in the individual but holds that they all arise in relationships between individuals. Far from reducing the importance of the individual, this perspective has the opposite effect in that the human person becomes the central ethical concern. Knowledge is not understood to be "property" at all but active relational processes between human persons. Knowledge is a reflection of human identity and it becomes aethical to talk of capturing, storing and owning "it."

Far from mistrusting informal exchanges between people, such ordinary communicative interaction in the living present is to be highly valued because this is the very process in which knowledge arises. This view leads, not to the search for alternatives to informal exchanges, but to attaching much greater importance to ordinary conversational life in organizations. In this, the complex responsive process perspective takes a similar position to some critics of mainstream thinking who point to the importance of informal communication in communities of practice and to the importance of conversation. However, the critics mostly continue, implicitly, to build their views on cognitivist assumptions about individual human psychology and on systems thinking about the social as a level separate from the individual. The prescriptions then follow that more importance be accorded to people talking "around the water cooler" and greater reliance placed on narrative forms of knowledge and storytelling. This can be understood as an addition to mainstream thinking, one that does not fundamentally contest its other prescriptions. In my view, the perspective of complex responsive processes goes further than these critics because it builds an understanding of knowledge creation on substantially different assumptions about the individual and the social. This leads not simply to increased emphasis on forms of knowledge not usually accorded much prominence, but to a fundamental questioning of mainstream prescriptions, particularly their ideological and ethical underpinnings.

In suggesting this fundamental questioning, however, I am in no way dismissing the importance of systems of recording and storing data or of systems and technology that change communication between people. However, from the perspective I am suggesting, these systems do not capture knowledge or store it because that is impossible. Instead, they are viewed as tools people use in their communicative interaction with each other. They are artifacts and technologies that store the only kind of symbol that it is possible to store, namely, reified symbols. What is stored is reified symbols as data, patterned as abstract systematic frameworks. As such, they are of enormous importance as tools in the modern world and the invitation is to explore their impact on human relating. These tools themselves, however, are not knowledge. What I am calling knowledge arises only when humans use the tools.

Hiring and retaining a professional elite

If one starts from the basic assumption that the origins of knowledge are located in tacit form in the heads of individuals, it is a natural step to advocate that organizations pay particular attention to hiring and retaining a professional elite. It is argued that professionals must be managed in a different manner to others to persuade them to stay in an organization. The call is for greater flexibility and empowerment because professionals require more autonomy. However, prescriptions of this kind tend to be immediately coupled with further prescriptions to do with the setting of stretch targets, monitoring of performance and linked financial reward systems. The autonomy of the professional is thereby heavily subscribed. Linked to this, there are prescriptions for "downsizing" and leaner organizations to be accomplished by the outsourcing of work, including non-core professional work. Self-employed professionals supposedly have greater autonomy too. However, their autonomy is also precarious because they must maintain networks of links with those still employed in organizations if they are to get work. The temporary nature of their work and their need to maintain a network of personal contacts become a form of control through the operation of the market (Blair, 2000). Again, I argue, the prescriptions to do with the management of knowledge reflect a particular ideology of corporate control of the individual's knowledge and competence.

How would one think of prescriptions of this kind from the perspective of complex responsive processes of relating? First, one would note the point I have already made, namely, that to do with ethics and ideology. Closely linked to this is the matter of power relations and the role these prescriptions about professional elites play in sustaining those power relations. It does not follow that simply hiring and retaining individual professionals has all that much to do with knowledge creation. If knowledge arises in communicative interaction, then what matters is the process of relating that individual professionals engage in, not simply how clever or competent they are as individuals. This conclusion leads to the focusing of attention on the dynamics of relating associated with carrying out the prescriptions for a core professional elite. The very notion of a "core" immediately excludes other members of the organization who are not "in" the elite and of course it excludes the non-core workers who have be "outsourced." In Chapter 7, I emphasized the fundamental importance of the dynamics of inclusion and exclusion in the process of communicative interaction and power relating in which knowledge arises. We simply do not know whether the kind of "in/out" dynamics generated by emphasizing a professional elite is conducive or otherwise to the generation of knowledge, but I would guess that it is not. Linked to this are the consequences of the "stretch" targets set for the supposedly autonomous professionals. From the perspective I am suggesting, one would want to explore how the consequent stress, frustration and anxiety impacts on the process of human relating in an organization, upon which the generation of knowledge so crucially depends. In short, is this prescription of hiring and retaining a professional elite really an effective way of creating knowledge in organizations?

Managing the quality of learning

Closely linked to prescriptions for hiring and retaining of professionals are those for training and developing people. Again, these prescriptions reflect the underlying assumption that knowledge is stored in individual heads. The aim of training and development follows, namely, to increase the competence, skill and knowledge of the individual, including the capacity to work as a member of a team. The emphasis is placed on managing not just the activities of training and development but the quality of the learning process itself. Again, management is understood in systemic terms and the prescriptions relate to the design and operation of a system to ensure the quality of the learning process. This is not just a prescription for the training and development functions of individual organizations but has been taken into government policies for the educational sector as a whole, at least in the UK.

Quality assurance in education closely follows models of quality management in manufacturing and commercial operations. A system is designed in which teachers are required to set overall objectives for any program they deliver, translated into the learning outcomes to be achieved in each teaching session they take. Each session must then be designed in terms of content and delivery method so that it delivers the outcome aims, so fulfilling the overall objectives of the program and the equal contract with students as consumers of knowledge. An audit trail must be established enabling others to follow just what the intended objectives and outcomes are and just how the events during the session and the material distributed to the students are supposed to meet the outcomes designed. Students can then know in advance what they are to learn, check that they have learned it, and sue the institution if they have not! This procedure entails keeping detailed records of course programs, session by session, and copies of all materials distributed. In addition to the traditional coursework and examinations, also forming part of the audit trail, other monitoring devices are put in place. Teachers monitor each other's classroom performance. Course leaders require students to fill in questionnaires on how they found the course. Reports on how well each session achieved its outcome must be prepared, as well as reports on student progress. Finally there is periodic monitoring of departments delivering courses in which the paper audit trail is inspected. The government in the UK has set up a Quality Assurance Agency to manage this monitoring process for universities and to rank them according to compliance. There are other monitoring bodies for other educational sectors. The cost in terms of money, and even more in terms of time throughout the educational sector, is enormous.

It is immediately clear how this entire project reflects systems thinking and the cognitivist psychological assumptions so consistent with it. Policy-makers seem to believe that operating this system manages the quality of learning throughout the educational sector. How would one think about it from the complex responsive process perspective? From that perspective, learning is a responsive relational process of communicative interaction. It is participative action rather than mimicry. Knowledge arises in that participative communicative interaction in the sense of themes patterning experience. The themes are continuously reproduced always with the potential for the transformation of identity, individual and collective. In any teaching session the patterning of communicative interaction reflects both continuity and potential transformation and is, therefore, unique to some extent, if learning is actually taking place. What the transformation will be cannot be predicted in advance. How the anxieties provoked by such transformation are to be lived with also cannot be known in advance. While participants do, of course, engage in the process with intention and foreknowledge, no one can predict how the experience will evolve or what will be learned, individually and collectively. It is, therefore, impossible to set learning outcomes in advance in any truly meaningful sense. The meaning will emerge in the session.

One would expect, therefore, that when teachers are compelled to adhere to the system outlined above, they will find it impossible to do other than articulate very bland objectives and outcomes, and do the paperwork required to create an audit trial that appears to comply with requirements. A great deal of effort will be directed to this paper process, to the detriment of the main task, namely teaching. The major monitoring exercises will be some kind of charade, but one that generates a great deal of frustration and anxiety. None of it will have much to do with authentic quality, that is, the quality of the learning experience. Instead, it will be a massive system for producing counterfeit quality. This pretty precisely describes my personal experience with quality assurance in the university sector of the UK. From the perspective of complex responsive processes, quality assurance systems of this kind are a massive waste of resource and even more a damaging source of frustration and anxiety that actually reduces the authentic quality of learning.

I know that I am not alone in holding this damning view of quality assurance in the UK educational sector. I have rarely spoken to anyone in the sector, apart from those employed by the agencies whose task it is to monitor, who does not share the view I have expressed. Yet, we all feel powerless to do anything about it. How have we come to this state? It seems to me that a powerful reason has to do with the taken for granted validity of mainstream systems thinking, supported by cognitivist psychology, reflecting a particular ideology of control. It seems impossible to challenge so powerful a way of thinking. For me, this is why the kind of perspective being suggested in this book is so important. It provides a coherent basis for challenging the whole way of thinking underpinning the kind of highly damaging policies just described.

Spreading knowledge around the organization

Next, there is a raft of prescriptions concerned with spreading knowledge around an organization. If knowledge is created in individual heads, and if human nature is such that individuals selfishly seek to keep it to themselves, then it becomes a prime management task to design structures, systems and behaviors to overcome these selfish tendencies and spread knowledge around the organization. The prescriptions relate to what a leader, manager or consultant should design and then implement. Typically the prescriptions relate to the following:

- Organizational structures. The prescription is to design structures that are more flexible. This means flattening the hierarchy and decentralizing decision-making and control in project-based, network or web-like structures. The call is for self-managing teams. These prescriptions are linked to those calling for downsizing and outsourcing.
- Behavioral change. Here the prescriptions are to empower people and articulate the values that should guide their behavior. New cultures must be engineered to support this.
- Inspiration. People need to be inspired by the visions of their leaders so that they will share their knowledge and work toward achieving the inspiring vision.
- Removal of obstacles to informal contact. Here the call is to take seriously the role of informal contacts in getting work done and undertake steps to make such contacts easier to form. Linked to this is the suggestion that narrative knowledge be taken seriously and storytelling in communities of practice encouraged.

How does one think about advice like this from the perspective of complex responsive processes of relating? If knowledge is not a thing but a process of meaning making where meaning is continuously reproduced and potentially transformed in the action of communicative relating between human bodies, then one cannot speak of sharing it, or of spreading it around an organization. Any concern with "improving" knowledge-creating capacity becomes a concern with the qualities and the dynamics of human relating in the living present. Attention is then focused on the power relations being sustained and shifted in communicative interaction and on the ideologies unconsciously making patterns of power relations feel natural. Attention is focused on the dynamical qualities of communicative interaction, for example, whether patterns of conversation feel fluid and spontaneous, holding the tension and the excitement of potential transformation, or whether those patterns feel stuck and repetitive. One becomes concerned with what it is that sustains any stuck patterns of conversation and this will probably have much to do with power relations and their underlying ideology, and the dynamics of inclusion and exclusion, as well as with ways people find to live with anxiety. In other words, attention is focused on the themes organizing the experience of being together and how they may or may not be changing. Furthermore, each situation is unique in some way and this makes it impossible to identify universal patterns across a whole organization at other than a very general and hence rather unreliable level.

Turning now to the kind of mainstream prescriptions briefly summarized above, the perspective of complex responsive processes immediately questions the universal nature of the prescriptions. The argument for such universal prescriptions to do, for example, with organizational structure, usually proceeds from a macro level analysis. This analysis leads to the conclusion that economic activity is moving from the industrial to the new information or knowledge age. This is then held to require flexible organizations and the empowerment of people. But is this universally so? An example sometimes quoted is the film industry. The macro analysis suggests that the structure of the film industry has moved from a pre-World War II pattern of global domination by the major film studios in the United States to a much more fragmented pattern of small production companies relying on self-employed professionals. The experience of participation in the actual production of a specific film in the UK (Blair, 2000) suggests otherwise. Blair describes the strict discipline and tight control employed in the production of a particular film she participated in and the anxiety-producing and controlling effect that self-employment had on professionals working on the film. This took place in a financial and marketing context where the major film studios still controlled the money required to make the film and the distribution networks required for it to earn any return. What looked from a macro perspective like increased flexibility turned out in specific micro situations to be simply a reconfiguration of the same power relations sustained by the same ideology of control. This points to the need to focus attention on local situations in the living present.

From the perspective I am suggesting, then, there is no necessary link between any of the prescriptions referred to above and an increase in knowledge creation. Changes in organizational structure, changes in attitudes and the removal of obstacles to informal contact between members of an organization may all contribute to the potential for change in patterns of communicative interaction by increasing the possibility of contact. However, the impact of each of the prescriptions has to be understood in local situations as part of the dynamic of interaction in those situations in the living present.

A major implication: accomplishing more by doing less

When one takes the perspective of complex responsive processes, one reaches a similar conclusion in relation to each of the groups of mainstream prescriptions referred to above. They are questioned because they are made from the stance of the outside observer making changes to a supposedly whole system of knowledge creation. Instead, it is argued that knowledge creation is not a system but a process that cannot be designed in advance nor manipulated from a macro, outside position. This suggests that following mainstream prescriptions will not yield what they promise. They will yield something, of course, but it will not be the distribution of knowledge across an organization or its capture and possession by that organization. A major implication of the shift in thinking that I am suggesting, then, has to do with the policies and initiatives governments and organizations might simply abandon, with enormous savings in money and time and reductions in stress and anxiety levels. The kind of thinking I am pointing to, suggests that we might be able to achieve a great deal more if we did less rather than more. If this is true, it has enormous practical implications.

Focusing attention on the evolution of knowledge as participative self-organization

So far, I have been pointing to what leaders, managers and consultants could stop doing because it cannot achieve what they hope it will. This immediately raises the question: what do we do instead? If by doing something instead we mean some replacement for the universal global prescriptions of mainstream thinking then the answer is "nothing." What the complex responsive process perspective does is focus attention on the specific, unique situations in which people are already creating and obstructing new meaning, new knowledge. In this regard the focus of attention shifts first to ethics.

Ethics

The essence of the complex responsive process perspective is the social as simultaneous cooperative and competitive relating, forming and being formed by power relations. The concern is with the specific processes human individuals are engaged in as they negotiate with each other what they do or do not do and the use they make of their systems tools and other technologies. From this perspective, accountability and responsibility do not mean achieving targeted consequences, they mean the ethical, moral requirement to take responsibility for one's actions and account to one's fellows for what one is doing. The requirement is to account for the next gesture or action, quite apart from the consequences because they cannot be known when they depend as much on what others do as on what one does oneself. Quality actions are not actions with known consequences where one takes responsibility for the consequences, irrespective of the actions. Quality actions are actions that both those carrying them out and those affected by them can accept as ethical and moral in themselves and such acceptance implies a process of negotiation. The social is cooperative and competitive interaction as moral order. Griffin (forthcoming) will take up this concern with the ethical implications of complex responsive processes of relating in a later volume in this series.

Communication and conversation in the living present

The perspective of complex responsive processes focuses attention more on what people are *doing* in the *living present* than on what they are imagining about the future. The question is not what is being intended as consequences at some point in the distant future but on what is intended as the next gesture, the next word, that is, the next action. The focus is on communicative interaction, the pattern of relating between human bodies in the living present, that is, on the patterns of turn-taking/turn-making in their interactions, on who is talking and who is being silenced, on who is being included and who is being excluded and how all of this is happening. The focus of attention is on the themes that are organizing this complex relational process of being together in order to undertake the joint actions for which organizations exist.

For example, when I was invited to run focus workshops at the health Trust in the UK mentioned in Chapter 8, I was asked to find out what people felt would be good leadership practices that should be taken from the existing organization to the new ones to be created from it. To do this they would have to imagine what the new organizations would be and specify how leaders in them should behave. This focuses attention on some imagined future. From the perspective I take, this was a defensive action that enabled people to avoid talking about the frustrating and distressing situation they found themselves in, not knowing how their organization would change and when it would happen. They were experiencing great difficulty in carrying out their joint action of taking care of the mental health requirements of those their organization was supposed to be serving. The instructions of senior management were explicit: they did not want to "open the can of worms," which is how they talked about the strong emotions people felt about the current situation. Instead, knowing that they must do something, they wanted to get people away from the present by imagining some global future. This would enable the maintenance of current power relations. From the complex responsive process perspective, I suggested that we talk together about the living present. My approach was to try to change the conversation, not globally throughout the Trust, but in that local situation I found myself in. Changing the conversation is not some major program but the act of participative engagement in the conversation, asking different kinds of questions and pointing to different kinds of issue.

On another occasion, I was working with a group of top managers in a major multinational conglomerate. These managers had flown in from around the world, ostensibly to talk about how, in the future, they were going to ensure that they met their performance targets. However, they made it quite clear in their dinner table conversation how the main issue preoccupying them was the deteriorating relationship with their chief executive. This was manifesting itself in many ways, including an inability to talk openly about the difficulties they were now experiencing in meeting their targets. My approach, drawing on the complex responsive process perspective, was to ask questions about this issue in the living present and to point to what seemed to me to be important themes patterning the experiencing of being together, themes to do with fear of the chief executive. Through one person participating in this way the conversation shifts. Since change in an organization, knowledge creation in an organization, is the same as change in patterns of communication, the kind of participation I am talking about holds out the potential for organizational change.

Forthcoming volumes in this series will explore in much greater detail the processes of organizational change as shifts in the patterns of conversation (Shaw, forthcoming) and innovation and knowledge creation as the emergence of new patterns of conversing together (Fonseca, forthcoming).

Relationships and the paradox of control

Focusing attention on the processes of relating between people encourages a different way of thinking about large organizations and the nature of control. Organizations of any kind, no matter how large are processes not things. They are continuously reproduced and transformed in the ongoing communicative interaction between people in the living present, both their formal members and people in other organizations. That communicative interaction is patterned as themes organizing the experience of being together, multifaceted themes of habit, tradition, value and belief sanctioned by custom and repetitive procedures, as well as spontaneous variations and potential transformations of those themes. Mostly, when we think about organizations, we tend to focus attention on the more visible habitual facets of the themes organizing experience and lose sight of the always-present spontaneous variations. We think of global financial institutions, monetary systems, multinational marketing and distribution systems, hierarchical reporting structures within organizations, as well as their bureaucratic systems for controlling resources, as vast impersonal "things" that constrain what we are allowed to do. From the perspective I am suggesting one would think of all of these "systems" as tools people have constructed to reify their habitual, customary, traditional interactions with each other. They are the tools of reified symbols that simultaneously enable highly sophisticated forms of communicative and other joint action, on the one hand, and constrain what it is possible to do on the other, at the same time.

Focusing attention on the tools alone leads to the belief that their function is to control actions so as to yield globally intended consequences.

However, when one holds in mind that all of the "systems" we construct are tools employed in a much wider process of communicative interaction, one takes a different view. The "systems," no matter how large, sophisticated and seeming to have a power of their own, are all tools used in the communicative interaction between people in their own local situations in the living present in which spontaneous communicative acts emerge as variations on habitual themes. Without this spontaneous activity, the "tools" cannot function. These spontaneous variations are potentially amplified into transformations of habitual interaction, ultimately transforming the systems tools themselves. The intention behind using systems as tools of communicative interaction is to reproduce communication with little variation, in other words, to control and so sustain existing power relations. The use of the tools in local situations in the living present, however, requires spontaneous variations and this makes it impossible for anyone outside the local situation to stay in control. Hence the paradox of control, the requirement that managers be "in charge" when they cannot be in "control." This paradox will be explored in specific situations in practice in a later volume in this series (Streatfield, forthcoming).

The emphasis placed on patterns of relating in the perspective I am suggesting has implications for how one thinks about mergers and acquisitions. In the "new knowledge age," one of the fastest ways of acquiring organizational knowledge, it is supposed, is to merge with or acquire another organization that has the knowledge. However, if knowledge is continuously replicated and potentially transformed in communicative interaction in local situations in the living present, what is an organization buying when it acquires another? What is it gaining when it merges with another? It cannot buy relationships. It cannot buy local processes of communicative interaction in the living present. Indeed, the very act of acquisition or merger immediately threatens and fragments patterns of communicative relating, especially as people are removed, and moved about, in post-merger/acquisition reorganizations. From a complex responsive process perspective it is likely that the act of acquisition or merger will itself immediately destroy much of what has supposedly been bought. It is widely accepted that some 70 per cent of acquisitions and mergers fail. Perhaps the cause of these failures has something to do with their adverse impact on the knowledge creating process. An implication of major importance, then, is the need to focus more attention on the impact of acquisitions and mergers on the patterns of ordinary communicative interaction between people in local situations in the living present. This is another matter to be taken up in the later volume in this series by Streatfield (forthcoming).

The importance of the ordinary

The complex responsive process perspective shifts the focus of attention, when thinking about learning and knowledge creation in organizations in another very important way. It focuses on the "ordinary" on the basis that it is in the ongoing communicative interaction between everyone in an organization, and with people in other organizations, that learning occurs and knowledge arises. Mainstream prescriptions on these matters are directed at a "you." "You" should design new structures and install systems to capture knowledge. But who is this "you"? That question is normally only answered in implicit form and in mainstream prescriptions the "you" is the leader, the manager, the consultant, the expert required to take some "extraordinary" action in relation to whole systems. From the perspective I am suggesting, organizational knowledge is an evolutionary process of communicative interaction in which "you" is every member of an organization as they go about their ordinary, everyday responsive, relational lives. The focus of attention is on the "ordinary" in the sense that it is on how "ordinary" people act in the living present of their "ordinary," local relating to each other. This by no means excludes the powerful, the expert, the leader, the manager, or anyone else. This perspective by no means denies the enormous power that some have and the little power others have. Instead, one understands these enormous power differences as arising in the communicative interaction in "local" situations between the more and the less powerful and seeks to understand their part in the knowledge creating process.

I should also add that the complex responsive process perspective is ordinary in another way. It is ordinary because it suggests focusing realistically on what we already do as we go about our lives in organizations in order to better understand it. It is thus not an automatic pointer to more democratic ways of behaving. Nor is the emphasis on relationship a call for humans to return to simpler ways of relating, back to an ancient wisdom. It is not a call for some special form of communication called dialogue. It is certainly not to be interpreted as a simple call for more caring and loving relationships. Instead, it is a perspective that focuses attention on the ordinary way in which themes patterning communicative interaction between people may be caring and indifferent, cooperating and competing, loving and hating, agreeing and conflicting in the context of the living present. The complex responsive process perspective does not imply that humans can avoid the negative and have only the positive. On the contrary, it suggests that the paradox of the negative and the positive at the same time is essential to the emergence of new knowledge. The invitation is to try to understand more clearly just how these paradoxical process do give rise to knowledge and provide obstacles to its arising at the same time.

That invitation means being open to the emergent themes, especially their shadow aspects, seeking to articulate them when this seems likely to shift the patterns of conversational life. It means questioning ourselves when we think that our role is to "get them" to think differently, when we ask what do "you do" about complexity, knowledge creation or anything else organizational. When one moves away from thinking that one has to manage the whole system, one pays attention to one's own participation in one's own local situation in the living present. Perhaps this humbler kind of "management" is what the "knowledge society" requires.

Appendix
Autopoiesis: an inappropriate analogy for human action

In exploring knowledge creation in organizations, some writers (for example, Roos *et al.*, 1997; Nonaka and Takeuchi, 1995; Broekstra, 1998) link theories of autopoiesis to those of complexity. This appendix describes the theory of autopoiesis, comparing it with complexity theories and the theory of complex responsive processes of relating developed in this book to argue that it is inappropriate to think of human action in autopoietic terms.

Autopoietic systems

The biologists, Maturana and Varela (1992), developed the notion of autopoiesis to account for what was distinctive about living systems, starting with a living cell. An autopoietic system is one whose components participate in production processes that produce those components and the boundary that separates the system from its environment. The system consists of a circular organization of production processes that continually replaces the components necessary for the continuation of that system. In other words, the system creates itself. What this means can be seen most clearly in relation to living cells. An autopoietic system has:

- identifiable components, such as the nucleus and mitochondria in a cell, which produce themselves, as a cell produces the nucleus and mitochondria;
- mechanistic interactions between components, such as the general physical laws that determine changes that occur within a cell;
- an identifiable boundary produced by the system itself. In other words, the boundary is determined by internal relationships, not imposed from outside. A cell has a boundary in the form of a plasma membrane

produced through proteins seeking or avoiding water. The cell produces lipid molecules in a double layer forming a selectively permeable barrier.

These properties have a number of distinctive consequences. First, in producing its own boundaries, an autopoietic system establishes its own autonomy, that is, its identity:

> Maturana and Varela pick out the single, biological individual (for example a single-celled creature such as an amoeba) as the central example of a living system. One essential feature of such living entities is their individual autonomy. Although they are part of organisms, populations, and species and are affected by their environment, individuals are bounded, self-defined entities.
>
> (Mingers, 1995, p. 10)

Maturana and Varela distinguish between the organization and the structure of an autopoietic system. The organization is the nature of the components and the relations between them required for an entity to belong to a particular category or type. It is thus an abstract generalization that determines the identity of a system and this identity must remain constant and invariant if the system is not to disintegrate. The organization of the system prescribes the properties of its components and the relationships between them that permit them to enter into a limited, but large, number of relations to each other while still preserving the fundamental form of the system. Organization is, thus, the dynamics of interaction within the system, the context within which the components interact. Structure is the mode of operation that produces the potential range of structural arrangements that retain identity. The structure, then, is an actual example of the organization. In other words, the structure embodies the abstract principles that define the organization, or identity, of the system. It is the specific arrangement of the components at any particular moment. So, the organization of a prokaryote cell, that which gives it its identity as this kind of cell, is the abstract features of cell membrane containing nucleoid material. The structure of a prokaryote cell is some living example that has the features just described. As Mingers (1995, p. 206) puts it: "An organism interacts locally through its components but this generates, and is constrained by, global properties that are emergent." The organization thus emerges from its component interactions, while those interactions flow from the organization so that the circular, self-referential process functions to sustain the organization.

Autopoietic systems are organizationally (operationally) closed. This means that the system's organization, or identity, is not determined by anything outside of it. It may import energy, materials or information and export waste but its identity is determined by its own operations. There are no instructive interactions with its environment so that it can receive no constructive instructions from outside of itself. This does not mean that it is isolated because it is structurally coupled to other systems in its environment. This means that change in other systems can perturb the system in question and so trigger internal change, but the nature of the change itself will be determined entirely by the production processes within the system.

The structural coupling between systems leads to evolution as structural, or natural drift rather than adaptation to the environment. Evolution is the history of structural coupling and it is this history that is referred to as structural or natural drift. It is the system's own nature/identity/operational processes that determine the structural shape it takes on, not the particular environmental perturbation it experiences. In this sense the system does not adapt to a unique pre-given environment. However, because it is structurally coupled to other systems, they together determine the history of structural coupling. Evolution is thus co-determined or co-created. Evolution is a reciprocal adjustment between structurally coupled entities that continually trigger changes in each other. Those changes that facilitate the process of autopoiesis, that is, the maintenance of identity, are maintained and conserved. The loss of identity is the destruction of the system. This leads to natural drift as the success of some groups maintaining their identity and the dying out of others through the loss of their autopoiesis.

Comparisons with other systems theories

General systems theory is concerned with open systems. It explains how living systems function through importing energy and materials from a pre-given environment, across the system's boundary with that environment, transforming the imports into a form of functioning, and then exporting waste to the environment. The boundary is a given and its formation is not due to the functioning of the system. The theory explains how the system sustains homeostasis, or equilibrium, through adaptation to the environment. The history of the system is not important in that what matters is the process of adaptation to the current environment. The principle of equifinality means that the state of homeostasis can be achieved from a large number of starting points and it is this that renders history unimportant. Autopoietic systems are substantially different. First, they are organizationally, or operationally closed, which means that the state of the system is determined by its own operations, triggered by changes in other systems constituting the environment. This means that the system cannot be said to be adapting to a current state of the environment but, rather, that its current state reflects the history of its structural couplings with other systems. There is a similarity with homeostasis in that all structural changes must be consistent with the conservation of system identity. The only alternative is system destruction. While general systems theory understands the dynamics as simple movement to stability, autopoiesis theory understands the dynamic as wide variations consistent with identity.

The cybernetic branch of systems thinking explains system stability in terms of negative feedback applied to information about the external environment with the system structure playing little part in the nature of change. A cybernetic system functions with reference to some state in its environment, adapting to that environment. Again, history is not important as far as the current adapted state is concerned, although it plays a part in movement toward that state. The internal structure of the cybernetic system is not considered to be important, only the gap between current state and the environmental state to which the system must adapt. An autopoietic system is substantially different in that it is the internal structure that determines how it changes in a way consistent with the conservation of its identity. History is important in the form of a history of structural coupling with other systems.

The systems dynamics branch of systems thinking understands systems change in terms of damping and amplifying feedback loops. Here the internal dynamic of the system determines the pattern of change. This is similar to autopoiesis, the difference lying in the emphasis the latter places on the conservation of identity, a concept lacking in systems dynamics.

Despite the significant differences between autopoietic systems theory and other systems theories, there is one important matter that they all have in common. This is the underlying causal framework, namely, that of Formative Teleology (see Chapter 2). The first volume (Stacey *et al.*, 2000) in this series explained the claim that general systems theory, cybernetics and systems dynamics all assume Formative Teleology, that is, they all assume that the future is the unfolding of what is already enfolded in the system or its environment. Thus, an open system moves toward its homeostatic state of adaptation to the current environment, a cybernetic system moves toward the stable state specified in the external reference point, and system dynamics identifies archetypal patterns of damping and amplifying feedback that a system realizes. Although autopoietic systems co-construct their environment rather than adapt to it, they also unfold an already enfolded identity.

The alternative causal framework, underlying the perspective of complex responsive processes of relating developed in this book, is that of Transformative Teleology. This assumes that the future is under perpetual construction as continuity and transformation of identity at the same time. Autopoiesis quite explicitly excludes transformation of identity. It is, therefore, not a dialectical theory, that is, one firmly based on paradox as is the case with complex responsive processes. As with other systems theories, autopoiesis cannot explain the emergence of novelty as the transformation of identity. Indeed, it quite explicitly excludes this possibility in its insistence on the conservation of identity.

This inability to explain the origin of novel identities is revealed in the concept of structural or natural drift. Natural drift is the history of structural coupling between systems, where each system either conserves its identity or that identity is destroyed. Natural drift discards those that do not manage to conserve their identities. It explains the history of the destruction of species but does not, as far as I can see, explain new speciation:

> The first step is to switch from a prescriptive logic to a proscriptive one, that is, from the idea that what is not allowed is forbidden to the idea that what is not forbidden is allowed. In the context of evolution this shift means that we remove selection as a prescriptive process that guides and instructs in the task of improving fitness. In contrast, in a proscriptive context natural selection can be seen to operate, but in a modified sense: selection discards what is not compatible with survival and reproduction. Organism and the population offer variety; natural selection guarantees only that what ensues satisfies two basic constraints of survival and reproduction.
>
> (Varela *et al.*, 1995, p. 195)

Natural drift is variations on a central theme:

> There is not a single case in the structural history of living beings which does not reveal that each lineage is a particular case of variations on a basic theme, over an uninterrupted sequence of reproductive changes with conservation of autopoiesis and adaptation.
>
> (Maturana and Varela, 1992, p. 107)

Evolution here is understood as variations on a central theme, some of the variations being destroyed as they lose their identity. This is not a view that understands evolution as the transformation of identity, as the emergence of the truly novel but as a continuing unfolding of an already enfolded central theme. Organisms are said to offer variety but, as far as I can see, there is no explanation of how they do so.

Autopoiesis and theories of complexity

The first volume in this series (Stacey *et al.*, 2000) distinguished between two strands of thinking in the natural complexity sciences. The first is an extension of systems theory and therefore continues within the causal framework of Formative Teleology. For example, simulations of birds flocking treat each entity in the system as identical and therefore can only unfold patterns already enfolded in the system's set of rules (Reynolds, 1987). The theory of autopoiesis is similar to and consistent with this strand of thinking in the complexity sciences. The other strand points toward Transformative Teleology because it models phenomena on the assumption of non-average variations in relations with the environment, that is fluctuations, and non-average entities comprising the model (Allen, 1998a, 1998b). The potential for the transformation of identity lies in the fluctuations, that is, non-average relations, and in non-average features of entities. This strand of complexity thinking is thus completely different to the theory of autopoiesis. The difference is this. Autopoiesis is built on the notion of the conservation of identity while the second strand of complexity thinking places dialectics, that is, paradox, at the center of its concern with the potential for identity transformation. Evolution is then seen not as the unfolding of some central theme but the continuous reproduction of continuity and potential transformation of identity at the same time. The theory of complex responsive process that this volume is concerned with draws its analogies from this second strand of complexity thinking, which is incompatible with the theory of autopoiesis.

There is another important difference. Autopoiesis takes the individual as its fundamental unit of analysis and presents the conservation of individual identity as the fundamental principle. The perspective of complex responsive process of relating takes the individual and the collective simultaneously seeing both as arising in the interaction between individuals. Here, individuals are not bounded, self-determining entities

Autopoietic systems and human action

Many believe that the notion of autopoiesis is useful in understanding the nature of single cells, but there is considerable disagreement as to whether other living systems are autopoietic. Maturana and Varela have not given definite or consistent views on whether multicell organisms are autopoietic. Varela claims that the human nervous and immune systems are operationally closed. Both he and Maturana have said that they do not believe that social systems are autopoietic.

However, some others, most notably Luhmann (Luhmann, 1984), have claimed that social systems are autopoietic. In Luhmann's formulation, a social system is a system of communicative events: one communicative event produces another. This satisfies the condition of an autopoietic system that it should produce the components that constitute it. Communications always refer to previous communications and lead on to others. Communicative events are not thoughts, behaviors or actions. They are utterances of information by one individual that have meaning for another individual. This system of communications is at a different level to people and their thoughts. In fact, people are the environment of a social system. The communicative events are separate from the people, who come and go, while the self-referring communication goes on. Mingers critiques the work of Luhmann, first of all, pointing out that he does not adequately solve the problem of boundaries because his system of communicative events cannot be said to produce a boundary between themselves and people. Second, he does not demonstrate how communicative events could emerge from the interactions of humans and yet constitute a domain independent of them. Communications require people to make them but in Luhmann's theory people disappear into the environment of disembodied communicative events.

The perspective of complex responsive processes developed in this book differs fundamentally from that of Luhmann. First, Luhmann splits communication off from human bodies, while complex responsive processes are communicative relations between human bodies. Luhmann talks about a communicative event as an utterance made by one that has a meaning for another. In complex responsive processes, communicative acts are gestures by one that call forth responses from another and meaning arises in the social act of gesture and response taken together. There is no notion of a system of communication at a different level to people and their thoughts as there is in Luhmann's formulation. From the perspective of complex responsive processes, the thoughts of people are communicative acts as gestures of their bodies calling forth responses from their bodies and the bodies of others. Without human bodies there are no communicative acts and it makes no sense to talk about a system of communication continuing while people come and go. There are no different levels of individual, social, communication systems, and so on. They are all the same level and the notion of boundaries around individuals preserving their autopoiesis, or boundaries around communication systems conserving their autopoiesis has no place. The very notion of boundary has little relevance from the perspective of complex responsive processes of relating. This is because the private role play or silent conversation of individual mind is the same process as the public communicative acts of gesture and response between people. The individual mind is then not functioning purely in terms of an identity on one side of a boundary constructing variations in itself, triggered by changes in other identities contained within their boundaries. This would be a definition of narcissistic personality formation. Instead, communicative acts between bodies are elaborated in communicative acts with themselves, that is, fluid conversational forms characterizing health.

The theory of autopoiesis, with its requirement for clear boundaries and conservation of identities, does not capture the sense of this healthy lived experience, but rather, contradicts it. The focus on the conservation of individual identity precludes the possibility of transformation of identity. Individuals and groups cannot be autopoietic systems because their identities are narrative themes organizing the experience of being together and the notion of boundaries around processes has little meaning. Identity, both individual and collective, arises in relationship between bodies. Individuals cannot be autopoietic systems because an individual alone cannot produce an identity and a boundary. Identity arises in communicative interaction and power relating between people. Since they mutually constitute each other, it follows that groups, and individual minds, cannot be operationally closed. Power differences between people mean that interactive instructions are possible. It is possible for another to compel, or persuade, one to do something that one would not otherwise do.

When Luhmann describes the social as an autopoietic system of communicative events he claims that these are different from the thought, feelings and speech of human beings. The implication seems to be that meaning lies above or beneath thoughts and speech, that the function of the latter is to convey the former. From the perspective I have been putting forward, thought and meaning is language. One does not convey the other. One is the other.

Bibliography

Allen, P. M. (1998a) "Evolving complexity in social science," in Altman, G. and Koch, W. A. (eds) *Systems: New Paradigms for the Human Sciences*, New York: Walter de Gruyter.

—— (1998b) "Modeling complex economic evolution," in Schweitzer, F. and Silverberg, G. (eds) *Selbstorganization*, Berlin: Dunker and Humbolt.

Archer, M. S. (1995) *Realist Social Theory: The Morphogenetic Approach*, Cambridge: Cambridge University Press.

Argyris, C. (1982) *Reasoning, Learning and Action: Individual and Organizational*, San Francisco: Jossey-Bass.

Argyris, C., Putnam, R. and Smith, D. (1985) *Action Science*, San Francisco: Jossey-Bass.

—— (1990), *Overcoming Organizational Defenses: Facilitating Organizational Learning*, Needham Heights, MA: Allyn and Bacon.

Argyris, C. and Schön, D. (1978) *Organizational Learning: A Theory of Action Perspective*, Reading, MA: Addison-Wesley.

Axelrod, R. (1984) *The Evolution of Cooperation*, New York: Basic Books.

Barrie, J. M., Freeman, W. J. and Lenhart, M. (1994) "Cross modality cortical processing: spatiotemporal patterns in olfactory, visual, auditory and somatic EEGs in perception by trained rabbits," *Society for Neuroscience Abstracts*, 414.10.

Bateson, G. (1973) *Steps to an Ecology of Mind*, St Albans: Paladin.

Bateson, G. and Bateson, M. C. (1987) *Angels Fear: Towards an Epistemology of the Sacred*, New York: Macmillan.

Bentley, D. (2000) "Control and emergence: the paradox of the construction industry," unpublished thesis, Hertfordshire University.

Bhaktin, M. M. (1986) *Speech Genres and Other Late Essays*, Austin, TX: University of Texas Press.

Bhaskar, R. (1975) *A Realist Theory of Science*, Leeds: Leeds Books.

—— (1989) *Reclaiming Reality: A Critical Introduction to Contemporary Philosophy*, London: Verso.

Bion, W. (1961a) *Experiences in Groups and Other Papers*, London: Tavistock Publications.

—— (1961b) "A theory of thinking," *International Journal of Psycho-Analysis* 43: 306–310.

Blair, H. (2000) "You're only as good as your last job: the relationship between labour market and labour process in the British film industry," unpublished thesis, University of Hertfordshire.

Boden, D. (1994) *The Business of Talk: Organizations in Action*, Cambridge: Polity Press.

Bohm, D. (1965) *The Special Theory of Relativity*, New York: W. A. Benjamin.

—— (1983) *Wholeness and the Implicate Order*, New York: Harper and Rowe.

Bohm, D. and Peat, F. D. (1989) *Science, Order and Creativity*, London: Routledge.

Boisot, M. (1998) *Knowledge Assets: Securing Competitive Advantage in the Knowledge Economy*, Oxford: Oxford University Press.

Boje, D. M. (1991) "The storytelling organization: a study of performance in an office supply firm," *Administrative Science Quarterly* 36: 106–126.

—— (1994) "Organizational storytelling: the struggle of pre-modern, modern and postmodern organizational learning discourses," *Management Learning* 25(3): 433–462.

—— (1995) "Stories of the storytelling organization: a postmodern analysis of Disney as Tamara-Land," *Academy of Management Journal* 38(4): 997–1055.

Broekstra, G. (1998) "An organization is a conversation," in Grant, D., Keenoy, T. and Oswick, C. (eds) *Discourse and Organisation*, London: Sage.

Brown, J. S. (1991) "Research that reinvents the corporation," *Harvard Business Review* Jan–Feb.

Brown, J. S. and Duguid, P. (1991) "Organizational learning and communities of practice: toward a unified view of working, learning and innovating," *Organization Science* 2(1): 40–57.

Bruner, J. (1990) *Acts of Meaning*, Cambridge, MA: Harvard University Press.

Burkitt, I. (1999) *Bodies of Thought: Embodiment, Identity and Modernity*, London: Sage.

Burton-Jones, A. (1999) *Knowledge Capitalism: Business, Work and Learning in the New Economy*, Oxford: Oxford University Press.

Butler, C. and Keary, J. (2000) *Managers and Mantras: One Company's Struggle for Simplicity*, Chichester: John Wiley.

Chomsky, N. (1957) *Syntactic Structures*, The Hague: Mouton.

Commons, J. R. (1934) *Institutional Economics: Its Place in Political Economy*, New York: Macmillan.

Craib, I. (1992) *Anthony Giddens*, London: Routledge.

Dalal, F. (1998) *Taking the Group Seriously: Towards a Post-Foulkesian Group Analytic Theory*, London: Jessica Kingsley Press.

Damasio, A. (1994) *Descartes' Error: Emotion, Reason and the Human Brain*, New York: Picador.

—— (1999) *The Feeling of What Happens: Body and Emotion in the Making of Consciousness*, London: Heinemann.

Dardik, I. I. (1997) "The origin of disease and health, heart waves: the single solution to heart rate variability and ischemic preconditioning," *Frontier Perspectives* 6(2): 18–32.

Davenport, T. H. and Prusak, L. (1998) *Working Knowledge: How Organizations Manage What they Know*, Cambridge, MA: Harvard University Press.

Deetz, S. and White, W. J. (1999) "Relational responsibility or dialogic ethics: a questioning of McNamee and Gergen," in McNamee, S. and Gergen, K. J. *Relational Responsibility: Resources for Sustainable Dialogue*, Thousand Oaks, CA: Sage.

Easterby-Smith, M. (1997) "Disciplines of organisational learning: contributions and critiques," *Human Relations* 50(9): 1085–2003.

Easterby-Smith, M. and Araujo, L. (1999) "Organisational learning: current debates and opportunities," in Easterby-Smith, M., Burgoyne, J. and Araujo, L. (eds) *Organizational Learning and the Learning Organization*, London: Sage.

Easterby-Smith, M., Burgoyne, J. and Araujo, L. (1999) *Organizational Learning and the Learning Organization*, London: Sage.

Elias, N. (1970) *What is Sociology?*, New York: Columbia University Press.

—— (1989) *The Symbol Theory*, London: Sage Publications.

Elias, N. and Scotson, J. (1994) *The Established and the Outsiders*, London: Sage.

Fonseca, J. (forthcoming) *Complexity and Innovation in Organizations*, London: Routledge.

Foulkes, S. H. (1948) *Introduction to Group Analytic Psychotherapy*, London: William Heinemann Medical Books Limited.

—— (1964) *Therapeutic Group Analysis*, London: George Allen and Unwin.

Forrester, J. (1961) *Industrial Dynamics*, Cambridge, MA: MIT Press.

—— (1969) *Urban Dynamics*, Cambridge, MA: MIT Press.

—— (1971) "The counter intuitive behavior of social systems," *Technology Review* Jan. 52–68.

Freeman, W. J. (1994) "Role of chaotic dynamics in neural plasticity," in van Pelt, J., Corner, M. A., Uylings, H. B. M., and Lopes da Silva, F. H. (eds) *Progress in Brain Research*, vol. 102, Amsterdam: Elsevier Science BV.

—— (1995) *Societies of Brains: A Study in the Neuroscience of Love and Hate*, Hillsdale, NJ: Lawrence Earlsbaum Associates Publishers.

Freeman, W. J. and Barrie J. M. (1994) "Chaotic oscillations and the genesis of meaning in cerebral cortex," in Buzsaki, G., Llinas, R., Singer, W., Berthoz, A. and Christen, Y. (eds) *Temporal Coding in the Brain*, Berlin: Springer.

Freeman, W. J. and Schneider, W. (1982) "Changes in the spatial patterns of rabbit olfactory EEG with conditioning to odors," *Psychophysiology* 19: 45–56.

Freud, S. (1921) "Group psychology and the analysis of the ego," in *Freud: Civilization, Society and Religion*, vol. 12, Harmondsworth: Penguin.

—— (1923) "The ego and the id," in *Freud: On Metapsychology*, vol. 11, Harmondsworth: Penguin.

Gabriel, Y. (1998) "Same old story or changing stories? Folkloric, modern and postmodern mutations," in Grant, D., Keenoy, T. and Oswick, C. (eds) *Discourse and Organisation*, London: Sage.

—— (1999) *Organizations in Depth*, London: Sage.

Gardner, H. (1985) *The Mind's New Science: A History of the Cognitive Revolution*, New York: Basic Books.

Garfinkel, H. (1967) *Studies in Ethnomethodology*, Englewood Cliffs, NJ: Prentice-Hall.

Garven, D. A. (1993) "Building a learning organization," *Harvard Business Review*, July–Aug.

Gedo, J. (1999) *The Evolution of Psychoanalysis: Contemporary Theory and Practice*, New York: Other Press.

Gell-Mann, M. (1994) *The Quark and the Jaguar*, New York: Freeman & Co.

Gergen, K. J. (1999) *An Invitation to Social Construction*, Thousand Oaks, CA: Sage.

Gergen, M. (1999) "Relational responsibility: deconstructive possibilities," in McNamee, S. and Gergen, K. J. *Relational Responsibility: Resources for Sustainable Dialogue*, Thousand Oaks, CA: Sage.

Giddens, A. (1976) *New Rules of Sociological Method*, London: Hutchinson.

—— (1984) *The Constitution of Society: Outline of the Theory of Structuration*, Cambridge: Polity Press.

Gleick, J. (1987) *Chaos: The Making of a New Science*, London: William Heinemann Limited.

Goffman, E. (1981) *Forms of Talk*, Philadelphia: University of Pennsylvania Press.

Goldberger, A. L. (1997) "Fractal variability versus pathologic periodicity: complexity loss and stereotypy in disease," *Perspectives in Biology and Medicine* 40(4): 543–561.

Goodwin, B. (1994) *How the Leopard Changed its Spots*, London: Weidenfeld and Nicolson.

Grant, D., Keenoy, T. and Oswick, C. (eds) (1998) *Discourse and Organisation*, London: Sage.

Griffin, J. D. (forthcoming) *The Emergence of Leadership: Linking Self-organization and Ethics*, London: Routledge.

Hayek, F. A. (1948) *Individualism and Economic Order*, London: George Routledge.

Hebb, D. O. (1949), *The Organization of Behavior*, New York: Wiley.

Hirschhorn, L. (1990) *The Workplace Within: Psychodynamics of Organizational Life*, Cambridge, MA: MIT Press.

Hodgson, G. M. (1999a) *Evolution and Institutions: On Evolutionary Economics and the Evolution of Economics*, Cheltenham: Edward Elgar.

—— (1999b) "Structures and institutions: reflections on institutionalism, structuration theory and critical realism," paper for the "Realism and Economics" workshop, King's College, January.

Huber, G. (1991) "Organizational learning: the contributing processes and the literature," *Organization Science* 2(1): 88–115.

Husserl, E. (1960) *Cartesian Mediations: An Introduction to Phenomenology*, London: Allen Unwin.

Isaacs, W. (1999) *Dialogue and the Art of Thinking Together*, New York: Doubleday.

Jefferson, G. (1978) "Sequential aspects of storytelling in conversation," in Schenkein, J. (ed.) *Studies in the Organization of Conversational Interaction*, New York: Academic Press.

Kauffman, S. A. (1993) *Origins of Order: Self-organization and Selection in Evolution*, Oxford: Oxford University Press.

—— (1995) *At Home in the Universe*, New York: Oxford University Press.

Kelso, J. A. S. (1995) *Dynamic Patterns: The Self-organization of Brain and Behavior*, Cambridge, MA: MIT Press.

Kilminster, R. (1991) "Structuration theory as a worldview," in Christopher, G. A., Jury, B. and Jury, D. *Giddens' Theory of Structuration: A Critical Appreciation*, London: Routledge: 74–115.

Klein, M. (1946) "Notes on some schizoid mechanisms," in Mitchell, J. (ed.) (1986) *The Selected Writings of Melanie Klein*, New York: Free press.

Kleiner, A. and Roth, G. (1997) "How to make experience your best teacher," *Harvard Business Review* Sept.–Oct.

Langton, C. (1993) "Artificial Life," in Boden, M. A. (ed.) (1996) *The Philosophy of Artificial Life*, Oxford: Oxford University Press.

Lannamann, J. W. (1999) "On being relational in an accountable way: the question of agency and power," in McNamee, S. and Gergen, K. J. *Relational Responsibility: Resources for Sustainable Dialogue*, Thousand Oaks, CA: Sage.

Lave, J. and Wenger, E. (1991) *Situated Learning: Legitimate Peripheral Participation*, New York: Cambridge University Press.

Leader, D. (2000) *Freud's Footnotes*, London: Faber and Faber.

Leonard, D. and Strauss, S. (1997) "Putting your company's whole brain to work," *Harvard Business Review* July–Aug.

Lewin, R. and Regine, B. (2000) *The Soul at Work*, London: Orion Business Books.

Losada, M. F. (1998) "The complex dynamics of high performance teams," *Mathematical and Computer Modeling*.

Luhmann, N. (1984) *Social Systems*, Stanford, CA: Stanford University Press.

McCulloch W. S. and Pitts, W. (1943) "A logical calculus of ideas imminent in nervous activity," *Bulletin of Mathematical Biophysics* vol. 5.

McNamee, S. and Gergen, K. J. (1999) *Relational Responsibility: Resources for Sustainable Dialogue*, Thousand Oaks, CA: Sage.

Marion, R. (1999) *The Edge of Organization: Chaos and Complexity Theories of Formal Social Systems*, Thousand Oaks, CA: Sage Publications.

Matte-Blanco, I. (1975) *The Unconscious as Infinite Sets: An Essay in Bi-logic*, London: Duckworth.

—— (1988) *Thinking, Feeling and Being*, London: Routledge.

Maturana, H. and Varela, F. J. (1992) *The Tree of Knowledge: The Biological Roots of Human Understanding*, Boston: Shambhala.

Mead, G. H. (1934) *Mind, Self and Society*, Chicago: Chicago University Press.

—— (1936) *Movements of Thought in the Nineteenth Century*, Chicago: Chicago University Press.

—— (1938) *The Philosophy of the Present*, Chicago: Chicago University Press.

Meadows, D. H. (1982) "Whole earth models and system co-evolution," *Co-evolution Quarterly* Summer: 98–108.

Miller, E. J. and Rice, A. K. (1967) *Systems of Organization: The Control of Task and Sentient Boundaries*, London: Tavistock Publications.

Mingers, J. (1995) *Self-Producing systems: Implications and Applications of Autopoiesis*, New York: Plenum Press.

Nonaka, I. (1991) "The knowledge-creating company," *Harvard Business Review* November–December: 96–104.

Nonaka, I. and Takeuchi. H. (1995) *The Knowledge Creating Company: How Japanese Companies Create the Dynamics of Innovation*, New York: Oxford University Press.

Oberholzer, A. and Roberts, V. Z. (eds) (1994) *The Unconscious at Work: Individual and Organizational Stress in the Human Services*, London: Routledge.

Owen, H. (1992) *Open Space Technology: A User's Guide*, San Francisco: Berrett-Koehler.

Piaget, J. (1954) *The Construction of Reality in the Child*, New York: Ballantine Books.

Pinker, S. (1994) *The Language Instinct: The New Science of Language and Mind*, New York: William Morrow.

—— (1997) *How the Mind Works*, New York: Penguin Books.

Polanyi, M. (1958) *Personal Knowledge*, Chicago: Chicago University Press.

—— (1960) *The Tacit Dimension*, London: Routledge and Kegan Paul.

Polanyi, M. and Prosch, H. (1975) *Meaning*, Chicago: University of Chicago Press.

Popper, K. R. (1945) *The Open Society and its Enemies*, London: Routledge and Kegan Paul.

—— (1983) *Realism and the Aim of Science*, London: Hutchinson.

Prange, C. (1999) "Organisational learning – desperately seeking theory," in Easterby-Smith, M., Burgoyne, J. and Araujo, L. (1999) *Organizational Learning and the Learning Organization*, London: Sage.

Pratt, J., Gordon, P. and Plamping, D. (1999) *Working Whole Systems*, London: Kings Fund Publishing.

Prigogine, I. (1997) *The End of Certainty: Time, Chaos and the New Laws of Nature*, New York: The Free Press.

Prigogine, I. and Stengers, I. (1984) *Order Out of Chaos: Man's New Dialogue with Nature*, New York: Bantam Books.

Quinn, J. B., Anderson, P. and Finkelstein, S. (1996) "Managing professional intellect: making the most of the best," *Harvard Business Review* March–April.

Ray, T. S. (1992) "An approach to the synthesis of life," in Langton, G. C., Taylor, C., Doyne-Farmer, J. and Rasmussen, S. (eds) *Artificial Life II, Santa Fe Institute, Studies in the Sciences of Complexity*, vol. 10, Reading, MA: Addison-Wesley.

Reynolds, C. W. (1987) "Flocks, herds and schools: a distributed behavior model," Proceedings of SIGGRAPH "87," *Computer Graphics* 21(4): 25–34.

Roos, J. and Oliver, D. (1999) "From fitness landscapes to knowledge landscapes," *Systemic Practice and Action Research* 12: 279–294.

Roos, J., Roos, G., Dragonetti, N. C. and Edvinsson, L. (1997) *Intellectual Capital: Navigating the New Business Landscape*, London: Macmillan Press.

Rose, S. P. R. (1995) "Memory formation: its molecular and cell biology," *European Review* 3(3): 243–256.

Sacks, H. (1992) *Lectures on Conversations*, Oxford: Blackwell.

Sampson, G. (1997) *Educating Eve: The "Language Instinct" Debate*, London: Cassell.

Saussure, F. de (1974) *Course in General Linguistics*, London: Collins.

Schön, D. (1983) *The Reflective Practitioner*, New York: Basic Books.

Schore, A. N. (1994) *Affect Regulation and the Origin of the Self: The Neurobiology of Emotional Development*, Hillsdale, NJ: Earlsbaum.

—— (1997) "Early organization of the nonlinear right brain and development of a predisposition to psychotic disorder," *Development and Psychology* 595–631.

Schutz, A. (1967) *The Phenomenology of the Social World*, Evanston, IL: Northwestern University Press.

Segal, D. J. (1999) *The Developing Mind: Toward a Neurobiology of Interpersonal Experience*, New York: The Guildford Press.

Senge, P. (1990) *The Fifth Discipline: The Art and Practice of the Learning Organization*, New York: Doubleday.

Shannon C. and Weaver, W. (1949) *The Mathematical Theory of Communication*, Urbana, IL: The University of Illinois Press.

Shapiro, E. R. and Carr, W. A. (1991) *Lost in Familiar Places*, New Haven, CT: Yale University Press.

Shaw, P. (forthcoming) *Changing the Conversation: Organizational Change from a Complexity Perspective*, London: Routledge.

Shegloff, E. A. (1991) "Reflections on talk and social structures," in Boden, D.

and Zimmerman, D. H. (eds) *Talk and Social Structure*, Cambridge: Polity Press.

Shotter, J. (1983) "'Duality of structures' and 'intentionality' in an ecological psychology," *Journal for the Theory of Social Behavior* 13: 19–43.

—— (1993) *Conversational Realities: Constructing Life through Language*, Thousand Oaks, CA: Sage Publications.

—— (1999) "Dialogue, depth and life inside responsive orders: from external observation to participatory understanding," paper presented at Dialogue in Performing Knowledge conference, Stockholm, Sweden.

—— (2000) "Wittgenstein and his philosophy of beginnings and beginnings and beginnings," paper for Wittgenstein Conference in honor of Rom Harre, American University, Washington, DC.

Shotter, J. and Katz, A. M. (1996) "Hearing the patient's 'voice': toward a social poietics in diagnostic interviews," *Social Science and Medicine* 46: 919–931.

Shotter, J. and Katz, A. M. (1999) "Creating relational realities: responsible responding to poetic 'movements' and 'moments'," in McNamee, S. and Gergen, K. J. *Relational Responsibility: Resources for Sustainable Dialogue*, Thousand Oaks, CA: Sage.

Skarda, C. A. and Freeman, W. J. (1990) "Chaos and the new science of the brain," *Concepts in Neuroscience* 1(2): 275–285.

Stacey, R. (1993) *Strategic Management and Organisational Dynamics*, London: Pitman.

—— (2000) *Strategic Management and Organisational Dynamics: The Challenge of Complexity*, London: Pearson Education.

Stacey, R., Griffin D. and Shaw, P. (2000) *Complexity and Management: Fad or Radical Challenge to Systems Thinking?*, London: Routledge.

Stern, D. N. (1985) *The Interpersonal World of the Infant*, New York: Basic Books.

—— (1995) *The Motherhood Constellation: A Unified View of Parent–Infant Psychotherapy*, New York: Basic Books.

Stolorow, R., Atwood, G. and Brandchaft, B. (1994) *The Intersubjective Perspective*, Northvale, NJ: Jason Aaronson.

Stolorow, R. Orange, D. M. and Atwood, G. E. (1998) "Projective identification begone! Comments on a paper by Susan H. Sands," *Psychoanalytic Dialogue* 8(5): 719–725.

Streatfield, P. (forthcoming) *The Paradox of Control in Organizations*, London: Routledge.

Sveiby, K. E. (1997) *The New Organizational Wealth: Managing and Measuring Knowledge-based Assets*, San Francisco: Berrett-Koehler.

Tsoukas, H. T. (1997) "Forms of knowledge and forms of life in organized contexts," in Chia, R. (ed.) *In the Realms of Organization: Essays for Robert Cooper*, London: Routledge.

Turner, S. (1994) *The Social Theory of Practices: Tradition, Tacit Knowledge and Presuppositions*, Cambridge: Polity Press.

Varela, F. J., Thompson, E. and Rosch, E. (1995) *The Embodied Mind: Cognitive Science and Human Experience*, Cambridge, MA: MIT Press.

Veblen, T. B. (1899) *The Theory of the Leisure Class: An Economic Study in the Evolution of Institutions*, New York: Charles Scribeners.

—— (1934) *Essays on our Changing Order*, ed. Ardzrooni, J., New York: The Viking Press.

von Bertalanffy, L. (1968) *General Systems Theory: Foundations, Development, Applications*, New York: George Braziller.

von Glasersveld, E. (1991) "Knowing without metaphysics: aspects of the radical constructivist position," in Steier, F. (ed.) *Research and Reflexivity*, London: Sage.

Vygotsky, L. S. (1962) *Thought and Language*, Cambridge, MA: MIT Press.

Watzlawick, P. (1976) *How Real is Real? Confusion, Disinformation, Communication*, New York: Random House.

Weick, K. (1979) *The Social Psychology of Organizing*, Reading, MA: Addison-Wesley.

—— (1995) *Sensemaking in Organizations*, Thousand Oaks, CA: Sage.

Weisbord, K. and Janoff, S. (1995) *Future Search: An Action Guide to Finding Common Ground in Organizations and Communities*, San Francisco: Berrett-Koehler.

Wittgenstein, L. (1980) *Remarks on the Philosophy of Psychology*, vols I and II, Oxford: Basil Blackwell.

Wright, K. (1991) *Vision and Separation: Between Mother and Baby*, Northvale, NJ: Jason Aaronson Inc.

Index

formal–conscious–legitimate themes
174–5, 179; and importance of history
135–6; mutual expectations of
associative response 131; narrative-like
experience 136–9, 147; public/private
134–5; rhetorical devices 132–3;
sequencing, segmenting, categorizing
actions 132; thematic experience
139–44; turn-taking sequences 132,
146–7, 148–51, 155–6
Piaget, J. 55
Pinker, S. 51, 75, 120, 121
Polanyi, M. 13, 35; and Prosch, H. 35
Popper, K.R. 43, 121
power 149–50, 163, 173; complex
responsive process view 214;
conversation as threat to 183; and
ideology 208–9; inclusion–exclusion
dynamic 151–3, 156, 214; and
micro-diversity 205; and novelty 205–6;
and preservation of differentials 151–3;
and role play 205; and social
unconscious 154–5; and use of symbols
151
Prange, C. 39
Pratt, J. et al., 178
Prigogine, I. 69; and Stengers, I. 13
protoconversations 104, 137–8
psychoanalysis 54, 207; Freudian 44–5;
key questions 46–8; Kleinian 45–6; and
nature of thinking 47; and the
organization 31–3; and the unconscious
161

Quality Assurance Agency 225
Quinn, J.B. et al., 14, 25

Rationalist Teleology 26–7, 28, 31, 33, 38,
39, 48, 93, 126
Ray, T.S. 69, 73–4
reflection-in-action 106–7
Reynolds, C.W. 241
Roos, J. et al., 33, 35, 218–19, 236
rule-based communication, global 120–3,
127–8; local 126–9

Sacks, H. 130, 132
Sampson, G. 121–2

Saussure, F. de 120
Schön, D. 13
Schore, A.N. 78
Schutz, A. 57
self, emergence of 88–92; evolution of
77–9
sender–receiver process 23, 26, 194–6;
systems thinking/complex responsive
process comparisons 196–8
Senge, P. 13, 18, 28, 178, 215, 216
shadow themes 155, 167–8
Shannon, C. and Weaver, W. 15
Shapiro, E.R. and Carr, W.A. 31
Shaw, P. 232
Shegloff, E.A. 130
Shotter, J. 36, 37, 57–8, 59, 112–13, 130,
132, 133–4, 173; and Katz, A.M. 113,
130, 131, 132
Skarda, C.A. and Freeman, W.J. 33, 199
social constructionism 91–2, 152, 202;
defined 55–6; key questions 59–60;
problems with 56–8; and responsibility
58; working assumptions 55
Stacey, R. 167; et al., 5, 22, 54, 59, 61, 70,
186, 239, 241
Stern, D.N. 103, 137–8
Stolorow, R. et al., 44, 47
stories 35–6, 38, 41, 123–6, 127, 204;
folklore 124; modernist 124;
postmodernist 124; purpose of 124
structuration theory 91, 202; criticisms of
61–3; described 61; and emergence
61–2; key questions 63–4
Sveiby, K.E. 14
symbols 118, 129, 173, 188–9, 211; as
associative 146–7; multiple aspects of
111–15; and power 151; protosymbols
102–6, 189; reified 108–11, 116, 221;
significant 81, 84, 106–7
systems thinking 12, 38, 129, 178; and
history 201; and human interaction 70;
moving on from 4–7; and notions of
causality 26–30
systems thinking/complex responsive
process comparisons 193–4;
dialogue/ordinary conversation in the
living present 215–17; individual
tacit-unconscious/unconscious processes